The gentleman's mistress

Manchester University Press

The gentleman's mistress

Illegitimate relationships and children, 1450–1640

Tim Thornton and Katharine Carlton

Manchester University Press

Copyright © Tim Thornton and Katharine Carlton 2019

The right of Tim Thornton and Katharine Carlton to be identified as the authors of this work has been asserted by them in accordance with the Copyright, Designs and Patents Act 1988.

Published by Manchester University Press
Altrincham Street, Manchester M1 7JA

www.manchesteruniversitypress.co.uk

British Library Cataloguing-in-Publication Data
A catalogue record for this book is available from the British Library

ISBN 978 1 5261 1406 8 hardback
ISBN 978 1 5261 1407 5 paperback

First published 2019
Paperback published 2019

The publisher has no responsibility for the persistence or accuracy of URLs for any external or third-party internet websites referred to in this book, and does not guarantee that any content on such websites is, or will remain, accurate or appropriate.

Typeset
by Toppan Best-set Premedia Limited

Contents

List of figures and tables	*page* vi
Acknowledgements	vii
List of abbreviations	ix
Explanatory notes	x
Introduction	1
1 Background and legal framework	16
2 The extent of bastardy among the elite	38
3 The role and status of the mistress	60
4 Gentlewomen and their lovers	80
5 The 'wronged' partner	99
6 The bastard children	115
Conclusion	136
Bibliography	144
Index	164

Figures and tables

Figures

1	Number of wills and illegitimate beneficiaries, 1450–1640	45
2	Simplified Hesketh family tree	53

Tables

1	Totals of wills by county and period	46

Acknowledgements

Any project of this kind is long in the making and the debts accumulated in the process are many, varied and inevitably too complex to be acknowledged in the detail they deserve. Conversations and discussions, comments and ideas have been contributed along the way by many friends and colleagues, among whom it is important, given the subject matter, to single out Chris Haigh, the late Gordon Forster and Martin Ingram. We are both fortunate to have the University of Huddersfield as a context in which to work: over the years, the warm collegiality and generous support, and the clear direction and leadership, offered by fellow historians and senior colleagues alike has been vital to the stimulation of this work. Especial mention must go to Professors David Taylor, Mike Russ, Keith Laybourn, and Vice-Chancellor Professor Bob Cryan. The book was completed in the week immediately after the University of Huddersfield won the *Times Higher Education* Leadership and Management Award for Outstanding Leadership and Management Team 2018, and it is one sign of the strength of the team that it could support the completion of this work in the midst of so many other exciting agendas. Many dozens of students who have been involved in modules on late medieval and early modern English social and polital history also, probably unwittingly, have played a major role, and deserve their share of the credit. None, of course, share the responsibility for any misjudgements and errors which remain.

Anyone working on a project of this kind is fortunate to have the opportunity of reading in some outstanding archives and libraries, and the staff of those particularly important to the evidence used here deserve mention: Carlisle Archive Centre (Cumbria Archive Service), Cheshire Archives; Durham University Library; West Yorkshire Archive Service in Leeds; Leeds University Library Archives and Special Collections; Leicester and Rutland Record Office; Lancashire Record Office; and Borthwick Institute for Archives at the University of York. Special thanks are also due to colleagues in Computing and Library Services at the University of Huddersfield, especially document delivery, for their unfailing patience and excellent service over the years. Much logistical and administrative support has come from Sam Arrowsmith, Claire White and Katie Baron.

Manchester University Press have provided an unusually positive and supportive environment for the completion of the work: particular thanks are due to Emma Brennan and her editorial and production team, and to anonymous reviewers for their helpful comments.

We are grateful for permission to refer to the unpublished theses of Helen Matthews, the late Jack Brierley Watson and the late Philip Tyler.

Woven through this book is the support we have received from our respective families, in their different ways: Tim Thornton is always aware how much this reflects the love, stimulation and inspiration provided by Sue Johns, Carys and Gwyn; Katharine Carlton would like to acknowledge debts to the late Edna Aynge, loving support from Jason Carlton, Alice Carlton, Robert and Vivienne Walker.

Abbreviations

BIA	Borthwick Institute for Archives, University of York
BL	British Library
Cheshire Arch	Cheshire Archives and Local Studies
CP	G. E. C[ockayne] & G. H. White, *The Complete Peerage* (14 vols. London & Stroud: St Catherine Press; Sutton, 1910–59, 1998)
DUL	Durham University Library
JRULM	John Rylands University Library of Manchester
LP	*Letters and Papers, Foreign and Domestic, of the Reign of Henry VIII, Preserved in the Public Record Office, the British Museum, and Elsewhere in England*, ed. J. S. Brewer, J. Gairdner and R. H. Brodie (London: HMSO, 1862–1910); Addenda, I (London: HMSO, 1929–32)
LPRS	Lancashire Parish Register Society
LRO	Lancashire Record Office
ODNB	H. C. G. Matthew and Brian Harrison (eds), *The Oxford Dictionary of National Biography* (61 vols. Oxford: Oxford University Press, 2004)
RSLC	Record Society of Lancashire and Cheshire
TE	*Testamenta Eboracensia, A Selection of Wills from the Registry at York*, parts II–VI, ed. J. Raine and J. W. Clay, Surtees Society, XXX, XLV, LIII, LXXIX, CVI (1855, 1865, 1868, 1884, 1902)
TNA	The National Archives of the United Kingdom
VCH Lancs	W. Farrer and J. Brownbill (eds), *The Victoria History of the Counties of England: The Victoria History of the County of Lancaster* (8 vols. London: [A. Constable], 1906–14)
YASRS	Yorkshire Archaeological Society, Record Series

Explanatory notes

All dates have been given new style with the year beginning on 1 January. Abbreviations have been silently expanded and punctuation modernised.

Introduction

Extensive work has been done since the 1960s to investigate the phenomenon of extra-marital sexual relationships and consequent illegitimacy in early modern England. This has primarily been undertaken in examining bastard-bearing at parish level and based around birth rates and financial provision for mother and infant, usually culminating in intervention to deal with the perceived moral failings of the parents and resulting social costs.[1] By focusing upon narrow geographical and social boundaries, historians imply that bastardy became a lifetime stigma from which neither mother nor child could escape and, as a result, they do not explore illegitimacy patterns at gentry level and above. Keith Wrightson and David Levine's path-breaking investigation of illegitimacy in the Essex parish of Terling in the period 1590–1640 identified only one man of gentry status fathering an illegitimate child out of a total of fifty putative fathers. Richard Adair's outstanding survey of illegitimacy in the parishes of early modern England makes only the briefest of passing mentions of elite involvement in bastardy, essentially in the form of the results of rape or coercion of lower-class women by gentlemen. Yet concern at the extent of sexual relationships outside marriage, and of the extent of bastardy arising from it, was not necessarily limited to commentators on the state of the poor and disadvantaged in parish society. And even the most cursory survey of those who exerted power and influence in late medieval and early modern England quickly reveals the names of men (and some women) of dubious parentage or questionable fidelity. Approximately one in ten gentlemen who made wills during the period in the north of England made some mention of illegitimate offspring, suggesting that illegitimate relationships and children were to be found in at least 10 per cent of gentle families. The illegitimate offspring of gentry and noble families participated in office-holding and local government, and their marriages formed part of the social landscape of the period.

Yet historians have never explored the extent and implications of this situation: just as historians of illegitimacy have shown little interest in the irregular relationships and offspring of the elite, so historians of the gentry, and to a slightly lesser extent nobility, have tended to pass over anything other than straightforward marriage and legitimate children.[2] The possible implications of a group of bastards born to at least one parent of gentle status in late medieval and early modern England are, however, great: the bastard offspring of gentlemen could have an education but were not tied by entails and landed settlements (for example for a widow's jointure) which governed the choice of marriage partners and the inheritances of their legitimate step-siblings. Furthermore, the relationship the illegitimate, adult family had with their legitimate half-brothers, half-sisters and other relations has not been investigated, prompting questions regarding their role in aristocratic/gentry family influence and honour. The attitudes to these individuals, whether illegitimate themselves or the parents of bastards (or both), also tells us something about the nature of socio-religious cultures at a time when the historiography suggests that companionate marriage, involving love between partners, within a closed, nuclear family was either on the rise or already well established.[3] Similarly they help to provide an alternative perspective on the limits to the licence allegedly allowed to men by the 'double standard' defined in recent work, the primary focus of which has been men of the middling and lower sort.[4] Further, in the rarer cases of well-evidenced illicit relationships conducted by gentlewomen, we are able to access indications of the behaviour of these women (and degrees of acceptance and condemnation/sanction) that shed light on the gendered expectations of elite females, before, during and after marriage, and go beyond some of the complexities of power networks identified as being negotiated by women on the basis of age and 'orderliness'.[5] Looking at both men and women, the book will provide a proper context and hinterland for the better-known mores of court, and the behaviour there of monarchs and courtiers, their mistresses and lovers, especially as represented in recent scholarship on courts and court literatures.[6]

In fact, the more closely these and other historiographies of the late medieval and early modern periods are considered, the lack of questions examining the illegitimate relationships and offspring of the elite becomes increasingly striking. The classic context for the study of illegitimate relationships and bastard-bearing is a demographic one, the ultimate assumptions of which relate to the control of resources, in an England experiencing significant economic and social change, characterised by 'social polarization'. Most significant here is Tony Wrigley's and Roger Schofield's argument that fertility was the main factor in the limitation of population in England in the early modern period. Even if this has been challenged by John Hatcher, it remains true that demographics and life cycle generally provided limiting forces. There is therefore a particular focus in this type of work on apprenticeship, service, and the expectation that couples should form a household before marrying and starting a family.[7]

These arguments tend to see behaviour, including sexual behaviour, as responding to implicit rules and to wage rates and economic conditions, rather than to regulation and more explicit determinants. Such approaches are largely inappropriate when applied to the elite, given the different ways in which resource constraints applied to them, or should be understood in very specific ways: for example, service affected the life experiences of young men and women of the gentry and nobility in particular ways, and arguments about access to resources apply differently, even during the leanest years of the 1590s. This explains why most studies with this methodological background pay little attention to elite involvement in illegitimacy beyond passing references to, for example, 'sexual exploitation by masters'.[8] Some of this argument will be addressed in our coverage of the fundamental demographics of levels of bastard-bearing in chapter 2, and the identity and experience of the mistress in chapter 3. There is no inherent incompatibility, however, between an essentially demographic approach, although generally previously focused on non-elite subjects, and an analysis which considers a wider social spectrum, given the importance of service in the life cycle of the elite. Service was for them, as it was for their inferiors, a period in which marriage and the creation of an independent household was not an option, but at the same time a phase of life and a manner of living which offered opportunities for young men and women to mix with others with whom they might form more or less lasting relationships outside the norms of regulated and legitimate marriage.[9] As will be seen in chapters 2 and 3, and also in chapter 4, which considers elite women and their lovers, there is a possibility that these constraints on elite household formation were a factor in some of the relationships formed and maintained by the gentry and nobility between the middle of the fifteenth century and the outbreak of the civil wars of the seventeenth.

By way of contrast, increasing attention has been paid since the beginning of the millennium to the 'reformation of manners', with its focus on the common weal and commonwealth. This effort at the regulation of behaviour and morality, with a particular concern at times with disorder and vice, led to action against many groups but especially labourers, apprentices and servants and their personal and sexual behaviour. Martin Ingram in particular has recently argued that the regulation of sexual behaviour was an increasingly intense phenomenon of life in most parts of England from the late fourteenth century onwards, as part of this 'reformation of manners'.[10] Ingram and others have described how the process might be led by various groups in society and impact increasingly widely, for example dominating the rhetoric of civic governance in London and other cities for much of the period. This force for change in modes of behaviour was potentially a challenge to elite behaviour as it was to non-elite, as in Ingram's formulation it was a movement which did not have particular social or religious roots. Changes to elite sexual behaviour in the north of England and the nature of challenges to it may therefore provide insights into this understanding of the 'reformation of manners' more generally. This will be a particular issue for consideration when we examine the mechanisms and structures of regulation in the north in chapter 1.

It is also hard to deny the role of state-building in changing and developing regimes of sexual regulation during the period covered by our study. Historians have identified this phenomenon in a variety of ways. For some, it has been as extensions of royal government intervention in the early modern period, with the crown's ministers' growing role in aspects of what might be categorised as social and economic policy which had been alien to it in previous centuries, and more specifically in some aspects of the 'reformation of manners' just described. The historiography of the 'commonwealth' movement is long-standing, of course, and has tended to emphasise aspects of novel intervention during the sixteenth century to address poverty, un- or under-employment, the impact of disease or economic change as manifest in the countryside in shifts from agrarian to pastoral systems (and enclosure) and in towns as expressed in types of urban decline.[11] More recently, the language of commonwealth as applied in circles around the crown has been discussed by John Watts in his paper on '"Common Weal" and "Commonwealth"' suggesting a situation with roots in the fifteenth century in which this new sense of responsibility might attach to aspects of community and individual conduct and morality.[12] This needs to be read in parallel with the understanding we have from, for example, Gerald Harriss, of the heightened understanding of royal rights and responsibilities seen in government from the late fifteenth century, and which he perhaps a little negatively described as 'arid Tudor legalism', bringing an enhanced sense of system and momentum to the nexus of government power.[13] Equally, however, this context of state-building has been presented as the creation of the state from the bottom up, as particularly espoused by Steve Hindle, as communities sought validation for their efforts to resolve disputes and address questions of resource-raising and control, but also for our purposes in particular to reform manners.[14] In the same spirit, developments as seismic as the Henrician reformation and within it the dissolution of the monasteries and consequent redistribution of wealth can now convincingly be seen not as the universally unpopular intervention of a powerful central state in the face of massive popular resistance, but as being successfully negotiated between a variety of actors, most of them local and many of them outside the conventional elite.[15] That 'reformation of manners' might have been particularly targeted at some elements of the poor, but it was not necessarily so, and Ingram and others have highlighted the extent to which in London and other cities in might produce a clash between a reforming group and some elite individuals or groups whose behaviour could now be categorised as unacceptable and challenged. Ingram notices, in particular, the tension between those associated with the court and court morality and a civic grouping who were increasingly willing to denounce and act against what they saw as disorder and immorality.[16] Once again, in this study, it will be in our consideration of the structures of regulation in particular, in chapter 1, that we will examine the possibility that either an increasingly assertive central state, or one growing at local instance, was part of a challenge to previously widespread mistress-keeping and bastard-bearing among the elite. It will also be possible to test whether 'wronged' partners were willing to use 'state' mechanisms to challenge immorality, or whether that behaviour was either tolerated or dealt with by other means – a subject addressed in chapter 5.

More obviously, but perhaps misleadingly if considered in isolation, this is a topic which has been considered in a religious context. The period under scrutiny here is one of dramatic religious transformation, and these centuries' reformations – whether towards Protestantism, and then in the search for further reformation in a Protestant vein, or under Catholicism as part of a reaction to Reformation that might take the form of reform or retrenchment – were ones which saw an increased religious focus on the regulation of personal behaviour and especially on challenges to sexual immorality. English Protestantism soon took on a distinct flavour of condemnation of personal sexual immorality, perhaps because of the importance of its roots in the attack on monasticism and the way this was initially framed, certain elements of anticlericalism, and the heightened atmosphere of preaching on the theme in the royal court late in Henry VIII's reign and under Edward VI. In England, the Protestant Reformation emphasis on the value of marriage was complemented by a denunciation of adultery, so in the translation of Heinrich Bullinger's work on marriage, as *The Christen State of Matrimony* in 1543, Thomas Becon added a preface on whoredom, adultery, and fornication. Elements were then reworked into the 1547 homily of whoredom and uncleanness.[17] Largely in response, English Catholicism was not slow to identify personal sexual immorality as one of clearest signs of hypocrisy and incoherence in the challenge it had been facing, and therefore to prioritise its own position as a virtuous alternative.[18] It will be argued through in this book, beginning in chapter 1, that the particular definition of the Protestantisation initiative in the north of England in the early years of Elizabeth was shaped by a challenge to sexual immorality, and especially elite sexual immorality, just as it was by a challenge to continuing Catholic religious practice, for example.

A further context for this study is the history of sexuality and gender, especially the debates that have taken place about the early modern view of the male as the sexually active party, but the woman as predominantly culpable, and defined by transgression. This applies whether woman is seen as primarily defined by transgression, as Laura Gowing would argue, in terms closer to a simple sexual double standard, or in a less stark sense as Bernard Capp has proposed, in a world in which male culpability might also be established and debated.[19] During our period in the north of England, as elsewhere, women were seen as strongly inclined to sexual activity but issues of reputation and sanctions were undoubtedly also questions for men, and in some case *more* a matter for men than for women, as will be explored in the discussions of the regulatory and jurisdictional frameworks and patterns of enforcement in chapter 1, and the patterns of male and female behaviour and experience in mistress-keeping and bastard-bearing in chapters 2 and 3. In the case of the male and female elite, these issues interacted powerfully with ideas of gendered individual and social responsibility and power, for those involved might not only act as male and female heads of households but also hold positions which involved them in relationships with wider groups of family members, servants (both gentle and menial), and other dependants and associates. Relative historiographical consensus has emerged since 2010 around a view of early modern manhood or masculinity as being related to sexual potency and dominance, but within complex bounds that meant that illicit sex was unlikely to be something which could be too widely acknowledged if honour and reputation were to be maintained.[20] Widespread and relatively overt mistress-keeping and acknowledgement of bastard offspring by the gentry and nobility of the north potentially stands in tension to this consensus view of early modern manhood and therefore warrants investigation. It is a particular theme of chapters 2 and 3. Gendered attributes such as the furtherance of lineage, property and honour can be posited as social aspects of paternity, yet it might be argued that becoming a father was the ultimate physiological expression of manhood. Some contemporary medical textbooks claimed a direct link between the male reproductive system and virility. Writing in the late sixteenth century, the anatomist and surgeon John Banister argued 'the substaunce of the Testicle, by his insited facultie, addeth vnto the bloud, and spirite, conteined in his vessels, the perfect Nature of seede. And this force, in men, is the cause of strength and manhode, and in women (if so we may say) of womanhode.'[21] The personal had implications for the social and political sphere. For King Henry VIII, being capable of fathering a healthy (male) child was a matter of national political well-being as well as a demonstration of his own personal strength. It is striking that at the trial of George Boleyn in 1536, it was alleged that his wife, Lady Rochford, was the centre of gossip which alluded to Henry VIII's lack of sexual prowess, that he 'nestoit habile en cas de soy copuler avec femme, et quil navoit ne vertu ne puissance.'[22] Ironically, four years after Boleyn's execution, Henry claimed that he was unable to consummate his marriage to Anne of Cleves. In conference with his doctors, the King shifted responsibility for his impotence to Anne, blaming the 'loathsomeness' of her appearance and emphasising that he 'thought himself able to the act with other but not with her'.[23] That sixteenth- and seventeenth-century medical authors examined the possible causes of male impotence without considering the physical imperfection of the female partner suggests that the King sought to protect the image of his own health as well as that of the body politic.[24] For the nobility and gentry, the idea that sexual immorality and potential siring of illegitimate children signified a failure of self-control stood at odds with their desire to present themselves as strong, virile and commanding. In her examination of Lord Herbert of Cherbury's autobiography, Christine Jackson acknowledges this tension. She identifies how Herbert's 'apologetic presentation of his marital infidelity appears cathartic and confessional in purpose, albeit a subconscious desire to affirm his sexual virility and attractiveness to women cannot be discounted.'[25] In a passage redolent of Henry VIII's justification one hundred years earlier, Herbert was able to blame his wife for his adultery when posted abroad, while emphasising his own version of masculine self-discipline. 'As my wife refused to come over and my Temptations were greate I hope the faults I committed were more pardonable; Howsoeuer I can say truly that whether in France or England I was never in Bawdyhouse nor vsed my pleasures intemperatly and much lesse did accompany them with that dissimulation and falshood which is comonly found in men addicted to love women.' He went on to claim 'if I transgressed sometimes in this Kynde It was to avoyde a greater ill, as abhorring any thing that was against Nature'.[26] Herbert was therefore able to construct his own behaviour within a frame which included unconventional sexual relationships, which were for him in some way legitimate and even contributed to his sense of manhood and masculinity, in the effectiveness of the sexual acts at their heart but also the ways in which they demonstrated avoidance of what he could describe as falsehood and unnatural activity. This understanding of elite masculinity is an important one when making sense of our evidence.

Patricia Crawford has also explored the idea that 'illicit paternity was an uneasy point where private or secret sexual relations intersected with public social relations … If the alleged father were already married his honour involved maintaining a boundary between his household and the world.'[27] This may be true to a point in some cases, but in many of the cases we have examined in the north there seems to have been a more nuanced situation than simple binaries of married monogamy equalling public acceptability versus extra-marital procreation equating to secretive affairs. Chapters 2 and 3 explore the ways in which mistresses were often more than marginal and victimised figures in a secretive isolation, and chapter 6 attemps to chart the experience of illegitimate sons and daughters in the ways in which they were accommodated within the legal and financial structures of family life and in many cases as active and visible participants in local and regional society. As Crawford has pointed out, paternity within marriage was discussed contemporaneously, with parenthood contrasting with childlessness, which was viewed as emasculating.[28] From the paternal point of view, it could be argued that lineage begotten within wedlock was an act of familial assertion; that begotten without wedlock, of self-assertion and of the assertion of alternative associations. The situation of noble- and gentlewomen who took lovers, or who were suspected of doing so, is explored in chapter 4, highlighting a far greater prevalence of illicit behaviour than might have been expected, revealing the degree of agency which existed for women within these gendered norms of sexual conduct and allowing us to address questions of the reactions this elicited, as well as the issues of regulation and more formal control already addressed and to be considered here. The scope of female honour ran far wider than simply the sphere of chaste self-control, meaning that there was more space for women and their connections to understand other relationships than might otherwise have been expected.[29]

This is also a story with other contexts, including those defined by historians of the family, who have in many cases seen the late medieval and early modern periods as ones of a major transition. While at the start the family was clearly still an extensive formation with at its core a marriage made around alliances representing family and especially landed power, most historians have seen it becoming, by the end of the seventeenth century, a more focused unit with a central role for an affective relationship between man and wife formed and maintained through love. While some such as Lawrence Stone were keen to argue for the significance of change over continuity, others such as Ralph Houlbrooke were more confident that strong elements of affective relationships were already present at the start of the period and became stronger.[30] The place of a mistress or mistresses, or lover(s) taken by a married woman, in such a setting can only suggest extreme and unusual disfunction of a marital model based on affection (especially in the latter formulation). Their presence on an extensive level would question major parts of the theory, and this will be something the discussion of the extent of mistress-keeping, and responses to it, especially in chapter 5 on the 'wronged partner' in the marriage will address.[31]

In all of these major historiographical contexts there has been a tendency to disregard the elite when exploring the continuing significance of illegitimate relationships and bastard-bearing; these debates have tended to be conducted in a way which places less emphasis on regional variation, with a more or less explicit assumption that national patterns of behaviour and attitudes were at work. Given the subject matter here, it is important, therefore, to foreground other, less directly specific, contexts for the study.

Among those other contexts which must be kept in mind are those relating to the historiography of the gentry and nobility, and the environments in which they lived, notably at court and in their localities. The first of these is discussion of the culture and politics of the court and the extent to which this is seen as distinct from the world of the 'country', as refracted through the particular prism of sexual activity which is the subject here.[32] One of the most immediate challenges raised by this project is the degree to which these cannot be seen as two separate worlds but as environments which overlapped and where attitudes and behaviours were always in a complex dialogue. No courtier lived exclusively within a court environment; even the city of London, for example, provided a contrasting moral sphere in which a courtier might operate at various points through the fifteenth, sixteenth and seventeenth centuries. A country home in perhaps Essex or Kent, or Yorkshire or Cheshire, too, represented a different moral setting in which to conduct him or herself. However abstract, in some contexts, might appear the ideas of courtly love by which courtiers seemed to be bound, the variety of settings in which they found themselves may well have given the opportunity for a freer range of interpretations of those 'rules'. There was evidently substance to the allegations of adultery made against Elizabeth Brooke, wife of the courtier and poet Thomas Wyatt. Wyatt's own long-term mistress, Elizabeth Darrell, was the servant of the marchioness of Dorset and then a maid of honour to Catherine of Aragon, and Wyatt established her at Allington Castle in Kent after separating from Brooke, with the relationship producing three children.[33] The culture of courtly love which pervaded the court of Henry VIII and which has formed the basis for so much of the discussion of the politics of the court of Elizabeth I has been controversially seen as associated with sexual activity at court, and it is important to understand how far it was of a piece with a world in which courtiers away from court kept mistresses and took lovers and were associated with adultery and fornication – but this is rarely addressed in the debate on life and politics at court.[34] Equally, those cultures defined by Paul Hammer in studies of Elizabeth's court, or in literary court cultures which were especially strong during the Elizabethan and Stuart periods as discussed by Johanna Rickman, might have had relevance in courtiers' activity away from London.[35] The courts of the archdeaconry of Buckingham in the final quarter of the fifteenth century handled allegations of adultery affecting senior gentlemen where it appears that court connections led to particular caution being exercised: in one case, care was necessary given the connections and protection being given to Sir Roger Dynham, brother of Henry VII's Lord Treasurer John, Lord Dynham. He was one of the most astute political survivors of the period, and Sir Roger was allegedly involved with the wife of one of his own servants.[36] Two other men who were active at court and particularly close to the king also demonstrate these issues: Matthew Baker had been with Henry in exile in Brittany and was trusted to guide him on his perilous escape to France, becoming an esquire for the body early in the reign. Indictments in King's Bench then show him keeping whores and bawds within the Palace of Westminster; in his will he left £20 and two feather beds to one Joan dwelling at Kenilworth, where he had established himself from early in the reign, 'and the childe she goth with all'.[37] An indication of the level of the king's trust in Baker was his appointment as captain of the strategically important island of Jersey in 1486. One of Baker's successors in that posting was Sir Hugh Vaughan, who like him had been in exile in Brittany with the king, and who was quickly appointed a gentleman usher and esquire of the body. Vaughan was misliked by many in the island, not least for a reputation for debauchery, which was seen to rest on his trust in the king's personal friendship: 'se confiant par trop en la faveur que le Roy luy portoit, s'oublia luy-mesme, s'abandonnant trop à son plaisir et s'adonnant à pailliardise et dissolution, il devint si débauché qu'il prenoit communément les jeunes filles par force, ensorte qu'elles n'ôsoient aller seulles par les chemins de peur de luy.'[38] Even the king's astrologer, William Parron, notorious for his inaccurately rosy predictions of the futures of the ill-fated Queen Elizabeth and Prince Arthur, was also part of the elite sexual moral climate at odds with the context in which he lived much of his life, facing action by the London court of aldermen, ignoring it, and eventually being imprisoned.[39] A better understanding of elite sexual cultures in the provinces will help us to understand the nature of sexual cultures and politics at court, and their interconnectedness.

Given that, there are also important contexts for this study in the historiography of gentry and noble society in the localities. Ever since the 1960s, most historians have built their view of the workings of local society from component elements made up of the family connections of the gentry, especially marriage alliances. This approach was pioneered by Alan Everitt in the 1950s: he saw Kent as an archetypal example of a 'partially independent county-state' built on strong relations between families with local connections and disntinguished by remarkably high levels of endogamy – what he called 'intense inbreeding and family feeling'. The assumption within this model is that the pattern of marriage was one which reinforced connections between families and enhanced their capacity to rely upon one another. At its historiographical high-point, this enabled an argument about the influence of what John Morrill called the 'mere country', epitomised by William Davenport of Bramall Hall in Cheshire and his fellows, as a driving force in the revisionist account of the outbreak of the English Civil War and the course followed by those conflicts through to Restoration and beyond.[40] This understanding of local society has been extended into the earlier part of the period and the later middle ages, notably through the work of Michael J. Bennett.[41] If this approach has been questioned, challenges in the earlier part of our period have been through an attempt to reassert the continuing power of lordship as a connective in society across administrative boundaries – and this has not necessarily been a tendency which has been any less prone to rely on marital alliances in understanding how lordship might have secured links between families.[42] This study is therefore once again at a pivotal point in that historiography: if we are to understand local societies' growing coherence at least in part as based on marital alliances, the extent to which these might be undermined by other relationships, or exist alongside them, needs to be considered. Such bonds – and possible tensions – are a theme in chapter 6, where the role of illegitimate offspring is discussed, and in chapters 2 to 5, which consider the impact of the role of mistress-keeping and the reactions of 'wronged' wives and husbands and their kin.

These were also local societies which, it has been argued, were shifting from being based on codes of honour to cohering more around the values of a 'civil' society and moralisation of politics. As espoused for the north of England with particular relevance to the sixteenth century by Mervyn James, this thesis might suggest that whatever role had existed for illegitimate relationships among the gentry and nobility would be reduced or eliminated, as part of a parallel modernisation narrative to those of the affective marriage.[43] The societies described in these studies were ones which have been described as experiencing disruptive changes in their political culture, especially in the eyes of historians who understand the period as one of a fundamental and relatively rapid socio-economic shift away from the regional dominance of a powerful nobility and their associates among the gentry, previously used to acting with relative impunity as the agents of a monarchy with no alternative allies there and with no meaningful competitors for power in the shape of an urban or other middle class. This disruption manifested itself most acutely in the rebellions of the sixteenth century, the Lincolnshire Rising and the Pilgrimage of Grace in 1536–37, and the Northern Rebellion of 1569, as the disciplines of civil society began to make themselves felt. Amid the cultures of honour which had governed northern society previously, it was argued by James and others, were codes of sexual behaviour which permitted the keeping of mistresses. This was a culture of 'virtue', in the sense of the unswerving exercise of the will, emphasising male autonomy asserted towards fate, significantly often imagined in female form. It was a world in which 'Men of honour could (and did) … seduce, and commit adultery, without incurring dishonour'. It was to be replaced by one with a tighter regulation of personal behaviours, under the guise of civility, Protestant religion and morality. It has been suggested by Richard Cust and others that the pattern of change identified by James is too stark, with a more complex understanding of honour required, which might allow for it reinforcing community and defusing tension; but these writers still tend to emphasise the growing incompatibility of 'lechery, incontinence, whoremongering and being cuckolded' with the capacity, right and responsibility to govern.[44] Once again, the testing of assumptions about the prevalence of mistress-keeping and bastard-bearing among the elite will allow for questions to be raised about these historiographies on the nature of regional political cultures in the north during the early modern period.

This book is, therefore, a study of far more than simply the regulation of illegitimate relationships and the children they produced. But, since it was the attempt to describe this behaviour, to define its limits, to proscribe it, to control it and to punish those who engaged in it which is so important in the way it was imagined at the time and in the way it is relevant to us in our consideration of these major debates on the late medieval and early modern past, it is with this that the book begins.

Notes

1 Peter Laslett, 'Long-term Trends in Bastardy in England', in *Family Life and Illicit Love in Earlier Generations: Essays in Historical Sociology* (repr. with corrections, Cambridge: Cambridge University Press, 1980), pp. 102–59; Peter Laslett, Karla Oosterveen and Richard M. Smith (eds), *Bastardy and its Comparative History: Studies in the History of Illegitimacy and Marital Nonconformism in Britain, France, Germany, Sweden, North America, Jamaica and Japan* (London: Edward Arnold for the Cambridge Group for the History of Population and Social Structure, 1980), Part I: Britain, esp. David Levine and Keith Wrightson, 'The Social Context of Illegitimacy in Early Modern England', pp. 158–75, at p. 163; Richard Adair, *Courtship, Illegitimacy and Marriage in Early Modern England* (Manchester: Manchester University Press, 1996).

2 E.g. Felicity Heal and Clive Holmes, *The Gentry in England and Wales, 1500–1700* (Basingstoke: Macmillan, 1994); M. L. Bush, *The European Nobility*, 2 vols. (Manchester: Manchester University Press, 1983–88). There are brief treatments of the situation in the nobility in T. H. Hollingsworth, 'The Demography of the English Peerage', supplement to *Population Studies*, 18 (1964), 47–49; Barbara J. Harris, *English Aristocratic Women, 1450–1550: Marriage and Family, Property and Careers* (Oxford: Oxford University Press, 2002); Michael Hicks, 'Heirs and Non-Heirs: Perceptions and Realities amongst the English Nobility, c. 1300–1500', in Frédérique Lachaud and Michael Penman (eds), *Making and Breaking the Rules: Succession in Medieval Europe, c. 1000–c. 1600* (Turnhout, Belgium: Brepols, 2008), pp. 191–200. It should be noted that this study is not concerned with one category identified by Hicks, the inadvertently illegitimate relationships and offspring of partners who discovered, too late, that their relationship fell within the prohibited degrees of consanguinity.

3 Lawrence Stone, *The Family, Sex and Marriage in England, 1500–1800* (Weidenfeld & Nicolson, 1977); Ralph A. Houlbrooke, *The English Family, 1450–1700* (London, New York: Longman, 1984). The latter shares the common concern with illegitimacy associated with non-elite courtship customs, and hence as evidence for freedom of courtship (pp. 82–3, 88), while briefly mentioning adultery among the peerage at pp. 116–17.

4 Keith Thomas, 'The Double Standard', *Journal of the History of Ideas*, 20 (1959), 195–216, esp. p. 196; Bernard Capp, 'The Double Standard Revisited: Plebeian Women and Male Sexual Reputation in Early Modern England', *Past & Present*, 162 (1999), 70–100.

5 Harris, *English Aristocratic Women*, pp. 84–6; Laura Gowing, 'Ordering the Body: Illegitimacy and Female Authority in Seventeenth-Century England', in Michael J. Braddick and John Walter (eds), *Negotiating Power in Early Modern Society: Order, Hierarchy and Subordination in Britain and Ireland* (Cambridge: Cambridge University Press, 2001), pp. 43–62, 255–7.

6 Chris Given-Wilson and Alice Curteis, *The Royal Bastards of Medieval England* (London: Routledge & Kegan Paul, 1984); Beverley A. Murphy, *Bastard Prince: Henry VIII's Lost Son* (Stroud: Sutton, 2001); Johanna Rickman, *Love, Lust, and License in Early Modern England: Illicit Sex and the Nobility* (Aldershot: Ashgate, 2008).

7 E. A. Wrigley and R. S. Schofield, *The Population History of England, 1541–1871: A Reconstruction* (London: Edward Arnold for the Cambridge Group for the History of Population and Social Structure, 1981); John Hatcher, 'Understanding the Population History of England 1450–1750', *Past & Present*, 180 (2003), 83–130; Keith Wrightson, *English Society, 1580–1680* (London: Routledge, 1982), esp. pp. 84–6, 140–2, 145–6.

8 Wrightson, *English Society*, p. 84.

9 Deborah Youngs, *The Life Cycle in Western Europe, c. 1300–c. 1500* (Manchester: Manchester University Press, 2006), pp. 107–8; Nicholas Orme, *From Childhood to Chivalry: The Education of the English Kings and Aristocracy 1066–1530* (London, New York: Methuen, 1984), pp. 44–60; Harris, *English Aristocratic Women*, pp. 39–41.

10 Martin Ingram, *Carnal Knowledge: Regulating Sex in England, 1470–1600* (Cambridge: Cambridge University Press, 2017); also, for example, Marjorie Keniston McIntosh, *Controlling Misbehavior in England, 1370–1600* (Cambridge: Cambridge University Press, 1998); Shannon McSheffrey, *Marriage, Sex, and Civic Culture in Late Medieval London* (Philadelphia: University of Pennsylvania Press, 2006).

11 Whitney R. D. Jones, *The Tudor Commonwealth, 1529–1559: A Study of the Impact of the Social and Economic Developments of Mid-Tudor England upon Contemporary Concepts of the Nature and Duties*

of the Commonwealth (London: Athlone Press, 1970); J. J. Scarisbrick, 'Wolsey and the Common Weal', in E. W. Ives, Robert J. Knecht and J. J. Scarisbrick (eds), *Wealth and Power in Tudor England: Essays Presented to S. T. Bindoff* (London, Atlantic Highlands, NJ: Athlone Press, 1978), pp. 45–67; G. R. Elton, *Reform and Renewal: Thomas Cromwell and the Common Weal* (Cambridge: Cambridge University Press, 1973).

12 '"Common Weal" and "Commonwealth": England's Monarchical Republic in the Making', in Andrea Gamberini, Jean-Philippe Genet and Andrea Zorzi (eds), *The Languages of Political Society: Western Europe, 14th–17th Centuries* (Rome: Viella Libreria Editrice, 2012), pp. 147–63.

13 Gerald Harriss, 'Political Society and the Growth of Government in Late Medieval England', *Past & Present*, 138 (1993), 28–57.

14 Steve Hindle, *The State and Social Change in Early Modern England, c. 1550–1640* (Basingstoke: Palgrave, 2000); *On the Parish? The Micro-Politics of Poor Relief in Rural England, c. 1550–1750* (Oxford: Clarendon Press, 2004).

15 Ethan Shagan, *Popular Politics and the English Reformation* (Cambridge: Cambridge University Press, 2003), esp. parts II and III.

16 Ingram, *Carnal Knowledge*, pp. 292–302, for the intense and broadly-focused moral enforcement campaign of the late 1540s and early 1550s in London.

17 *The Christen State of Matrimony: Moost Necessary [and] Profitable for all the[m], that Entend to Liue Quietly and Godlye in the Christe[n] State of Holy Wedlock Newly set Forth in Englyshe* (London: printed in the house of John[n], Mayler for John[n] Gough, '1546' [i.e. 1543]); *Certain Sermons or Homilies (1547): And, A Homily against Disobedience and Wilful Rebellion (1570): A Critical Edition*, ed. Ronald B. Bond (Toronto: University of Toronto Press, 1987); Ingram, *Carnal Knowledge*, pp. 268–70; Ian W. Archer, *The Pursuit of Stability: Social Relations in Elizabethan London* (Cambridge: Cambridge University Press, 1991), pp. 251–3.

18 The language of whoredom was almost immediately associated with Anne Boleyn, and sexual immorality with the bishops who associated with her: G. W. Bernard, *Anne Boleyn: Fatal Attractions* (New Haven CT, London: Yale University Press, 2010), pp. 184–8. For the situation under Mary: Ingram, *Carnal Knowledge*, pp. 271–2.

19 Laura Gowing, *Domestic Dangers: Women, Words and Sex in Early Modern London* (Oxford: Clarendon Press, 1996); Capp, 'Double Standard Revisited'.

20 Originating in particular with Elizabeth A. Foyster, *Manhood in Early Modern England: Honour, Sex and Marriage* (London, Harlow: Longman, 1999); and Alexandra Shepard, *Meanings of Manhood in Early Modern England* (Cambridge: Cambridge University Press, 2003).

21 John Banister, *The Historie of Man Sucked from the Sappe of the most Approued Anathomistes, in this Present Age, Compiled in Most Compendious Fourme, and Now Published in English, for the Vtilitie of all Godly Chirurgians, within this Realme* (London: printed by Iohn Daye, 1578), fo. 87v.

22 ['is not capable of copulating with women, and that he has neither the strength nor the staying power for it'] *LP* x. 908; David Starkey, *Six Wives: The Queens of Henry VIII* (London: Vintage, 2004), p. 580; G. W. Bernard, *Anne Boleyn: Fatal Attractions* (New Haven CT, London: Yale University Press, 2010), p. 168.

23 Anne's pre-contract with the duke of Lorraine was also referenced. *LP* xv. 850; Starkey, *Six Wives*, p. 632.

24 See Eucharius Roeslin, *The Byrth of Mankynde, Newly Translated out of Laten into Englysshe. In the Which is Entreated of all suche Thynges the which Chaunce to Women in theyr Labor, and all suche Infyrmitees whiche Happen vnto the Infants after they be Delyuered. And also at the Latter Ende or in*

the Thyrde or Last Boke is Entreated of the Conception of Mankynde, and Howe Manye Ways it may be Letted or Furtheryd, with Diuers other Fruytefull Thynges, as doth Appere in the Table before the Booke, translated from Latin by Richard Jonas (London: printed by LR, 1540), fo. lxxxii: 'maye there be defecte and lacke in the man as yf the seade be over hote ... or to cold & others whyche shall not nede here to be rehearsed'; Ambroise Paré, *The Workes of that Famous Chirurgion Ambrose Parey Translated out of Latine and Compared with the French. by Th: Johnson* (London: printed by Th: Cotes and R. Young, 1634), also suggests problems with the condition of the seed, physical injury or illness and 'defects or imperfections of the yard', including how to diagnose a 'palsie'.

25 Christine Jackson, 'Memory and the Construction and Experience of Elite Masculinity in the Seventeenth-Century Autobiography of Lord Herbert of Cherbury', *Gender & History*, 25(1) (2013), 107–31.

26 *Ibid.*, p. 101.

27 P. Crawford, *Blood, Bodies and Families in Early Modern England* (London: Routledge, 2014), pp. 124–8.

28 *Ibid.*, p. 114.

29 Compare the approaches to understanding female honour in Phillipa Maddern, 'Honour among the Pastons: Gender and Integrity in Fifteenth-Century English Provincial Society', *Journal of Medieval History*, 14 (1988), 357–71; Felicity Heal, 'Reputation and Honour in Court and Country', *Transactions of the Royal Historical Society*, 6th ser., 6 (1996), 161–78; Linda A. Pollock, 'Honor, Gender and Reconciliation in Elite Culture, 1570–1700', *Journal of British Studies*, 46 (2007), 3–29, at pp. 21–6.

30 Stone, *Family, Sex and Marriage*; Houlbrooke, *English Family*.

31 In Houlbrooke's account, for example, it is notable that it is particularly to matches hastily made through love, or at least physical infatuation, that the acts of 'the very small minority of married people [who] broke their bonds' are ascribed: *English Family*, pp. 114–15.

32 This is a hugely influential historiography originating in the work of Norbert Elias on court society. The court as a focus for the control of the aristocratic behaviours through processes of self-constraint, emphasising particularly the control of physical violence through its channeling into codes of etiquette and conduct of e.g. duelling, might apply equally to previously untrammeled expression of aristocratic sexual appetites: *Die höfische Gesellschaft: Untersuchungen zur Soziologie des Königtums und der höfischen Aristokratie* (Neuwied: Luchterhand, 1969). This underpins key English historiography from David Starkey *et al.* (eds), *The English Court: From the Wars of the Roses to the English Civil War* (London: Longman, 1987).

33 Susan Brigden, *Thomas Wyatt: The Heart's Forest* (London: Faber and Faber, 2012), p. 495; Kenneth Muir, *Life and Letters of Sir Thomas Wyatt* (Liverpool: Liverpool University Press, 1963), pp. 3, 37, 41, 83ff, 95, 177, 209, 211.

34 E. W. Ives, *The Life and Death of Anne Boleyn: 'The Most Happy'* (Malden MA, Oxford: Blackwell, 2005), esp. pp. 20–2, 68–72; Retha M. Warnicke, 'The Conventions of Courtly Love and Anne Boleyn', in Charles Carlton, Robert L. Woods, Mary L. Robertson and Joseph S. Block (eds), *State, Sovereigns and Society in Early Modern English History: Essays in Honour of A. J. Slavin* (Stroud: Sutton, 1998), pp. 103–18; Bernard, *Anne Boleyn: Fatal Attractions*; Retha M. Warnicke, *The Rise and Fall of Anne Boleyn: Family Politics at the Court of Henry VIII* (New York: Cambridge University Press, 1989); Greg Walker, 'Rethinking the Fall of Anne Boleyn', *Historical Journal*, 45 (2002), 1–29.

35 Paul E. J. Hammer, 'Sex and the Virgin Queen: Aristocratic Concupiscence and the Court of Elizabeth I', *Sixteenth Century Journal*, 31 (2000), 77–97; Rickman, *Love, Lust, and License*.

36 *The Courts of the Archdeaconry of Buckingham 1483–1523*, ed. E. M. Elvey, Buckinghamshire Record Society, 19 (1975), no. 94; noted by Ingram, *Carnal Knowledge*, pp. 105–6.

37 Polydore Vergil, *Anglica Historia*, ed. Denys Hay, Camden Society, 3rd ser., 74 (1950), p. 198; S. J. Gunn 'The Courtiers of Henry VII', *EHR*, 108 (1993), 23–49, at p. 37; C. S. L. Davies, 'Richard III, Henry VII and the Island of Jersey', *The Ricardian*, 9 (1991–94), 334–42; Ingram, *Carnal Knowledge*, p. 153.

38 ['trusting too much in the king's favour, forgot himself, abandoning himself too much to pleasure and indulging in sexual immorality and dissolute behaviour, he became so debauched that he commonly took girls by force, such that that they did not travel the roads alone for fear of him'] *Materials for a History of the Reign of Henry VII.*, ed. William Campbell (2 vols. London: Longman & Co., 1873–77), i. 320; *Chroniques, des îles de Jersey, Guernesey, Auregny, et Serk: auquel on a ajouté un abrégé historique des dites îles*, ed. George S. Syvret (Guernsey: Thomas James Mauger, 1832), ch 19, p. 42; Gunn, 'Courtiers', pp. 37–8.

39 C. A. J. Armstrong, 'An Italian Astrologer at the Court of Henry VII, in E. F. Jacob (ed.), *Italian Renaissance Studies: A Tribute to the late C. M. Ady* (London: Faber and Faber, 1960), pp. 433–54; Ingram, *Carnal Knowledge*, p. 226. S. McSheffrey, 'Men and Masculinity in Late Medieval London Civic Culture: Governance, Patriarchy and Reputation', in J. Murray (ed.), *Conflicted Identities and Multiple Masculinities: Men in the Medieval West* (New York, 1999), p. 262. See also the behaviour and condemnation of court physicians William Hobbys and Lewis of Caerleon, the latter of whom shared astrological interests with Parron: McSheffrey, *Marriage, Sex, and Civic Culture*, pp. 166–73, 182.

40 Alan Everitt, *The Community of Kent and the Great Rebellion, 1640–60* (Leicester: Leicester University Press, 1966), pp. 13, 15, 42–3, 328; Peter Clark, *English Provincial Society from the Reformation to the Revolution: Religion, Politics, and Society in Kent, 1500–1640* (Hassocks: Harvester Press, 1977), esp. pp. 118–32. J. S. Morrill, *The Revolt of the Provinces: Conservatives and Radicals in the English Civil War, 1630–1650* (London, New York: Allen and Unwin; Barnes & Noble, 1976), esp. pp. 19–51; Anthony Fletcher, *Reform in the Provinces: The Government of Stuart England* (New Haven CT, London: Yale University Press, 1986), e.g. p. 368: 'Localism ... mastered and subsumed by the country gentry for the purposes of government'.

41 Michael J. Bennett, 'A County Community: Social Cohesion amongst the Cheshire Gentry, 1400–25', *Northern History*, 8 (1973), 24–44; *Community, Class, and Careerism: Cheshire and Lancashire Society in the Age of Gawain and the Green Knight* (Cambridge: Cambridge University Press, 1983).

42 For example in the challenges to these arguments made by Christine Carpenter, in *Locality and Polity: A Study of Warwickshire Landed Society, 1401–1499* (Cambridge: Cambridge University Press, 1992); esp. ch. 17 'Conclusions'.

43 Esp. Mervyn James, *English Politics and the Concept of Honour, 1485–1642* (Past & Present Supplement, 3) (Oxford: Past & Present Society, 1978), esp. pp. 28, 59–60, reprinted in *Society, Politics and Culture: Studies in Early Modern England* (Cambridge: Cambridge University Press, 1986), pp. 308–415. Note the prominence in these accounts of Henry Medwall's *Fulgens and Lucrece*, in which (it is argued) virtuous humanist is preferred to debauched nobleman.

44 Richard Cust, 'Honour and Politics in Early Stuart England: The Case of Beaumont v Hastings', *Past & Present*, 149 (1995), 57–94, esp. pp. 92–4; Pollock, 'Honor, Gender and Reconciliation'; William Palmer, 'Scenes from Provincial Life: History, Honor, and Meaning in the Tudor North',

Renaissance Quarterly, 53 (2000), 425–48; Brendan Kane, *The Politics and Culture of Honour in Britain and Ireland, 1541–1641* (Cambridge: Cambridge University Press, 2010); Raoul Fievet, 'L'ambivalence de l'honneur dans l'Angleterre de la fin du Moyen Âge: une force compétitive ou modératrice?' *Médiévales*, 70 (2016), 215–32. See also the emphasis of R. W. Hoyle, 'Faction, Feud and Reconciliation amongst the Northern English Nobility, 1525–1569', *History*, 84 (1999), 590–613, on frequent small disputes and attempts to arbitrate them, rather than large-scale, more extreme and uncontrolled violence.

1

Background and legal framework

'[I]T IS NOT (AS I do take it) to be lightly regarded, yt we have in so short a time so many examples of those that have entered upon that libertie in these parts of ours more I think … than any where els in al England … in which case the censure of the Church is drawn forth against them to their own reformation and example of others.'[1] Thus Edmund Bunny, the rector of Bolton Percy in 1595, referred to the incidence of adultery-driven divorce followed by remarriage in Yorkshire during the late sixteenth century. His subsequent discussion of doctrinal arguments was informed by thinkers such as Calvin, Bucer and Erasmus and reflected Protestant debates centred upon the dissolution (or not) of marriage bonds. Such debates had been given political significance in England by the matrimonial difficulties of Henry VIII, but arguably the pace of religious change, in terms of reforms to ritual and the suppression of monasticism, for example, have masked the fact that throughout the sixteenth and early seventeenth centuries canon law in relation to adultery and marriage remained conservative.[2] Essentially, the legal position in 1630 was the same as it had been in 1530, and hence as it had been a hundred years before that. The definitions of adultery and fornication, and the treatment of their consequences remained the same. Efforts to reform canon law with specific implications for sexual immorality made no progress in the middle years of the sixteenth century, and suggestions that the criminal law might be brought into play, for example in making adultery a secular crime punishable by death, were similarly unsuccessful.[3] And yet in the north of England the phenomena represented by sexual relationships of the elite outside the conventional bounds of marriage and the offspring that resulted produced new regulatory responses in the early modern period in new and revised court structures and varying patterns of enforcement through those structures. Although the behaviour of the elite was not the sole target of this regulation, it was of leading significance; it is important to consider how elite behaviour prompted these changes, how it was shaped by them, and the other consequences of these efforts to reform elite sexual behaviour. This chapter therefore assesses some of the arguments for the way that the regulation of manners, broader questions of state-building, and more specific ones of religious change might intersect with the pattern of elite immorality and bastard-bearing during the period.

The theoretical definitions at the heart of the largely unchanging legal and judicial understanding of what constituted sexual immorality are, in their most essential aspects, relatively simple. Fornication was sexual intercourse by a man with an unmarried woman and adultery was committed with a married woman, irrespective of the marital status of the man.[4] In two Durham cases, separated by nearly a century, Robert Liddell was accused of adultery with his 'harlot' in 1532, while in 1620, John Errington was charged with adultery 'with _ the wife of _ Lawley of Symondburne', with the marital status of the woman clearly more important than any other aspect of her identity.[5] Yet, while Helmholz argues that there was a delineation between adultery and fornication, he admits that 'incontinence' was used to cover most sexual offences.[6] As Ingram has asserted, the wording used in court documents can be inconsistent, with adultery and fornication used interchangeably, along with references to living arrangements and further outrageous behaviour.[7] It was said of Ralph Elstobb in court that he 'keepeth Ann Martindell suspiciously in his house' resulting in the birth of a child.[8] The case against Michael Dixon that 'he had the use of the bodie of the wife of Sir John Smith, curat there 19 severall tymes, And that the bastard she did beare some 13 years agoe was his the said Dixons and not Henry Liddells who took to be the father thereof', did not specify adultery, fornication or bastardy at all, although the general immorality is clear.[9]

Incest cases involving blood relationships were rare, but did occur. Edward Paylor and Elizabeth Bulmer were uncle and niece cited to appear before York High Commission in 1631–32, and Anthony Huddlestone was accused of 'incontinency with Anne Latus, wief of Rauff Latus being the naturall sister of the said Anthony' and ordered to abstain from her company in 1571–72.[10] In Durham, the problem seems to have been on a similar scale, with William Orde accused of incest with his wife's sister's daughter, Agnes Mathew, in 1591, and John Collingwood summoned for incest with an unnamed partner in 1622.[11] Yet there was another, more frequently occurring, type of case which bordered between incest and matrimonial and that was marrying the sister of a deceased wife. Technically, this fell under the degrees of prohibition, but a remarkable number of gentlemen pursued such relationships, and were prepared to go to some lengths to defend them. One of the first cases heard by York High Commission in 1562 considered the allegation that

> Thomas Standish was first married to one Elizabeth Houghton ... And that he and she continued and dwelt together as man and wife by the span of two or three years ... he had carnal knowledge with her. And after her death [Thomas] was likewise married to one Margaret Houghton being her natural sister to the aforesaid Elizabeth and both born of one woman called Elizabeth Warmsley and hath continued with her as his wife by the space of four years last past or thereabouts and hath sundry children with her, whereby he hath committed the horrible crime of incest not only against God's Laws and the Laws Ecclesiastical established and set forth by ancient fathers in all Council's times and ages since the birth of Christ as well when this realm of England as in all other realms and dominions throughout all Christendom. But also against all good order and custom frequented and used when the same and specially when this realm of England and the dominions of the same to the great danger of his own soul and most perilous example of others.

Despite the attempts of Archbishop Thomas Young, this case was still in High Commission ten years later.[12] At the same time, Henry Neville, fifth earl of Westmorland faced the same charge, appearing in court to account for his marriage to Margaret, widow of Sir Henry Gascoigne – and sister of his previous wife, Jane (this being pursued with greater vigour than his paternity of his bastard daughter Margaret Watson).[13]

Apart from adultery, fornication, incest and their consequences in bastard-bearing, the church courts also sought to prosecute those who enabled or sanctioned immorality, a category of offence referred to as 'bawdry'. Two cases involved extreme examples of husbands actively encouraging their wives' liaisons with other men. William Nelson initiated a suit against his wife Frances for her adultery with Charles Barnby, only to find himself having to perform penance for bawdry. Edward Awde was prosecuted for allowing his wife Margery to dwell with Peter Maddyson, gentleman. Awde's comment in court 'that neither Bishop nor Chancellor should nor coulde call or have anything to doe with his wif so longe as he himself is not displeased therewithe and shall permit the same', could be construed as contempt.[14] More typical of this type of offence was the archdeaconry of Richmond's prosecution of Leonard Richardson in November 1577 for harbouring Margaret Whytwell and her base child by Robert Layton, gent. The court was not effective in bringing him to justice, as four years later, the archdeaconry court was still pursuing Richardson for his support of Whytwell, which it was alleged took place eleven years previously.[15] Even churchmen could be prosecuted: in October 1592 George Clerk, the vicar of Featherstone faced accusations that 'he had secretly baptised a bastard child begotten by one Paul Hamerton, gent of the body of Elizabeth Stanford alias Peniston, in one John Packington's house in Featherstone, not brought to the Church', and this was closely followed by action against Hamerton himself for fathering the child.[16]

Others aspects of definition and categorisation were inevitably more complex, however. Judicial separation or divorce *a mensa et thoro* could be granted by the ecclesiastical courts on the grounds of adultery, cruelty or heresy, but the parties could not remarry.[17] This was reinforced by *The Constitutions and Canons Ecclesiastical of the Church of England*, issued in 1604, which declared 'that the parties so separated will live chastely and continently; neither shall they, during each other's life contract matrimony with any other person.'[18] Edmund Bunny's choice to write about the incidence of adultery causing the dissolution of marriages and the dedication to Archbishop Matthew Hutton in the passage which began this chapter is significant; as chaplain to Archbishop Grindal, he had been at the centre of ecclesiastical power in the province of York, and was therefore in a unique position to comment upon the moral welfare of the north of England, knowing that, whatever the theoretical arguments, it was one of the responsibilities of the ecclesiastical courts to impose the church's authority upon the moral welfare and conduct of the local population, including the nobility and gentry.

The legal position surrounding the dissolution of a marriage might have been consistently unequivocal across the period in question, but it was difficult to sustain in reality as it left the parties free from each other while unable to form an intimate relationship with another. If the formal termination of a valid marriage in order to pursue a subsequent union was impossible, a litigant might, however, attempt to discover a reason why that marriage was invalid. A divorce *a vincula* (from the chains of matrimony) was a formal recognition that there was a pre-existing impediment to the marriage, rendering it invalid, thus enabling 'remarriage'. This might be due to the minority of the bride and/or groom, consanguinity or affinity, mental incapacity, failure to fulfil a conditional marriage contract or lack of consent (although in the latter case, consensual sex and cohabitation might validate a coerced marriage).[19] Where matrimonial litigation and immorality could collide, however, was in terms of pre-contract, and it is worth examining the law in relation to marriage formation in order to understand how one relationship might be put aside to make way for another.

While the church might prefer a process of the couple making a future (*de futuro*) promise to marry, banns read in church followed by a witnessed, consensual, ceremonial exchange of present-tense (*de praesenti*) vows in church and consummation, an unsolemnised, unwitnessed, irregular or clandestine marriage was still binding, particularly if followed by sexual intercourse. A *de futuro* promise followed by consummation also formalised the union irrespective of banns, *de praesenti* vows or church ceremony. The issue of consent was central to the validity of a marriage, but in terms of immorality litigation, the key point was whether sexual relations had taken place. An unconsummated *de futuro* arrangement could be terminated at any time with both parties free to negotiate other relationships, but the ambiguous nature of the wording of vows, absence of a formal setting or need for witnesses presented a huge legal grey area which blurred the boundaries between confused attempts at marital conformity, adultery and fornication. In terms of pre-contract, vows made *de praesenti* could not be superseded by a later marriage, but the absence of a standard series of promissory words left room for misunderstandings and litigation. An apparently straightforward case of adultery could have a more complex back-story, rooted in a belief in sexual continence. For example, when Gervase Steele was prosecuted by the church courts for immorality in 1605, it was against the background of his attempts in the York Consistory to prove that his marriage to the higher-status Yorkshire gentlewoman Margaret Savile was lawful and, as such, had been consummated.[20]

Particularly problematic were unsolemnised but consummated *de futuro* agreements that were not translated into *de praesenti* settlements, but which could provide a framework to assert matrimony on the one hand, or identify fornication on the other. These matrimonial cases could be brought by either the husband or wife as instance cases, or by the church court itself as an office case – and given that the church did not have a dedicated moral policing service, office cases depended upon presentations by ecclesiastical personnel (often churchwardens) backed up by the 'common voice and fame' of the local population and witness statements from at least two people.

In 1562–63, William Constable, a member of the extensive gentry family based in the East Riding of Yorkshire, launched a validity suit against his wife Katherine Hamerton, in which evidence was given that they had solemnised matrimony according to the Book of Common Prayer in a church and dwelt together subsequently as man and wife at bed and board. Possibly in order to pre-empt further suits, Constable proved the validity of his marriage to Hamerton, just as Matthew Usher initiated legal proceedings claiming to be her husband. However, Usher's case rested upon vague promises made in her father's kitchen at three o'clock in the morning, 'she responding sayd yea by my trouthe I love you above almen and I can well fynd in my harte to forsake al men for you and tayke you to my husband … Mathew sayd to the sayd Katherin, Katherin I am contente to tayke you to my wyf and to forsake all women for you and never to have other woman to my wyf but you and therto I plight you my trothe.'[21] The marriage publicly celebrated in church followed by cohabitation as man and wife defeated the private verbal contract, although deposition evidence given in the Usher case also points to the disapproval of Hamerton's parents which may have had a bearing upon her marriage to Constable. While the Hamerton / Constable / Usher litigation did not imply adultery, other cases tipped from matrimonial validity into immorality.

In 1575–76, the triangular relationship between Jane Roberts, Gabriel Fairfax and Henry Doughtie came under scrutiny, initially via litigation for adultery initiated by the office against Roberts (to whom Doughtie claimed to be married) and Fairfax in York High Commission.[22] However, some kind of matrimonial contract between Fairfax and Roberts was referenced in April 1577, when Henry Doughtie launched a suit for Restoration of Conjugal Rights, also in High Commission: 'he did demand restitution of the said Jane now departed from his companie and from cohabitacion with him which demand althoughe the said Commissioners did thinke to be lawfull nevertheles for the matter of matrimonie pretended betwene the said Jane and Gabriell Fairfaxe esquire', stressing that they had solemnised the marriage in church. Doughtie's Restoration of Conjugal Rights suit was a possessory action, initiated by the plaintiff in which the marriage had already been proved valid and, as such, was a method of legally forcing a wayward spouse to return to the marital home.[23]

It is rare to find pregnant gentlewomen initiating litigation in order to enforce matrimony, but in July 1610 Margaret Huntley sued Anthony Hall in the Durham Consistory. The court was told that negotiations for a marriage between Huntley and Hall had been ongoing the previous year, but in the meantime Huntley had also formed a relationship with Thomas Hudson, they

> being in love together with intent to contract mariage betwixt them them were present in this examinants house together with divers of both their frends & neighbours requested to beare witnes of the said contract when Anthonie Hall came into the house and called Margaret Huntley unto him & said if she refuse … Thomas Hudson he would taike her to his [wife] forthwith marie her whereuppon … Margaret did withdraw her love from … Thomas Hudson & after that would not afford him eyther her love or good[will].[24]

Her mother Isabella Johnson admitted that Margaret 'att this instant is great with childe', but did not specify who the father was. While the outcome of this case is unknown, the pregnancy was important here insofar as it was probably the catalyst for litigation.

In the north there were, therefore, consistently many contexts in which sexual relationships could be formed which were considered illegitimate. Some of those contexts might have produced issues that were, to a degree, accidental, but in most cases it was their restrictiveness and inflexbility which meant they prompted a purposeful effort to establish a substantial relationship which the participants knew was illegitimate. Frequently this was in situations which were unlikely in the near term to be resolved into a more legitimate form.

However consistent those legal concepts and categorisations might have been, the mechanisms by which prosecutions were attempted and the vigour with which cases were pursued varied across time and geographical location in the north of England. The ecclesiastical administration of the north of England saw much business centred upon the seat of the Northern Province at York, and the archbishop or his deputy carried out visitations. In each diocese there were consistory courts, and again a system of visitation operated. Appeals came to the York courts from those consistory courts, and from the inferior courts of the York diocese itself, as well as from Hexhamshire within Durham. Archdeaconry courts, unusually absent in most of the diocese of York, but otherwise generally important jurisdictions, also dealt with immorality in each diocese, although the number of gentry cases presented there was tiny. The exceptions in the York diocese were the important court of the archdeacon of Nottingham, and that of Richmond which was absorbed into the diocese of Chester as one of two episcopal consistory courts there after its creation.[25]

In this period the mechanisms to deal with moral questions, rather than simply issues of religious conformity, in relation to both the elite and the masses, were extended. In the Northern Province a new diocese was created in 1541, seated at Chester, and this might have helped to address issues of physical separation between the centres of ecclesiastical authority and what could previously be isolated communities, thanks to long distances and challenging topography.[26] And in this and other dioceses, Ecclesiastical Commissions and a High Commission were appointed. The approach of creating a commission made up of a mixed body of laymen and ecclesiastics with the power to arrest, impose bonds and fine the contumacious was initiated in 1543 for Lancashire very specifically to tackle adultery, to which its successor in 1550 added fornication, incest and bawdry.[27] We have a fragmentary record of the activity of the 1543 commission, relating to a sitting during June in Wigan. The business for which we have evidence is dominated by the names of prominent Lancashire gentlemen being pursued for adultery: Thomas and William Gerard of Bryn, Sir Thomas Butler of Bewsey, Gilbert Assheley gent., John Wynstanley gent., Gilbert 'Millenax' (probably a member of the Molyneux family of Sefton), William Bradshaw gent., Sir James Stanley (1486–1562; third son of George Lord Strange, younger brother of the second earl of Derby, and founder of the Bickerstaffe line[28]), and a gentleman with the surname Dilworth; as well as, possibly, one Thomas Mathew, for whom the status description is not clear.[29] The other business of the commission was limited to addressing the condition of churches of Standish, Eccles and Crofton, along with a further two or three similar cases.[30]

The actions of the 1543 Commission usually resulted in a straightforward recognisance with a requirement to put away concubines; these were specified as Margaret Warren in the case of Dilworth; one Mary in that of Butler; and one Elizabeth in Mathew's possible case. The efforts of the commissioners to resolve the wider family issues represented by a case of marriage break-down are clearest in the case of Thomas Gerard of Bryn and his wife Jane. The recognisance in their case not only required them to be friends and forget past transgressions, but included her brother Piers Legh in the bond. It further specified that Piers and his wife, and Jane, were to come to Thomas's house at Windleshaw on 3 July next 'and make merye' with Thomas, and on the morrow Thomas and Jane were to hunt and make merry with Piers at Bradley. Thomas was then to return with his wife to Bryn or wherever he pleased, and cohabit with his wife.[31]

The men addressed by the 1543 commission were some of the most prominent individuals in the area: Thomas Gerard would serve as sheriff of Lancashire in 1548, and Sir James Stanley as Marshal of Ireland. The indications were already clear, therefore, that ecclesiastical commissions would be a means of challenging mistress-keeping among gentlemen whose position had previously protected them from challenges to their behaviour. With their hybrid character, involving both clerics and laymen, they gave an early indication of the character of this change too, which might be seen as representing an extension of state power in the broadest sense, with strong central iniative but also involving many local men.[32]

Then, in 1561, York High Commission was established. As well as being, as Philip Tyler particularly emphasised, the successor to the Marian heresy commissions, High Commission was part of this growing response to immorality. Its jurisdiction in religious affairs is the most extensive part of each successive High Commission patent, but this is in part a product simply of the way until 1604 that they reproduced at length the parliamentary statutes for the suppression of nonconformity. From the start, the commissions were also charged, among other things, with addressing notorious adulteries and fornications. Incest was added to the list in 1577.[33] The overall pattern of the commission's activities quickly showed how important these responsibilities were, accounting as they did for a third and more of overall business.[34]

High Commission at York was an ecclesiastical court which derived its authority from royal letters patent, and as such can be seen as an extension of Tudor state control.[35] Philip Tyler and Christopher Haigh have examined the creation of these and similar new agencies of the reformation regimes, but though the latter in particular has noted that the context of their creation was one of moral, social and religious disorder and that their purpose was to achieve conformity in all aspects, in most historians' work it is the religious agenda which is seen to predominate, with particular emphasis upon Catholic recusancy in Lancashire and Cheshire.[36] An analysis of York High Commission's business and range of responsibilities suggests that this should be read alongside the evidence for a parallel priority to challenge some aspects of elite immorality.

Other jurisdictional change potentially impacted on the definition and regulation of sexual and moral conduct that might be defined as fornication and adultery, and their consequences in children born to the women involved. The Council in the North also held some authority over the intimate lives of the northern gentry and in 1561, in parallel with the distinctive direction in York High Commission of the same year, was given an additional instruction 'that the said Bishops and Ordinaries be assisted in the punishment of such as do dayley marry unlawfully and against the law of God and the Realm and of such others as notoriously lyve and contynue in adultery to the slander and infamy of God's people.'[37] The complete absence of records from this important jurisdiction means that the historian is dependent upon references elsewhere to gain any sense of its day-to-day involvement in punishing immorality, but evidence is available. In 1605, for example, John Thornton was keen to point out to the York Consistory court that the charges of adultery and fornication with numerous women they were endeavouring to establish against him had already been proved before the Council in the North.[38] As Rachel Reid has pointed out, the Council in the North and York High Commission worked together very closely, with the President of the Council appointed to the Ecclesiastical Commission and the archbishop serving on the Council. This took on a particular significance with the appointment of Archbishop Matthew Hutton as President of the Council in 1595, a role in which he continued until 1600, but we should also note the close working relationship between Henry Hastings earl of Huntingdon when the earl was President of the Council (1572–95) and Archbishop Grindal during his time at York (1570–75), when the courts showed a particular interest in elite immorality.[39]

At a much more local level, peculiar jurisdictions were important in the regulation of elite sexual morality in localities across the north of England. For example, that of the Cistercian House at Whalley exercised independent authority over a large portion of East Lancashire, particularly the forest areas of Bowland, Trawden, Pendle and Rossendale. Its court operated in a similar way to a visitation, meeting in Clitheroe Castle, or in Clitheroe or Whalley parish churches, with representatives from each area presenting the defendants for judgement. The surviving Act Book covering the years 1510–37 notes 156 cases of fornication or adultery, the most prominent defendant being Hugh Shirburn esquire, who 'holds in adulterous embrace … daughter of Ralph Dobson.'[40] Prosecution seems to have been initiated in April 1518, but exactly a year later, Joan Dobson was reportedly pregnant. This may have been behind Shirburn's donation of twenty shillings to the abbey in 1521.[41] Also from a prominent Lancashire family was Agnes Towneley, accused of adultery with Hugh Whitacre in 1535 and sentenced to undergo penance.[42] Elizabeth Nutter was censured for her fornication and resulting child with Laurence Nowell in 1525, although he was not brought before the court.[43] Admittedly, the suppression of Whalley Abbey after the Pilgrimage of Grace brought an end to its peculiar jurisdiction, which does not appear to have been reconstituted within a Reformation framework, and it might be considered to constitute part of what some have seen as a jurisdictional 'winnowing' over the course of our period.

It must be remembered, however, that the early modern legal landscape remained a patchwork of overlapping jurisdictions, each with some potential claim to oversee the moral welfare of society. To modern eyes, the ecclesiastical courts appear to be the natural home of morality litigation, but many secular courts sought to punish or otherwise manage the impacts of adultery, fornication or bastardy. These covered a number of jurisdictions, from national agencies of state control, to local forums dealing with neighbourhood matters including those belonging to trade guilds. It was in the urban environment that we see some of the clearest examples of the trend to the regulation of manners occurring in the north, for example. After increasingly tough regulation in the latter years of the fifteenth century, Chester in the 1530s–1540s saw attempts to prevent women between the ages of 14 and 40 selling ale and efforts to cleanse the streets of prostitutes, in the context of wider measures to address social and moral questions especially associated with the mayoralties of Henry Gee in 1533–54 and 1539–40. This was not particularly connected with either a Protestantising or reforming Catholic agenda in the city elite.[44] Similar steps were being taken to the far north east of the region. The Newcastle Merchant Adventurers had extensive powers to regulate the behaviour of their apprentices and members. Before a young man could be considered for an apprenticeship, his father had to prove he held landed property of a certain value, ensuring membership was limited to the wealthier members of society.[45] The conduct of the apprentices was a continual cause of concern for the fellowship, seemingly because they had access to ready cash, which they spent on fine clothes, gambling, 'typlinge, daunseng, and braseng of harlots'; and the penalties laid down by Ordnances issued by the Adventurers in 1554, 1562 and 1655 became successively more draconian. In each case the apprentice caught in fornication had to start their term of years from the beginning, irrespective of length of time already served, and pay a fine of £3 6s 8d (1554), increased to £13 6s 8d in 1562 and to £100 in 1655.[46] The apprentices were not permitted to marry during their apprenticeships, and the Adventurers controlled the marriages of its fellows and their families. On 10 November 1575, the Fellowship ordered that 'no maner of apprentice of this said Feoloship shalbe permitted to marrie with anie maner of woman, before the expiracion of his yeres wherin he remaineth so bounden, upon pain all the terme of yeares that he hath so served, before his suche marriage, to be utterlie voide and of none effect.' By 1575–76, Thomas Crome was fined £40 for various offences against the Fellowship. He had already paid £10, but the Governor decreed that if he married Elizabeth Brigham, daughter of a deceased member, before the end of August, he could keep the remaining £30. If he did not marry Elizabeth, the Merchant Adventurers would keep the money (he paid the £30 on 28 August).[47] Arguably, the Guild did try and regulate some of the same types of ill conduct that the church courts tried to deal with among the wider population. Marriage itself, sexual conduct outside it, and other such crimes as 'absurd and filthye languishe' among the ranks of the fellowship and their apprentices could bring the whole organisation into disrepute, although it is impossible to gauge how successful the Adventurers were in policing illicit behaviour. The York Merchant Adventurers took a more relaxed approach to the behaviour of their apprentices and brethren. While they were keen to stamp out 'dicyinge, carding, mummynge or any other unlawful games, whereby he doth waist and imbasell his masters goodes', sexual impropriety is not mentioned explicitly in the 1603 York ordinances.[48] In a different sphere, and one more likely to be directly encountered by the gentry, the palatine courts of Lancaster, Durham and Chester might find a relevant role. In the Duchy of Lancaster court in 1545–46 Thomas Molyneux sued his father-in-law Sir Thomas Boteler for assault. Boteler claimed his daughter Elizabeth had been the victim of slander spoken by Molyneux's father Roger, who had called her a whore and accused her of adultery with John Hyndley (for which she had already made purgation).[49] It is highly likely that this was the same Thomas Molyneux who sued Elizabeth Butler alias Molyneux for a divorce in the Chester Consistory in 1560 on the grounds that they were aged six and eight years at the time of their marriage.[50]

These jurisdictions added a degree of richness and complexity to the environment in which illicit sexual behaviour might be defined and challenged in the north and provided routes through which a climate of hostility to immorality typical of the movement for reformation of manners might express itself. That climate was somewhat less intense than that to be found in London or the south east of England, however. Such a richness and complexity also inevitably produced dangers of conflicts between authorities and scope for avoidance of decision, but there does not appear to have been much effective outright particularism or isolationism in operation. The palatinate jurisdictions in Lancashire, Chester and Durham may have offered immunity from some impositions from Westminster and retained a high degree of autonomy, elements of which were even enhanced during the early modern period.[51] It is not surprising, therefore, that some defendants tried to rely on palatinate jurisdiction when challenged: one prominent offender who appeared before York High Commission attempted to claim immunity from prosecution there on the basis of his residence in Cheshire. In 1574, Sir Rowland Stanley of Hooton 'did allege that he was persuaded that he [is] priviledged not to appear because he is of the County Palatinate of Chester', and there were fears in some quarters that jurisdictional issues might stand in the way of addressing immorality. But what is consistently significant is that in these cases particularism was overruled: Stanley's argument got short shrift from the archbishop of York and the earl of Huntingdon, who were sitting in judgement upon him.[52] The jurisdiction of the commissions did not permit this to develop; if there was an ongoing pattern of diversity across England in elite sexual relationships, it was not straightforwardly correlated with jurisdictional barriers and boundaries.

The northern courts also intersected with jurisdictions based around London, such as Star Chamber and southern High Commission, in their treatment of the northern elite. For example the Scrope bigamy case appeared before the York Consistory in December 1626 and in Star Chamber in 1632.[53] While at first sight a pre-contract or validity case initiated by the first Mrs Scrope, Star Chamber officials recorded that when he was aged seventeen or eighteen, Henry Scrope married Anne Scrope at St Clements Eastcheap, with a Dr Spight officiating. By contrast, his subsequent marriage to Anne Plumpton was conducted late at night by a Romish priest, in Sir Edward Plumpton's house 'and was contrived in the hope of getting the earl of Sutherland's [sic – for *Sunderland's*] estate.'[54] Arguably, it was the King's interest in a case against Sir Robert Constable that meant it was also heard in Star Chamber, under Henry VIII. Constable was accused of 'the ravishing and taking away of the body of Agnes Grissacre, the King's Ward; affiancing her to Thos. one of his sons, without the King's consent', but most importantly he 'suffered' Thomas to have carnal relations with Agnes despite them both being unmarried.[55] Constable was forced to beg for the King's mercy on his knees, and was pardoned in 1525. In 1621, the State Papers include a record of the pardon granted to Richard Shirburn and Ellen Gregson for their incontinency, but they were summoned before York High Commission in 1622 for the same offence.[56] In 1636, Thomas Hesketh appeared before southern High Commission, despite being resident in Lancashire. Accused of adultery with seven women, he was fined the enormous sum of £1,000 (later mitigated to £500) and ordered to perform penance in York Minster, Chester Cathedral and Croston parish church, as well to avoid the company of his former lovers.[57] Sir Ralph Ashton of Whalley also appeared before southern High Commission, a couple of months later, for incest with Alice, wife of John Kenyon and her niece Joan Whiteaires and adultery with Elizabeth Holmes. Initially, Ashton was sentenced to penance in Whalley church and Chester Cathedral, but he argued that as a gentleman of ancient family with a virtuous wife and ten children, such a punishment would be to their disparagement, particularly with regard to their future marriages. The judges were somewhat sympathetic and commuted his penance to the payment of £300 towards the repair of the west end of St Paul's and a £600 bond; he was also ordered to avoid the company of Kenyon, Whiteaires and Holmes and provide a 1,000 mark bond for this.[58]

Surveying the range of jurisdictions that might impact on the sexual behaviour of gentry and nobility, it was, therefore, in practice not any specific regional particularism that included or excluded our subjects from a court. On rare occasions, cases relevant to sexual morality were brought against some members of the gentry in local magistrates' courts, as is evidenced, for example, in some church court records. Grace Flower was, for instance, forced to appeal to the East Riding Justices of the Peace when the gentleman father of her child, George Burfitt, failed to provide for them.[59] In the proceedings of the York ecclesiastical court, reference was made to Burfitt's failure to pay for his child and treatment of Flower within a context of his general 'wickedness', which included bragging about fathering a male child with Joan Ridley, drunkenness, problems with tithes, conflict over the profits of the vicarage of Hornsey and allowing the miller to grind corn on Sundays and Holy Days. It must be noted, however, that the East Riding Justices were concerned with the maintenance of the child rather than Burfitt's immorality, which was dealt with in the ecclesiastical court. And such circumstances were relatively unusual given the capacity of gentry and noble fathers to support children or to avoid responsibilities before the bench when they chose not to. Michael Dalton in *The Countrey Iustice* was particularly concerned with bastardy chargeable to the parish, yet it is not only from a twenty-first-century perspective that it is hard to escape the ironies of the fact that many of those punishing others for bastardy were guilty of immorality themselves.[60] When Edwin Sandys, archbishop of York gave his views about the character of the justices of the peace in Yorkshire in 1587, he claimed 'there be many gentlemen in Yorkshire, yet very hard choise of fit men for that purpose.'[61] Robert Lee was noted as 'an open adulterer', Peter Stanley 'noted to be a great fornicator. Of small wisdom and less skill'. Later, Sir John Vavasour and Sir Richard Hawkesworth were deprived of office due to litigation surrounding their marital problems.[62] Even more dramatically, those presiding over the Ormskirk Assizes in April 1592, and who decided the fates of 'women of ill fame' and those who harboured them, were themselves fathers of at least seven illegitimate children between them. Henry, earl of Derby was the father of four illegitimate children; Richard Bold's heir Thomas was illegitimate; Robert Hesketh had an extensive base-born collateral family as well as two base sons of his own; Edward Scarisbrick included his bastard brother Henry in an enfeoffment of 1574, and William Faringdon may have had an illegitimate brother Henry and a sister Margaret, leaving only Sir Richard Molyneux, Richard Wrightington and John Cuerden with no immediate illegitimate dependants or relatives.[63]

Politics was a factor in many of the elite prosecutions which did emerge in these courts. In 1631, Nicholas Bacon was accused of an 'inordinate and lascivious' course of living, during which he had attempted the chastity of Elizabeth Tomlinson, seduced a servant of William Pepper and was often to be found in the company of lewd women. However, the crux of the argument seems to have been his 'divers scandalous and unchristian speaches' against Sir Henry Anderson, formerly of Newcastle and by then of East Cowton in the North Riding, who was a somewhat aggressive opponent in a dispute.[64] Ultimately, Bacon's representative 'exhibited a petition with reference thereunto from the King's Majesty declaring His Highness' pleasure that for some causes in the said petition mentioned the Court should surcease to proceed any further in this cause as by the reference aforesaid … whereupon the Court decreed suspended.' The records of Star Chamber reveal that Anderson and his son were each fined £60 for their attempts to conspire against Bacon in 1632, and £500 each in 1633 for their attempts to set fire to Bacon's hay.[65] In this case, an apparently malicious prosecution ended up in the Ordinary York Court and York High Commission before the intercession of the King and resolution in Star Chamber.

One factor specific to the north of England which did relate to jurisdictional boundaries and provide for a persistently distinctive character to illegitimate relationships among some of the elite was the proximity of the Anglo-Scottish border. This applied even after the accession of James VI of Scotland to the throne of England. Prior to 1603, marriage between Scots and English nationals was illegal, although repeated attempts to stamp out the practice met with failure. In 1565, a note on the regulation of the borders highlighted the proscription of cross-border marriages.[66] By 1583, Sir Simon Musgrave wrote that they caused 'the greatest occasion of the spoiles and robberies upon the Borders'.[67] Even in the early 1590s the Warden of the Eastern March, Sir John Carey, wrote to Lord Burghley that as a result of fraternising between English soldiers and Scottish women, 'Marye! the countrey is full of Scottes (as I will certifye your honour at more leasure).'[68] Lord Scrope wrote of 'the grievous murders, &c., done both by the Liddesdales and Kinmont, his sons and complices, of which there is no redress from their friendship and intermarriages with the English borderers.' The intermarriage of Anglo-Scots borderers meant that ties of loyalty (and disloyalty) spanned the border, bringing into question the trustworthiness of locally based government officials.[69] That the English state was weakened by the immorality and personal ties of those who were charged with enforcing the laws was highlighted by a description of the Captain of Bewcastle, Thomas Musgrave, of whom it was said in 1599 that among the Scots, none but outlaws were in favour with, the chief of these being one Sym of Whythaugh, whom Musgrave had married to an English woman who it was alleged was his bastard daughter. The letter writer indicated that he personally could vouch for the fact that Musgrave provided an evil example to his neighbours as a senior officeholder, in keeping a 'very unhonest and an unworthy' woman in his house, 'by whome he hath had dyvers children: she is hatefull to God and man'. Strikingly, this mistress was seen as the cause of Musgrave's friends all forsaking him: neither the bishop nor any other officer was seen to be able to influence him positively, and his mistress was thought to be the chief cause of his lewdness.[70]

Even after the disarmament and pacification of the border, there are hints of continued suspicion of international fraternisation. The 1609–10 records of the Durham Consistory refer to Jane Carr's adultery 'with a Scotts man' in terms of his national origin rather than his home parish.[71] The courts also seemed suspicious of the small number of clandestine marriages for which English couples crossed into Scotland. In 1633, Durham High Commission called Roger Wooderington to explain his marriage to Rosamund Revely, which from the evidence supplied seems to have been celebrated 'at a place in Scotland called Cuthberthoope'.[72] Adulterers or fornicators escaping over the border and evading the courts' jurisdiction was also a concern, as in the case of George Hume and Margaret Mitton in 1633.[73] The former pleaded that he was too ill and infirm to attend Durham High Commission, but by 1636 was reported to have absconded to Scotland and could not be found.

The pattern of jurisdiction was complex, and interacted with a fluctuating impetus to apply it in pursuit of gentry and noble mistress-keeping and bastard-bearing. The most significant impact of this kind is associated with the influence of Archbishop Grindal in York. A survey of the records of York High Commission demonstrates that, beginning in the 1560s with an average of just over one case per year, the pattern of cases saw a very significant peak in the 1570s, with sixty-three cases being dealt with in that decade.[74]

This analysis also provides clear evidence of patterning in the data in terms of the nature of the offences prosecuted. Claire Cross argued that many of the cases represented family resistance to commitments informally made between men and women who wanted to be married in the eyes both of the church and at least some of their neighbours. Our sampling suggested this was the case in some instances: in 1582 William Tattersall was the subject of action because he had contracted matrimony with Mary Bell without the knowledge of her father, Richard Bell, while in the same year Katherine Savile, unmarried daughter of Thomas Savile, gentleman, was dealt with for already having given birth to one illegitimate child by Christopher Warren, and being pregnant with another fathered by one Watson.[75] There were also cases in which conflicting claims about marriage to one or both parties were raised, as with the complex of litigation relating to Ralph Rishton, Elizabeth Rishton alias Parker, and Anna Stanley alias Rishton in the 1570s.[76] The vast majority of cases, however, related to relationships between married men or women and others in situations where there are no signs that an attempt to marry against parental / family wishes was involved. Most typically, this was married gentlemen who were identified as keeping mistresses: for example Sir Thomas Venables and his mistress Jane Varnam in 1571–72, or Laurence Tetloe of the Chambre in 1571–73, who 'hath kepte a Whore this xxtie yeres and hath had dyvers children by her and disheryted his lawful children'.[77] It did also include women in similar positions: Elena Bostock may in 1571–72 have initially pursued her husband Ralph for his relationship with Elen Huxley, but she found herself enjoined in turn to abstain from the company of William Sompner, except in church, market and open places. In the same year, Anna, wife of William Staveley faced action for adultery with John Gill.[78] This focus of the court on mistress-keeping needs to be understood alongside its chronology. The peak of activity in the 1570s clearly correlates with the archiepiscopate of Edmund Grindal, and with his arrival in the city in March 1571.

It is noteworthy that Grindal carried many of his senior colleagues with him in this campaign, in particular Bishop Richard Barnes of Carlisle. Barnes was more effective than William Downham of Chester, who was rebuked by the Privy Council for his inefficiency in 1570 and 1575,[79] and Grindal took advantage of his energy. The archbishop delegated the 1571 visitation of the diocese of Chester to Barnes, stating 'it is so far from me that I cannot do so much as otherwise I could'. At least sixteen of the nineteen gentry immorality cases before York High Commission between 1570 and 1572 originated west of the Pennines (seven in Cheshire) and all were initiated by the office. Barnes was at this point engaged in a vigorous campaign against the relics of Catholic practice and the vestiges of political resistance in the aftermath of the 1569 rebellion, and in building a body of effective Protestant clergy; his efforts also extended to this widespread challenge to gentry immorality in some of the most intractable parts of the province.[80] Margaret Clark has indicated the vigorousness of Barnes' regime in the diocese of Carlisle, noting that the Reformation in Cumbria really began in the 1570s, with his appointment to the bishopric.[81] Yet while the ecclesiastical leadership and High Commission personnel demonstrated unprecedented enthusiasm for tackling immorality, these cases involved notorious offenders and relationships that were well known within their respective local communities, requiring little detective work on the part of the authorities.[82] By plucking such easily prosecuted cases, High Commission was able to impeach a large number of prominent plaintiffs relatively quickly, while apparently leaving other contemporary fornicators or adulterers untouched.[83]

There are, in fact, signs that the urgency of Grindal's challenge to elite immorality was waning even by the middle of the decade. In his visitation of 1575, while begetting illegitimate children and adultery/fornication were the most commonly identified offences, the proportion of those targeted who were of gentry status was very small. Only four were accused: John Kaye of Oakenshaw ('Okenshay') near Dewsbury, esquire; Henry Burdet of Penistone; Robert Thwaite of Bossall; and Thomas Bulmer of Scarborough, all of them gentleman.[84] It was Grindal's expected return to the south which seems to have undermined the impetus for the campaign, and this was being promoted by William Cecil as early as May 1575. In subsequent years not only did the total number of elite cases coming before York High Commission decline, but the higher elite almost disappear completely: with the exception of Sir John Vavasour, Sir Richard Hawkesworth and Sir Francis and Lady Elizabeth Foljambe, all defendants were gentlemen or esquires.

This is not to say, however, that Grindal's assault on gentry immorality had no impact: evidence from wills shows a decline in the numbers of noble and gentry wills acknowledging bastard children, and in the numbers of bastards acknowledged there, in the 1570s.[85] This should be read in the light of widespread scepticism about the efficacy of ecclesiastical justice in general and the Commissions in particular. It is undoubtedly true that their main weapons, in particular excommunication, had limited impact on most potential targets. Haigh describes the situation where, by the 1590s, as many as 1,000 Lancastrians were being excommunicated at each visitation for failure to attend the correction courts, and very few among them are known ever to have submitted.[86] For nobles and gentry, however, as Haigh acknowledges, their dependence on the machinery of state and church administration meant that they were less able simply to completely ignore such sanctions.[87] The evidence of High Commission, therefore, illustrates the way in which the court was used, briefly but powerfully, to intervene against married gentlemen who openly kept mistresses. The focus of previous accounts, drawing chiefly from John Strype, has been on Grindal's confrontation with gentry influence and conservative religion.[88] What this investigation has indicated is that associated with this was a challenge, in some instances, to gentry adultery.

The effects of this challenge must not be overestimated, however. The observed effect may be more about the manifestations of mistress-keeping and bastard-bearing in the records and especially their appearance in the courts than about a complete reformation in the conduct of the elite. First, gentlemen may have been drawn into the ecclesiastical courts but most even in the 1570s avoided sterner sanctions unless other aspects of their behaviour eroded the tolerance of their peers. Second, in the 1580s and into the 1590s evidence from wills suggests the number acknowledging illegitimate offspring plateaus.[89] The celebrated Cheshire case of Sir Randle Brereton and Lady Dorothy Townsend soon after the turn of the century, he 'a notable libertine' and she 'a courtesan of no mean talent', spectacularly shed light on the mores of the gentry which High Commission did not touch.[90] With fears being voiced in the 1590s that the prevalence of bastardy in Lancashire might infect neighbouring counties, Chester's ecclesiastical commission was remodelled in 1598, with more lay members, in an attempt to bolster its effectiveness in imposing discipline, at a point when commissions in many other dioceses had reduced their activities or ceased to act; and in 1600, Bishop Robinson of Carlisle voiced his concern that the full weight of lay punishment was required to bolster ecclesiastical authority in the face of what he considered 'impious … licentiousnes, one husband having divers wives now living, one wife divers husbands'. Such people took little notice of ecclesiastical censures, he wrote, but if they felt 'the smart of Civill iustice', they might be humbled.[91]

While the Reformation may generally be acknowledged to be a process of challenge to some aspects of English plebeian culture through the imposition of discipline, the degree to which it might have been a challenge by some of the elite to the morality of other elements of their number has been relatively underestimated. Being, and becoming, Protestant, did not just mean adopting a set of religious beliefs and practices, but taking on certain moral values and associated behaviours and rejecting others which had been very common and remained widespread.[92] Arguments about the 'revolutionary' impact of discipline, most prominently seen in the work of Michael Walzer, are rightly less common than they once were, particularly in relation to England.[93] Attempts to apply such an analysis to our evidence would miss the significance of discipline as an issue *within* the elite (in the form in particular of the church hierarchy and their lay allies), rather than challenging the elite from below. Yet it is important to reassert the Reformation as a process which involved changes and challenges to religious identities that included ways of living by elements of the elite against other elements of the elite, and not just against the poor and middling sort. Hypocrisy undoubtedly existed, but many Protestant gentlemen and noblemen were less tolerant of sexual immorality among their peers, as they were of it among their inferiors. This was particularly true of the ways in which formal means of discipline might be deployed, through the Commissions and church courts. These and other courts also worked to express the developing expectations of sexual conduct that manifested the 'reformation of manners', to an extent independent of specific religious change, which impacted the north of England as it did the south, if less dramatically. Defining oneself against others operated across these spheres as well as in theology and worship. The period also saw the north of England experience a growth of state power which injected new instruments of moral regulation, most directly the commissions and in their support the Council in the North, against a background of what continued to be relatively secure particular jurisdictions, such as the palatinates. But none of these developments appear to have created the conditions for a dramatic transition in the behaviour of the overwhelming majority of the elite during this period. This highlights the dangers and the frustrations of studying elite sexual conduct primarily through the lens of regulation and enforcement. It is, therefore, to the evidence for the illegitimate offspring of the elite and their fathers that the book turns to next.

Notes

1 Edmund Bunny, *Of Diuorce for Adulterie, and Marrying Againe: That There is no Sufficient Warrant so to do. VVith a Note in the End, that R.P. Many Yeeres Since was Answered* ('Oxford' [i.e. London]: printed by Ioseph Barnes, 1610) (STC 4091), p. 1.

2 Alan Macfarlane, *Marriage and Love in England: Modes of Reproduction 1300–1840* (Oxford: Basil Blackwell, 1986), pp. 224–5; Claire Cross, 'Sin and Society: The Northern High Commission and the Northern Gentry in the Reign of Elizabeth I', in Claire Cross, David Loades and J. J. Scarisbrick (eds), *Law and Government under the Tudors: Essays Presented to Sir Geoffrey Elton, Regius Professor of Modern History in the University of Cambridge, on the Occasion of his Retirement* (Cambridge: Cambridge University Press, 1998), pp. 195–205.

3 *Tudor Church Reform: The Henrician Canons of 1535 and the* Reformatio Legum Ecclesiasticarum, ed. Gerald Bray, Church of England Record Society, 8 (2000); Martin Ingram, *Carnal Knowledge: Regulating Sex in England, 1470–1600* (Cambridge: Cambridge University Press, 2017), pp. 278–82.

4 Johanna Rickman, *Love, Lust, and License in Early Modern England: Illicit Sex and the Nobility* (Aldershot: Ashgate, 2008), p. 23.

5 DUL, DDR/EJ/CCA/1/1, partially surviving fos. 32v, 33 (Liddell); DDR/A/ACN/1, fo. 107 (Errington).

6   R. H. Helmholz, *The Oxford History of the Laws of England*, volume 1: *The Canon Law and Ecclesiastical Jurisdiction from 597 to the 1640s* (Oxford: Oxford University Press, 2004), p. 628.
7   Martin Ingram, *Church Courts, Sex and Marriage in England, 1570–1640* (Cambridge: Cambridge University Press, 1987), p. 239.
8   DUL, DDR/EJ/CCA/2/7A, fo. 35.
9   DUL, DDR/A/ACN/1, fo. 122.
10 BIA, HC.AB 18, fos. 19, 28, 33, 34, 49, 52, 59 (Pailor / Bulmer); HC.AB 6, fos. 161–2, 182, 183, 184; HC.AB 7, fos. 4, 17, 45 & 9 (Huddleston). See also Cross, 'Sin and Society', p. 207, and below, pp. 65–6, 104.
11 DUL, DDR/EJ/CCA/2/2, fo. 40; DDR/EJ/CCA/2/3, fos. 8, 11 (Orde / Mathew); DDR/A/ACN/2, fo. 107v (Collingwood).
12 BIA, HC.AB 1, fos. 16, 34–5; HC.AB 7, 32v, 41, 91v, 113, 121v–122v, 126, 152v, 162v.
13 *Wills and Inventories from the Registry at Durham*, ed. W. Greenwell, Surtees Society, XXXVIII (1860), ii. 1–6; BIA, CP.G 863 and CP.G 1033. See also TNA, SP 12/19, fo. 47 (*Calendar of State Papers, Domestic Series, of the Reigns of Edward VI., Mary and Elizabeth, 1547–80*, ed. Robert Lemon (London: Longman, Brown, Green, Longmans, & Roberts, 1856), p. 183 (17 Aug. 1561)) where Elizabeth I personally ordered Archbishop Young to proceed against Westmorland. Keith Dockray, 'Neville, Ralph, Fourth Earl of Westmorland (1498–1549), *magnate*', *ODNB*, xl. 522–4, at p. 524; R. R. Reid, *The King's Council in the North* (London: Longmans, Green and Co., 1921), p. 188; Eric Josef Carlson, 'Marriage Reform and the Elizabethan High Commission', *Sixteenth Century Journal*, 21 (1990), 437–52, at p. 445.
14 BIA, HC.AB 13, fo. 240 for Office c William Nelson; *The Injunctions and Other Ecclesiastical Proceedings of Richard Barnes Bishop of Durham from 1575 to 1587*, ed. James Raine, Surtees Society, XXII (1850), p. 123. On bawdry, see Ingram, *Carnal Knowledge*, pp. 103–4.
15 West Yorkshire Archive Service, RD/A/1, fo. 45v; /2, fo. 77.
16 BIA, HC.AB 12, fo. 82.
17 Helmholz, *The Oxford History of the Laws of England*, p. 554.
18 *Ibid.*, p. 555; *The Constitutions and Canons Ecclesiastical (Made in the Year 1603, and Amended in the Year 1865) to which are Added the Thirty-Nine Articles of the Church of England* (London: S.P.C.K., 1900), p. 55.
19 Helmholz, *Oxford History of the Laws of England*, pp. 529–33. Consanguinity was a blood relationship between bride and groom, affinity between couples related by marriage. This could also cover godparents or sexual relationships outside marriage. Prior to the Reformation, papal dispensations could overcome distant consanguinity / affinity. An example of a conditional marriage contract might be that matrimony was dependent upon lands or goods being given to the bride and groom; if these were not provided the marriage would be deferred.
20 BIA, CP.H 288 for Steele's validity case against Savile in 1603; CP.H 156 for his unsuccessful attempt to enforce a marriage contract in 1604 and CP.H 200 for the adultery / fornication case against him in 1605. The background to the series of litigation seems to have been familial disapproval from Savile's family.
21 BIA, CP.G 1138 William c Katherine Constable; CP.G 1142 Mathew Usher c William & Katherine Constable; CP.G 924 Mathew Usher c Katherine Constable. Whilst Usher did not claim to have consummated his relationship with Hamerton, the case does illustrate the flimsy nature of a plaintiff's view of admissible evidence for clandestine marriage.
22 BIA, CP.G 1473; HC.AB 9, fos. 30, 32, 36, 43, 52, 54, 65, 76 and 77v.

23 BIA, HC.AB 9, fos. 30, 32, 36, 43, 52, 54, 65, 76 and 77v. The implications for the elite of a possible survival of traditional marriage customs in the north-west are discussed further below, pp. 48–51.
24 DUL, DDR/EJ/CCD/1/9, fos. 236–v.
25 Ronald A. Marchant, *The Church under the Law: Justice, Administration and Discipline in the Diocese of York, 1560–1640* (Cambridge: Cambridge University Press, 1969), chs 2–6 (5 being an account of the archdeaconry of Nottingham).
26 Peter Heath, 'The Medieval Archdeaconry and Tudor Bishopric of Chester', *Journal of Ecclesiastical History*, 20 (1969), 243–52; Christopher Haigh, *Reformation and Resistance in Tudor Lancashire* (Cambridge: Cambridge University Press, 1975), pp. 1–19.
27 Cheshire Arch., EDA, 12/1; TNA, DL 42/96, fo. 33v; Haigh, *Reformation and Resistance*, pp. 19, 21, 46–7; C. A. Haigh, 'Slander and the Church Courts in the Sixteenth Century', *Transactions of the Historic Society of Lancashire and Cheshire*, 78 (1975), 1–13, at pp. 6–7. On the emergence of this approach to imposing discipline by commission in specific dioceses, see Roland G. Usher, *The Rise and Fall of the High Commission* (Oxford: Clarendon Press, 1913), p. 31, who, however, emphasises a slightly later period.
28 Peter Draper, *The House of Stanley; Including the Sieges of Lathom House, With Notices of Relative and Co-Temporary Incidents, & etc.* (Ormskirk: T. Hutton, 1864), p. 260.
29 Cheshire Arch., EDA, 12/1, pp. 2–13, 24.
30 Cheshire Arch., EDA, 12/1, pp. 14–21.
31 Cheshire Arch., EDA, 12/1, p. 4.
32 We might see echoes of a tradition of historiography which viewed the sixteenth century as one in which central authority is stamped on the locality (a classic example of which would be Reid, *King's Council*), as well as one in which certain local interests participate in, and even actively sponsor, this change, exemplified by Steve Hindle, *The State and Social Change in Early Modern England, c. 1550–1640* (Basingstoke: Palgrave, 2000).
33 *Calendar of Patent Rolls, 1560–1563*, pp. 170–1; *Calendar of Patent Rolls, 1566–1569*, pp. 172–3; *Calendar of Patent Rolls, 1572–1575*, no. 975; *Calendar of Patent Rolls, 1575–1579*, no. 2599. Cf. Philip Tyler, 'The Ecclesiastical Commission for the Province of York 1561–1641' (unpubl. D.Phil. diss., Oxford University, 1965), ch. 2, which discusses briefly the commissions' elements regarding immorality (pp. 94–6) while emphasising aspects relevant to religious nonconformity.
34 Tyler, 'Ecclesiastical Commission', pp. 416–18.
35 Carlson, 'Marriage Reform', pp. 437–52; Emma Watson, 'The Court of High Commission and Religious Change in Elizabethan Yorkshire', in Christopher Dyer, Andrew Hopper, Evelyn Lord and Nigel Tringham (eds), *New Directions in Local History since Hoskins* (Hatfield: University of Hertfordshire Press, 2011), pp. 172–85, at p. 173; C. Hill, *Society and Puritanism in Pre-Revolutionary England* (London: Secker and Warburg, 1964), pp. 344–53.
36 C. B. Phillips and J. H. Smith, *Lancashire and Cheshire from AD 1540* (London: Longman, 1994); C. A. Haigh, 'Finance and Administration in a New Diocese: Chester, 1541–1641', in Rosemary O' Day and Felicity Heal (eds), *Continuity and Change: Personnel and Administration of the Church of England, 1500–1642* (Leicester: Leicester University Press, 1976), pp. 145–66; K. R. Wark, *Elizabethan Recusancy in Cheshire*, Chetham Society, 3rd ser., XIX (1971); Watson, 'Court of High Commission'; David Marcombe, 'The Durham Dean and Chapter: Old Abbey Writ Large?' in O' Day & Heal (eds), *Continuity and Change*, pp. 125–45.

37 Reid, *King's Council*, p. 188.
38 BIA, CP.H 154.
39 See below, pp. 28–30.
40 Margaret Lynch, *Life, Love, and Death in North-east Lancashire, 1510 to 1537: A Translation of the Act Book of the ecclesiastical court of Whalley*, Chetham Society, 3rd ser., XLVI (2006), pp. 84, 89, 95.
41 Charles Davies Sherborn, *A History of the Family of Sherborn* (London: Mitchell and Hughes, 1901), p. 23.
42 Lynch, *Life, Love and Death*, pp. 208, 212, 215. Whitacre was a serial offender, fathering children with Katherine Botheman and Margery Cronkehay alias Parker, both of whom claimed to be married to him. See also *The Act Book of the ecclesiastical court of Whalley 1510–1538*, ed. Alice M. Cooke, Chetham Society, n.s., 44 (1901).
43 *The Act Book of the ecclesiastical court of Whalley 1510–1538*, ed. Alice M. Cooke, p. 129. Nowell was presumably a member of the gentry family from Read, very close to Whalley.
44 Tim Thornton, *Cheshire and the Tudor State, 1480–1560* (Woodbridge: Boydell, 2000), p. 48; Jane Laughton, *Life in a Late Medieval City: Chester, 1275–1520* (Oxford: Windgather Press, 2008), pp. 160–1; B. E. Harris, C. P. Lewis and A. T. Thacker (eds), *The Victoria History of the County of Chester* (4 vols. in 5 parts, continuing; Oxford / Woodbridge: published for the Institute of Historical Research by Oxford University Press / Boydell & Brewer, 1979–), v/1. 63–4 (the emphasis here, of Jennifer Kermode, on Gee's 'puritanism', if read in strictly religious terms, should be qualified).
45 *Extracts from the Records of the Merchant Adventurers of Newcastle-upon-Tyne*, ed. F. W. Dendy, vol. 1, Surtees Society, XCIII (1895), pp. xxvi, 258.
46 *Ibid.*, pp. 26, 27. Although note at p. 192 that Cuthbert Wilkinson, apprentice to Thomas Maddison, was fined £13 6s 8d in June 1658, suggesting that the higher fine was unworkable.
47 *Ibid.*, pp. 97–8.
48 M. Sellers, *The York Mercers and Merchant Adventurers 1356–1917*, Surtees Society, CXXIX (1918), p. 269.
49 *Pleadings and Depositions in the Duchy Court of Lancaster in the Time of Henry VIII*, ed. H. Fishwick, RSLC, XXXV (1897), pp. 206–8.
50 Cheshire Arch., EDC 5/1560/4. The outcome of this case is unknown.
51 Thornton, *Cheshire and the Tudor State*; 'Fifteenth-Century Durham and the Problem of Provincial Liberties in England and the Wider Territories of the English Crown', *Transactions of the Royal Historical Society*, 6th ser., 11 (2001) 83–100; Edward Baines, *The History of the County Palatine and Duchy of Lancaster*, ed. James Croston (5 vols. Manchester: John Heywood, 1888–93), i. 82–98; Robert Somerville, 'The Duchy and County Palatine of Lancaster', *Transactions of the Historic Society of Lancashire and Cheshire*, 103 (1951), 59–67, at pp. 64–5.
52 BIA, HC.AB 7, fo. 204; BL, Lansdowne MS 17, fos. 113r–v (reference to 'Chesshyer practises' being used to obstruct action; printed in *The Cheshire Sheaf*, 3rd ser., IV (1902), 111–13; 121). For more on this case, see below, pp. 72–3, 82, 106–10, 136–9. See also HC.AB 10, fo. 151v: in Feb. 1581/82, Rauff Lawson tried to claim that as a resident of the diocese of Durham he was not subject to the rule of the York High Commission. He had already appeared in Durham as a defendant in 1580: DUL, DDR/EJ/CCA/1/3, fos. 240, 244v; DDR/EJ/CCA/1/4A, fo. 11.
53 BIA, CP.H 1736; John Southerden Burn, *The Star Chamber: Notices of the Court and Its Proceedings, with a Few Additional Notes of the High Commission* (London: J. R. Smith, 1870), pp. 114–15.

Despite being the plaintiff in the Star Chamber case, Sir Edward ended up being sent to the Fleet prison whilst enquiries were made into the identity and whereabouts of the priest who conducted the marriage.

54 Emanuel Scrope, first earl of Sunderland (1584–1630), for whose illegitimate family see below, pp. 119, 121.

55 Southerden Burn, *Star Chamber*, p. 45. See also TNA, C 1/563/15 Ralph Rokeby c Robert Constable & Brian Hastynges, who were accused of the abduction of Anne 'daughter and heir of Edward Cresacre' and the detention of her rents. For Constable's submission, see *LP* iv. 1115.

56 *Calendar of State Papers Domestic: James I, 1619–23*, ed. Mary Anne Everett Green (London: HMSO, 1858), pp. 239, 362. BIA, HC.AB 16, fos. 282, 282v, 284, 288, 290, 291. In his will Shirburn left 1000 marks to 'Margaret Shereburn als Stegson [sic], my reputed daughter', she presumably being his daughter by Gregson: *Lancashire and Cheshire Wills and Inventories, 1572 to 1696, Now Preserved at Chester, with an Appendix of Lancashire and Cheshire Wills and Inventories Proved at York and Richmond 1542 to 1649*, ed. J. P. Earwaker, Chetham Society, NS, 28 (1893), pp. 199–200.

57 *Calendar of State Papers Domestic: Charles I, 1635–6*, ed. John Bruce (London: HMSO, 1866), pp. 475, 496, 500.

58 *Ibid.*, pp. 500–1.

59 BIA, CP.H 1870.

60 Michael Dalton, *The Countrey Iustice Containing the Practise of the Iustices of the Peace out of their Sessions. Gathered, for the Better Helpe of such Iustices of Peace as Haue not been much Conuersant in the Studie of the Lawes of this Realme. Newly Corrected and Inlarged* (London: printed [by Adam Islip] for the Societie of Stationers, 1619), p. 32.

61 John Strype, *Annals of the Reformation and Establishment of Religion and Other Various Occurrences in the Church of England During Queen Elizabeth's Happy Reign: Together with an Appendix of Original Papers of State Records and Letters* (4 vols. in 7; Oxford: Clarendon Press, 1824), iii/2. 463.

62 J. T. Cliffe, *The Yorkshire Gentry from the Reformation to the Civil War* (London: Athlone Press, 1969), p. 247. For the litigation involving Vavasour in 1617, see BIA, HC.AB 16, fo. 174v; for Hawkesworth, HC.AB 17, fos. 112, 117, 139. Sandys may have been influenced in his view by an encounter with a Doncaster innkeeper's wife six years earlier. Carrying out his visitation, Sandys stopped at the Bull Inn, but was surprised to wake up with the innkeeper's wife in bed with him, and her husband threatening him with a dagger. Sir Robert Stapleton was present at the inn at the time, and the archbishop, believing him to be guilty of plotting to ruin his reputation, launched a suit against him, initially in York but later in Star Chamber: Sarah Bastow, 'An Abortive Attempt to Defend an Episcopal Reputation: The Case of Archbishop Edwin Sandys and the Innkeeper's Wife', *History*, 97 (2012), 380–401; Southerden Burn, *Star Chamber*, p. 75.

63 For Bold, see *Lancashire Inquisitions Returned into the Chancery of the Duchy of Lancaster and now Existing in the Public Record Office, London, Stuart Period Part I, 1–11 James I*, ed. J. P. Rylands, RSLC, III (1879), p. 257; Hesketh, *Lancashire and Cheshire Wills and Inventories, 1572 to 1696*, ed. J. P. Earwaker, Chetham Society, NS, 28 (1893), pp. 21–4; Farington, Henry Fishwick, *The History of the Parish of Preston in Amounderness in the County of Lancaster* (Rochdale: J. Clegg, 1900), p. 282; Scarisbrick, LRO, DDSC 28/17.

64 BIA, CP.H 5200; HC.AB 18, fos. 25, 44, 49; William Page (ed.), *The Victoria History of the County of York: North Riding* (3 vols. London: Constable and Co., 1914), i. 160–2; Andrew Thrush

and John P. Ferris (eds), *The House of Commons, 1604–29* (6 vols. Cambridge: Cambridge University Press, 2010), iii. 37–40.

65 There seems to have been some very complicated litigation running through the courts at the time regarding Long Cowton: Southerden Burn, *Star Chamber*, pp. 91, 124.

66 *The Border Papers: Calendar of Letters and Papers Relating to the Affairs of the Borders of England and Scotland Preserved in Her Majesty's Public Record Office London*, ed. Joseph Bain (2 vols. Edinburgh: H. M. General Register House, 1894–96), i. 3.

67 Ibid., p. 105.

68 Ibid., p. 454.

69 For example, Thomas Carleton, the Constable of Carlisle Castle, was related to the notorious Scottish reiver 'Kinmont' Willie Armstrong, who escaped from the castle whilst in Carleton's custody. It is possible that Scrope was referring to Carleton in his letter. See P. W. Hasler, *The House of Commons, 1558–1603* (London: HMSO for the History of Parliament Trust, 1981), i. 554–5, for details of his career and in particular his collaboration with the Scottish Graham family, to whom he was also related.

70 *Border Papers*, ii. 1084. See also Whitehaven, Cumbria Archive Service, Whitehaven RO, DPEN/216, fo. 157: in a letter dated 22 Nov 1606 from Carlisle, the Bishop of Carlisle, Sir W[ilfred] Lawson, and J[oseph] Pennington wrote to the Council, describing how Musgrave had allied his daughter to 'that bloodie and theevish clanne' [the Armstrongs].

71 DUL, DDR/EJ/CCD/1/9; see also DDR/A/ACN/2, fo. 84v, for Matthew Heron's fathering a child with a Scots woman, Katherine Hambleton. Also noteworthy is a rare jactitation case in DDR/EJ/CCD/1/2, fo. 334v, which alleged marriage in Edinburgh.

72 DUL, Hunter MSS, vol. 17, fo. 98. At about the same time, High Commission sought to prosecute Edward Gray for the same offence. In both cases the proximity of their houses to the border was noted.

73 DUL, Hunter MSS, vol. 16, fos. 76v, 77, 78, 83v.

74 The totals for each period are: 1560–69 – 13; 1570–79 – 63; 1580–89 – 24; 1590–99 – 28; 1600–09 – 2; 1610–19 – 11; 1620–29 – 10; 1630–39 – 6. The act books of the court are lacking for the years 1604–7 and 1634–38.

75 BIA, HC.AB 10, fos. 145, 168, 183; Cross, 'Sin and Society', pp. 197–8, 205.

76 BIA, HC.AB 6, fos. 88, 89–89v, 162, 181, 182; HC.AB 7, fos. 26, 27, 28, 32, 56, 61.

77 BIA, HC.AB 6, fos. 75, 81, 106v, 107, 108v, 147; HC.AB 7, fo. 78; Cross, 'Sin and Society', pp. 202–3.

78 BIA, HC.AB 6, fos. 32, 34v–35, 147, 152.

79 Wark, *Elizabethan Recusancy*, p. 13, argues that the 'final shame' for Downham was Barnes' appointment to hold a visitation in Chester.

80 Patrick Collinson, *Archbishop Grindal 1519–1583: The Struggle for a Reformed Church* (London: Jonathan Cape, 1979), p. 200 (it was only later that the two fell out over allegations relating to Barnes' behaviour in 1572: p. 194).

81 Margaret Clark, 'Northern Light? Parochial Life in a "Dark Corner" of Tudor England', in Katherine French, Gary G. Gibbs, and Beat A. Kümin (eds), *The Parish in English Life 1400–1600* (Manchester: Manchester University Press, 1997), pp. 56–73. Carlisle, Carlisle Record Office, DRC3/1, an unpaginated (and incomplete) court book from 1571, shows that in Dec. 1571 alone Barnes presided over proceedings involving 9 individuals charged with failure to cohabit with their spouses and a further 4 who failed to cohabit and were also involved in extra-marital

sexual activity. These were not members of the gentry, but the cases do suggest a determination to prosecute immorality.
82 A point also made in *Archbishop Grindal's Visitation, 1575: Comperta et Detecta Book*, ed. W. J. Sheils (York: Borthwick Institute of Historical Research, University of York 1977), p. x.
83 For example, the three generations of the Halsall family from Lancashire: *VCH Lancs.* iii. 191–7.
84 *Archbishop Grindal's Visitation*, pp. 22, 36, 43, 82.
85 See below, pp. 44–6. Cf. Cross's conclusions: 'too much should not be claimed for the court's control over the gentry'; the commission 'may have tightened its grip a little over gentry morals': 'Sin and Society', pp. 208–9.
86 Haigh, *Reformation and Resistance*, pp. 235–6.
87 *Ibid.*, pp. 235–6.
88 Collinson, *Archbishop Grindal*, pp. 187–215; R. L. Arundale, 'Edmund Grindal and the Northern Province', *Church History Quarterly* CLX (1959), 182–99.
89 Katharine Carlton and Tim Thornton, 'Illegitimacy and Authority in the North of England, c. 1450–1640', *Northern History*, 48 (2011), 23–40, at pp. 32–3.
90 TNA, STAC 8/14/7; Thomas G. Barnes, 'A Cheshire Seductress, Precedent, and a "Sore Blow" to Star Chamber', in Morris S. Arnold *et al.* (eds), *On the Laws and Customs of England: Essays in Honour of Samuel E. Thorne* (Chapel Hill NC: University of North Carolina Press, 1981), pp. 359–82, at pp. 359–60.
91 Diarmaid MacCulloch, *The Later Reformation in England, 1547–1603* (2nd edn, Basingstoke: Palgrave 2001), pp. 137–8; TNA, SP 12/240, fo. 222 (*Calendar of State Papers Domestic Series, of the Reign of Elizabeth, 1591–94*, ed. M. A. E. Green (London: Longmans, Green, Reader, & Dyer, 1867), p. 158); TNA, SP 12/275, fo. 111 (*Calendar of State Papers, Domestic Series, of the Reign of Elizabeth, 1598–1601*, p. 468).
92 Examples of 'Protestantisation' (and resistance thereto) seen chiefly in terms of personal religious devotion, formal practice, or in relation to a limited range of popular customs and pastimes: Patrick Collinson, 'Elizabethan and Jacobean Puritanism as Forms of Popular Religious Culture', in Christopher Durston and Jacqueline Eales (eds), *The Culture of English Puritanism, 1560–1700* (Basingstoke: Macmillan, 1996), pp. 32–57; Alexandra Walsham, '"Yielding to the Extremity of the Time": Conformity, Orthodoxy and the Post-Reformation Catholic Community', in Peter Lake and Michael C. Questier (eds), *Conformity and Orthodoxy in the English Church, c. 1560–1660* (Woodbridge: Boydell, 2000), pp. 211–36.
93 Michael Walzer, *The Revolution of the Saints: A Study in the Origins of Radical Politics* (Cambridge MA: Harvard University Press, 1965); Henry Heller, *Iron and Blood: Civil Wars in Sixteenth-Century France* (Montreal; Buffalo: McGill-Queen's University Press, 1991).

2

The extent of bastardy among the elite

IN SPITE OF HISTORIANS' extensive efforts to assess the extent and scope of illegitimacy among the population outside the gentry and nobility, there has been very little consideration of the scale of the phenomenon as it affected these groups in the elite. It may be argued that this relative neglect is a consequence of an underlying assumption, that bastardy was relatively insignificant and declining, or that it was effectively no more than a dimension of the more widely studied field of non-elite social history. One of the limited range of examples of this is T. H. Hollingsworth's straightforwardly demographic account of the English peerage, which proposes, after a relatively high point for illegitimacy of almost 5% of all recorded births in 1550–75, a consistently very low rate below 2% through to the late seventeenth century. Another, from an immediately preceding period, is Helen Matthews' estimate for the fourteenth and fifteenth centuries that no more than 1.5% of men fathered bastards.[1] That said, there are some starting points for our discussion in the existing literature. In her pioneering work exploring the Elizabethan High Commission, Claire Cross explored the evidence for the extent of gentry sexual immorality in the late sixteenth century provided by the group of church courts with the fullest range of surviving documents, those of the province of York.[2] She sampled the records of the courts of chancery and particularly High Commission and came to some clear conclusions, claiming that the cases she examined suggested an extensive tendency to engage in extra-marital relationships: 'by far the largest number of gentry morals cases to come before High Commission related to fornication or adultery', both with servants and other inferiors and with other gentry, she suggested. Cross even suggested there was a relative willingness to engage in such relationships, including fornication and adultery, on the part of female members of gentry families – and by implication at least some wider acceptance of the inevitability, if not the full respectability, of such engagements. 'Clearly both before and after marriage these gentlewomen felt able to behave with surprising freedom.'[3] In spite of Cross's emphasis on the extensive nature of the evidence she encountered, her own estimate of the numbers of cases relating to gentry adultery and fornication was that they accounted for approximately 60 out of a total of about 120 gentry 'morality' cases she identified between the creation of High Commission and the death of Elizabeth I. Although she does not specify this precisely, the implication is that an average of only one or two such cases might come before High Commission in any one year, which in itself does not bear out the allegedly pervasive nature of the phenomenon.

If, for a moment, we focus on the evidence for the extent of bastardy provided by this unusually full set of church court papers, it is possible to test and extrapolate Cross's conclusions about the extent and pattern of prosecution by examining those immorality and matrimonial cases which came before High Commission between 1560 and its demise in 1640. As discussed above, the court initially saw an average of just over one case per year, experiencing a very significant peak in the 1570s, with sixty-three cases being dealt with in that decade, but the figures plateau in the later sixteenth century and decline in the early seventeenth.[4] The indications that this evidence is shaped very significantly by the pattern of enforcement rather than providing easily legible indications of the character and level of certain behaviours is evident here, and reinforced by further investigation. Unfortunately the often sparse information that these entries provide means that it is rarely possible to identify whether the production of bastard children is part of the accusation of immorality being laid. Maurice Ashton's case in 1572–73 definitely involved the production of 'dyvers children' by his mistress of eight or nine years' standing. Twenty years later in 1593, Thomas Roos was prosecuted as he had 'with divers women comitted adultery and got six bastards'.[5] That he had to perform penance in Laxton and Egmanton parish churches and Retford and Newark market places with a paper on his head stating the number of illegitimate children he had begotten (rather than the names of his mistresses for example), suggests that the Commissioners viewed the fathering of those children as excessive behaviour. In contrast, in the 1620s Ellen Gregson did not have to have a paper on her head stating her four children by Sir Richard Shirburn to be bastards when she performed her penances in Mitton parish church and Skipton market place.[6]

The Act Books alone can therefore provide evidence for only part of this argument, given the often sparse information on the essential aspects of each case that they contain. The greatest detail is available in those cases for which cause papers survive, providing as they do a fuller set of documentation relating to the issue. An examination of the marital and immorality litigation in the York ecclesiastical courts between 1450 and 1640, which has left material among the cause papers, indicates 141 relevant cases involving participants who described themselves as of gentry status or above.

There are, however, still very few cases in this group which make explicit reference to bastard children, a total of fifteen, and even here the existence or status of a child might be contested. The cases involved six female and three male plaintiffs (one man presenting two suits against his wife), while seven were ex-officio. Considering the defendants in cases where base-born children resulted from adultery or fornication, the cases produce seventeen individuals: five women and twelve men were prosecuted independently (one woman twice) and two couples were cited in two joint actions. Where individual women were the defendants, two out of the three women had left the marital home, with further gendered implications which will be examined later. In both cases where there were joint defendants, the parties denied any impropriety at all. In one of these, an immorality case brought by the court in 1572, Edward Holme and Anne Constable alias Holme defended themselves against the charges of adultery, fornication and thus begetting a child by arguing that they were actually married, although in their evidence they did not provide any details of where and when the ceremony took place, who conducted it and who was present.[7] In the other, in her action for Restitution of Conjugal Rights, Anne Wormley accused her husband Simon of adultery and conceiving a child with Elizabeth Sparrow (as well as cruelty and violence), which they denied.[8] While the birth of a child might, prima facie, have been solid proof of sexual impropriety, even the actual existence of such children could be a source of debate: Simon Wormley and Elizabeth Swallow denied the existence of any child born to them as they said they were innocent of the adultery/fornication charge. The surviving evidence of a case involving Matthew and Bridget Redman refers to a child who may have been born to Bridget or fathered by Matthew (but not conceived by them jointly) and whose welfare was organised by Matthew Redman's sister, Mary Gargrave. The practice of fostering children enabled the concealment of births, particularly to married elite women, who could not sanction financial settlements or purchase estates for their own illegitimate children independently.[9] Alongside fostering, technically illegitimate children born of a wife's adultery may have been concealed by the husband's acknowledgement of the child, wittingly or unwittingly, for some time after the birth. To a very limited extent, the paternity of an adulterous wife's child could be established by her period of absence from the marital home and reports of the 'vicious and offensive life' reaching the courts.[10]

While confirming the likely extensive nature of gentry and noble mistress-keeping, the evidence from other courts also suggests both the limited impact of elite bastardy on the system and its relative invisibility there. In the diocese of Chester, the short-lived Ecclesiastical Commission of 1543 tackled ten cases of high-profile gentry immorality in one month, but evidence for bastardy has not survived in this context.[11] The inefficiency of the Chester courts has already been noted, with the bulk of York High Commission immorality cases of the early 1570s originating with Cheshire gentlemen. Whereas in 1562, Chester High Commission heard that William Heiton kept Alice Eccles his servant, but did not refer to any children he may have had, by 1572, when he appeared before York High Commission his mistress's name was left blank, but it was noted that he 'hath dyvers children with her'.[12] The number of bastardy cases appearing in the Chester courts between 1541 (the formation of the diocese) and 1640 is similar to that of York over a slightly longer time span – fifteen.[13]

Meanwhile, in Durham, references to bastardy in High Commission and Consistory courts (including that for the archdeaconry of Northumberland) are more frequent than in York and Chester, although still rare in themselves. Thirty gentry cases reference bastardy between 1531 and 1640, some of which were clearly designed to enforce paternity and subsequent financial arrangements. In 1611, Janet Dixon initiated two cases; one of matrimonial enforcement and another of filiation against the serial offender Christopher Athie.[14] The archdeaconry of Northumberland prosecuted a miller, Andrew Dawson, and Agnes Lawson for their sexual relationship, but, it was argued, Lawson lived in the house of a gentleman, Mark Collingwood, and it was he who had the sexual relationship with Lawson but 'hath caused the milner to take to be the father of it'.[15] The limited surviving material for the Carlisle diocese does not contain any explicit bastardy cases but, as shown in chapter 1, the loyalty of those gentlemen keeping order along the Anglo-Scottish border was brought into question by their choice of sexual partners and the Anglo-Scottish marriage alliances of bastard offspring.[16]

While the church courts of Carlisle, Durham, York and Chester therefore assist us in understanding the boundaries of illegitimate and legitimate relationships, they provide relatively little assistance in developing our understanding of the prevalence of bastard-bearing among the elite. Unlike in some other social contexts, in most gentry immorality litigation the bastard child was not the primary focus. We must therefore turn to other sources. Although the primary focus of much of the earlier work on illegitimacy has been on parish registers and records generated by the poor law and associated mechanisms, these too are intrinsically less likely to reveal a trace of gentry involvement in bastardy. The gentry's capacity for concealment arising from social status and the immunity from financial pressures consequent on relative wealth had obvious effects on the records. One of the most focused of earlier studies touching on this subject, Keith Wrightson and David Levine's investigation of illegitimacy in the parish of Terling (Essex) between 1590 and 1640, discovered only one man of gentry status fathering a child out of fifty putative fathers.[17] While the adoption of parish registers for baptisms, marriages and burials became a legal requirement in 1538, there was no standard method of recording parentage, status or illegitimacy. The surviving parish registers of as large a town as Stockport, for example, on the Mersey crossing in Cheshire, do not specify any children as being base-born at all for a significant part of this period.[18] Then in the parish of Mirfield, over the Pennines in the West Riding, the record of the baptism of 'Alexander son of Ellynn Foster baze begotten by Rodger Nowell, gent' from 1605, contains very full information about the child, his mother and the gentry status of his father, while in Lancashire, at Croston in 1552 that for 'Robert Blundell nothus' simply confirms the bastardy with no references to either parent.[19] Between these extremes, a record might identify the child's name and either that of the mother ('Margaret Rosthorne, base daughter of Alice Rosthorne') at Burnley, or father (such as Elena, Anna and William, illegitimate children of Henry Barcroft, gentleman), at Colne, both in Lancashire.[20] These inconsistencies reflect the different approaches to record keeping by parish officers, but do mean that registers have to be used with caution when identifying gentry bastardy and are particularly problematic as sources for a quantitative approach.

As with the ecclesiastical courts, so too with other courts: quantification of elite bastardy is extremely problematic. While manorial courts were not necessarily concerned with the morality or otherwise of the population, the implications of such behaviour might manifest themselves in relation to these jurisdictions. The Court Rolls of the honor of Clitheroe, for example, during the 1550s, record Richard Towneley's transfer of property in the forest of Rossendale to feoffees to hold for the use of Anne, Ellen and Mary Towneley, 'daughters to the late Alice Brunley deceased otherwise called bastard daughters of the said Richard Towneley.'[21] On a larger scale, inquisitions *post mortem* returned into the Duchy of Lancaster Chancery court reveal the extensive base-born family for which Sir Robert Hesketh was responsible.[22] The Duchy court had an equity jurisdiction over its properties, which again did not touch directly upon the moral behaviour of the residents, but did arbitrate in inheritance disputes and therefore could reveal bastardy, for example in a dispute involving land at Sutton, Rainford and Whiston (Lancashire) and the extensive brood of illegitimate children fathered by Rauf Atherton.[23] In none of these categories, however, can we approach a sense of a quantifiable set of data.

Other types of sources, which might be thought more likely to allow us to access elite behaviour, are either strikingly opaque or unlikely to help us to come close to a quantitative response to our questions. Gentry correspondence, for example, is highly suggestive, but the body of evidence for our period is not extensive enough for confident extrapolation and its nature is also dependent upon the nature of the correspondents involved. John Chamberlain, an observer reporting the court gossip in 1596, passed on the news of one of the queen's ladies: 'Mrs [Elizabeth] Vernon [daughter of John Vernon of Hodnet, Shropshire] is from the Court, and lies in Essex house; some say she hath taken a venew under the girdle and swells upon it, yet she complains not of fowle play but sayes the Erle of Southampton will justifie it'. Lady Anne Bacon wrote to the earl of Essex (also in 1596) to condemn his affair with her great niece, the countess of Derby. There is, however, no surviving evidence to suggest that she wrote to Lady Derby.[24] The Plumpton letters and associated papers provide some evidence for the activity of the illegitimate offspring of Sir William Plumpton (d. 1480), and insights into the attitudes of the father of one of the more successful bastard lines in the early modern north, the Plumptons' neighbour Sir Henry Savile (d. 1558). As to the early lives of these bastard children (or their mothers), however, this material is entirely obscure.[25] This lack of comment is apparently typical, as it is mirrored in the major collections of correspondence from outside our region: from the beginning of our period, the Paston letters suggest the existence of illegitimate offspring fathered by at least two members of the family – but despite the exceptionally rich texture of their evidence for many aspects of moral and social behaviours and attitudes, these bastard children appear in only the briefest hints in the evidence. John Paston III referred to his 'lytyll man', and Edmund seems to have fathered a child by one 'Mistress Dixon'; but these references are extremely brief, and the bastard daughter fathered by John II, and mentioned by Margaret, the child's grandmother, in her will, does not appear in the correspondence at all.[26] The Cely correspondence (from an urban context) is slightly more forthcoming, suggesting that male members of the family customarily kept mistresses in Calais before marrying, but only in one instance is there very direct evidence there of a child being conceived.[27] The Paston material also allows some insights into the lives of their neighbours. We therefore know of the marital difficulties of both John Heydon and Sir Thomas Tuddenham and the apparently illegitimate offspring of their wives, but even here the subject is elusive.[28] There might be an indication of shame or sensitivity in this, which will be explored below in chapter 6, but not necessarily: it must simply be accepted that correspondence of this kind, even when it is as extensive as the Paston material, does not necessarily include extensive reference to bastard children. Diaries can also be just as discreet. Lady Anne Clifford, for example, often referred to her extended family of aunts, uncles, cousins and other, more distant connections, but her illegitimate half-siblings Frances and George Clifford are absent from her diary. Her father's mistress is not referred to by name, but is described as 'a lady of quality'; she was probably easily identifiable by contemporary late Tudor/early Stuart society but less so by twenty-first-century historians.[29] Lady Anne did comment upon her husband's relationship with Lady Penistone, her visit to them at Knole in Kent, and the condemnation of it by local members of the gentry. She did not record any children born to Lord Dorset and Lady Penistone, however.[30]

Other apparently promising sources are also problematic in any attempt to approach a quantitative analysis of bastardy in the elite. The genealogical sources, especially the heraldic visitations which proliferated in the later sixteenth and seventeenth centuries, even if we accept that any objectivity on the part of the heralds involved was severely qualified by their dependence on the families with whom they worked, turn out to be unhelpful. The purpose of their work was to understand claims to armorial status, and so illegitimate children might conveniently be ignored entirely, or their status might be left ambiguous in other contexts. At best, this is made clear by the treatment of some illegitimate daughters; 'Izabel Percy, natural daughter of Sir Ingram Percy' features in the Yorkshire visitation material of 1563–64 in the Tempest entry as the wife of Henry and mother of Stephen, but not in the Percy family pedigree as her father's daughter. The same is true of Elizabeth Stanley, illegitimate daughter of the second earl of Derby, who features in the Lancashire visitation of 1567 as the wife of Thomas Scarisbrick and mother of James, but is not present within the Stanley family entry. By contrast, the illegitimate Clifford children (sons and daughters of Henry, 10th Lord Clifford and the second earl of Cumberland) do not feature in the 1563–64 visitation of Yorkshire at all.[31]

By studying the prevalence of illegitimate relatives in the wills of the English nobility and gentry it is, however, possible to broaden the scope of investigation and to gain some better sense of the prevalence of bastardy among the elite. A sample drawn from the published wills of testators of noble, knightly, esquire and gentry status from Northumberland, Durham, Yorkshire, Lancashire, Cheshire, Cumberland and Westmorland has been examined, covering the years 1450–1640.[32] This maps, with some exceptions, onto the sphere of influence of northern High Commission and therefore allows for a comparison between the evidence from the church courts and that produced for other reasons. Of a total of 876 wills examined, ninety-six (11 per cent) contained explicit references to illegitimate beneficiaries.[33] Of these ninety-six wills, eight testators were members of the nobility, twenty-seven were knights, twenty-three were esquires and thirty-eight were other members of the gentry. Given that the gentry were far more numerous than the nobility, it is not surprising to find a correspondingly larger number of testators within the gentry group. However, if the wills are examined within the context of social peer groupings alternative factors begin to emerge. For example, of the 876 wills in question, just forty were made by members of the nobility, but of these eight (20 per cent) mentioned illegitimate beneficiaries. These included the wills of two Lords Monteagle, Edward and Thomas, who were father and son, and two women, Lady Elizabeth Scrope and Katherine, countess of Northumberland.[34] By contrast, when the wills of men describing themselves as gentlemen are examined, of 371 in total, only thirty-eight (10.2 per cent) contain references to illegitimate beneficiaries. Therefore, in terms of social groupings, provision for illegitimate relatives was a disproportionately significant issue for noble as opposed to lesser gentry testators. We might initially speculate that this reflected a combination of a greater propensity to father, willingness to acknowledge, and capacity to support illegitimate offspring.

Plotting the results of the study of wills across time, it is clear that there are three notable peaks for the number of illegitimate beneficiaries, in 1521–30, 1561–70 and 1591–1600. It appears, however, that these are influenced by a handful of people providing for a large number of illegitimate dependants in each of these decades: Laurence Dutton referring to five in 1527, Thomas Forster eight in 1587, and Luke Ogle and Thomas Legh twelve between them in 1595–97. If, instead, we graph the numbers of testators making mention of illegitimate offspring by decade, the results are smoothed, to a fairly consistent level, albeit still with a noticeable peak in 1561–70. This might imply a greater readiness to acknowledge bastardy in those years, and a greater propensity to produce them in perhaps the three decades before that. There is an interesting comparison to be made here with Richard Adair's figures for lower-status bastardy, which start with 3.5% of births in 1538–50 then see a reduction to 2.3% between 1551 and 1560, and are at their lowest for our period in the decade 1561–70, at 2.2%. Hollingsworth's figures for the British peerage, on an admittedly very small sample, also see a drop from 4.7% of all recorded births in 1550–75 to consistently a very low figure below 2% through to the post-Restoration period.[35] The turbulence around the religious, cultural and social changes of the period therefore seems to have enhanced rather than diminished the bastardy culture of the elite in the north. It may be possible, for example, to propose a link between the peak in elite testators mentioning bastard offspring in 1561–70, on the one hand, and the evident debate around the same time about marriage and 'divorce' for the gentry on the other. There is little sign, for example, that this ferment of ideas about the legitimacy of remarriage passed far beyond the gentry, and it is clear that in some cases it was precisely the (in)ability to pass on landed inheritances that was cited as the reason for a review of the existing bar to a new marriage that might produce an heir, and the existence of well-placed connections that gave some gentlemen hope of success.[36] While, too, Adair's figures might allow for a correlation to some degree between bastard-bearing and periods of economic and social stress, mainly because of the way such stresses might break a previously firmly agreed intention to marry, economic conditions do not seem to have had an impact on gentlemen's willingness to father and (if in a limited way) acknowledge bastard children.

While the wills are not necessarily easy to plot geographically, some sub-regional patterns are evident.[37] In absolute terms, the county with the largest number of wills citing illegitimate beneficiaries is Yorkshire with thirty-two, a phenomenon which may be accounted for by it being a significantly larger area and population. Proportionately, however, it is the counties to the west of the Pennines which are best represented in the sample of

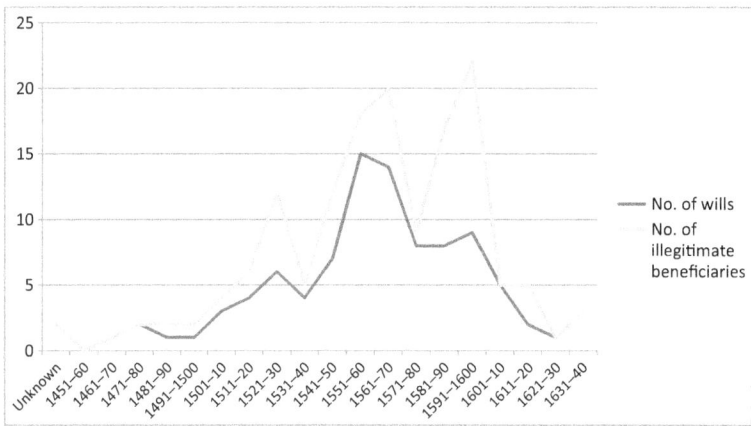

Figure 1   Number of wills and illegitimate beneficiaries, 1450–1640
Note: For a complete list of sources, see p. 55, n. 32.

wills, Cheshire and Lancashire being most prominent. Some of this regional patterning is also chronologically distinctive: prior to 1550, Lancashire produces only one such will, while after 1550 the county produces twenty-three. Even more striking is the peak in wills from Lancashire occurring during the 1590s, when the general trend across the whole of the north may have been of stability or even decline. Curiously, Lancashire's western neighbour, Cheshire, may have reached its peak in the 1550s.

The evidence of the wills of the gentry and nobility in some other areas outside the north, by contrast, provides no mention of bastard offspring. For example, a sample of published wills from Somerset and Lincolnshire produces no examples at all of explicit mentions of illegitimate offspring. Bedfordshire produces only one case out of thirty-one wills.[38] Yet other evidence from precisely these areas suggests that illegitimate offspring were far from unknown there; for example, some time during the years 1518–29, William Stafford, the bastard son of Thomas Stafford esquire of Tattenhoe in Buckinghamshire, felt confident enough to sue Robert Hobbes, abbot of the well-connected abbey of Woburn, in Chancery over the detention of deeds relating to manors and lands in Buckingham, Bedford, Wiltshire and Worcester, as part of a dispute with his legitimate kin.[39] It is likely, therefore, that a regional pattern of reticence affects the identification of illegitimate offspring in wills in some areas, a possibility that will be explored in greater depth in chapter 6 below.

There is an interesting contrast between the chronological patterning of this material from wills and that from the church courts considered in chapter 1 and at the start of this chapter. There, in northern High Commission, it was established that the levels of prosecution of gentlemen fell away after the initial period of activism associated in particular with Archbishop Grindal. Men and women of the highest status became effectively exempt

Table 1 Totals of wills by county and period

Date	Yorkshire	Lancashire	Cheshire	Northumberland	Durham	Notts	TOTAL
1450–60	1	0	0	0	0	0	1
1461–70	1	0	0	0	0	0	1
1471–80	2	0	0	0	0	0	2
1481–90	1	0	0	0	0	0	1
1491–1500	1	0	0	0	0	0	1
1501–10	3	0	0	0	0	0	3
1511–20	4	0	0	0	0	0	4
1521–30	4	1	1	0	0	0	6
1531–40	4	0	0	0	0	0	4
1541–50	5	0	1	0	0	1	7
1551–60	6	3	5	0	0	0	14
1561–70	5	2	2	2	3	0	14
1571–80	0	3	2	2	1	0	8
1581–90	0	2	1	3	2	0	8
1591–1600	0	6	2	1	0	0	9
1601–10	0	3	0	2	0	0	5
1611–20	0	1	0	1	0	0	2
1621–30	0	1	0	0	0	0	1
1630–40	0	2	0	0	1	0	3
unknown			2				2
TOTAL	37	24	16	11	7	1	96

Note: For a complete list of sources, see p. 55, n. 32.

from the rigour of the church's discipline; with a handful of exceptions, only those from the minor gentry remained potentially open to challenge in the courts (and even there it was often other factors, such as other aspects of conduct or religious affiliation which were responsible for making such action possible or likely). In this the court became more like other ecclesiastical courts. For example, the evidence of the Chichester diocesan courts in the sixteenth century suggests a lack of engagement with elite bastardy. Houlbrooke confirms that offenders of substantial wealth and gentle birth were seldom dealt with in Norwich and the other dioceses he studied. Bishop Thomas Thirlby in Norwich was exceptional in this regard – in August 1552 he personally exhorted the mistress of Sir Roger Woodhouse of Kimberley (Norfolk), and his chancellor punished an alderman of Norwich for his adultery with a servant, but this was very unusual.[40] Ingram suggests that churchwardens were unwilling to present gentry offenders due to their rank; he also traced an early seventeenth-century decline in bastardy cases in Salisbury commensurate with an increase in more lucrative cases brought against those labouring on Sundays and Holy days.[41] One of the starkest examples of this is to be found in the extremely detailed and conscientious record of the visitation of the archdeaconry of Suffolk in 1499. The level of engagement in the process was exceptionally high; the prevalence of sexual issues in the minds of those presenting and the officials who handled their complaints is plainly evident; and yet while authority figures in the clergy were challenged, gentlemen were not.[42] Yet the evidence of wills would suggest continuing relatively high levels of bastard-bearing on the part of the mistresses of the gentry, especially in the areas of the north just mentioned. An interplay in the mid-sixteenth century between more evident tolerance of bastardy and mistress-keeping among significant parts of gentry and aristocratic society and a concomitant desire on the part of other elements of lay and clerical elites to control it, most notably through the Commissions beginning in Lancashire in 1543, produced a relatively short-lived crop of evidence from an 'enforcement wave'.[43] This should not however distract us from the underlying behaviour of the elite. While recent studies of elite bastardy in the thirteenth, fourteenth and fifteenth centuries have tended to downplay overall rates of bastardy, both then and in the subsequent two centuries it is necessary to affirm the illegitimate relationships and offspring of the elite as a significant part of social and political history. Matthews' suggestion that 1–1.5% of men fathered bastard children is almost certainly an underestimate;[44] the likelihood is that the bastardy rate through the sixteenth and probably into the seventeenth centuries ran above that level, and perhaps twice as high, with significantly higher levels still in some areas.

What this striking finding also opens up is a set of questions about the nature of bastardy itself in the north of England among the elite. Implicit within the understanding of the term 'bastard', to twenty-first century eyes at least, is the marital status of the parents of the child. An illegitimate child may have been born in a pre-, extra-, or post-marital relationship (e.g. during widowhood), but factors surrounding marriage formation or the continuation of an informal relationship are important here, as differing intentions of participants, and therefore attitudes towards bastardy, can be detected. This has an influence upon consideration of the extent of bastardy, which in the sixteenth and seventeenth centuries could be a more nebulous idea than straightforward birth outside marriage. Any quantitative analysis of the extent of bastardy therefore must reflect upon the circumstances surrounding conception and the nature of the parents' sexual conduct.

Premarital fornication, subsequent pregnancy or bastard-bearing may have led to wedlock, as in the case of Alice Nelson and Robert Mawdesley who, in a bond dated 1589, referred to his son 'William Mawdysley, his bastard son by Alice his now wife.'[45] The capacity to conceal or to some extent cancel *de facto* illegitimacy through marriage was not guaranteed, as is evident in Mawdesley's case, but, as will be demonstrated, the status of a child could alter over time. This type of behaviour was one of the more typical underlying non-elite bastard-bearing. It was, however, relatively rare in this form among the elite. Matrimony was not a path taken by all parents; Sir John Pilkington, Sir John Byron and Sir Ingram Percy remained single throughout their lives, while fathering two sons and a daughter between them. The sons of Pilkington and Byron inherited property by will in 1478 and 1558 and as such were legally legitimate successors ahead of collateral, legitimate relatives.[46] There were unquestionably adulterous couples within established marriages who could not wed before the death of their respective spouses but who evidently had this intention, with some, such as Bridget Redman and William Gascoigne, waiting many years before they could marry each other.[47] Some parents were unable to marry, forcing their children to remain irrefutably illegitimate. The fourth earl of Derby, for example, died in 1593, his wife Margaret Clifford in 1596, meaning he was unable to marry Joan Halsall, the mother of his four illegitimate children. Post-matrimonial relationships, after the death of a spouse, are also in evidence with Thomas Pykerynge providing money for the 'funding' and legitimation of his son Anthony and any future child begotten with his servant Jane.[48] Perhaps Pykerynge's insistence that the inheritance be spent upon a legitimation suggests an intention, never fulfilled, to marry Jane, but at any rate he took steps to ensure Anthony's bastard status could be altered. Post-matrimonial bastard-bearing was not restricted to men. Elizabeth Leigh, widow of Thomas, was named in the court of High Commission as the mother of Edward Middleton's illegitimate child in 1597, although she does not appear to have been prosecuted.[49]

The extent to which some of the apparently straightforward benchmarks of matrimonial legality were openly questioned during the late medieval and early modern period in the north west, with subsequent implications for the status of any children, has led Jennifer McNabb to challenge what has become one of the most widely accepted orthodoxies in the social history of late medieval and early modern England. Using evidence from matrimonial litigation in the church courts at Chester, she argued that too much emphasis has been placed on the unidirectional nature of change in patterns of marital relationships and their formation, in essence the church's success in insisting on the reading of banns, or a marriage licence process, and an open ceremony in church, with the priest / minister officiating, and the partners over-age, exemplified by the work of Martin Ingram, Ralph Houlbrooke and David Cressy.[50] Among sparse marital litigation, the element relating specifically to annulment and separation was consistently extremely limited: these authorities would argue that if the making of a marriage was not open to contest, then subsequent issues in the relationship between partners were even less likely to be explored and resolved through the church courts.[51] By contrast, McNabb pointed in particular to evidence from the north west of England to suggest that in some areas at least it was possible in the late sixteenth and seventeenth centuries for marriages to continue to be made between partners in their early youth through negotiation between their kin, and for more mature individuals to be accepted as married on the basis of present-tense matrimonial consent outside church. The validity of these marriages rested more in the willingness of kin, neighbours and friends to accept them than did the allegedly more pervasively accepted church wedding between consenting adult partners. This, she argued, meant that 'residents' were able to apply their own standards in judging the reputation of couples whose children were born outside church-sanctioned wedlock.[52]

McNabb argued that the language of solemnisation was used for child-marriage arrangement or 'any event expressing marital consent', and that present-tense matrimonial consent was associated with rituals and signs such as the exchange of handkerchiefs, scarves and other gifts, and associated 'words and demeanor'. She associated this continuing tendency with the high levels of bastard-bearing identified by Adair in the 'highland' region of England, since she identified it with the practice of commencing sexual relations once serious courtship had begun, probably, and certainly once present-tense matrimonial consent had been confirmed. It was also the context for a phenomenon which Adair identified as occurring only in the north and west: that of 'stable, consensual unions that produced a string of children who were nonetheless deemed illegitimate by the church'. Unwed women and men producing children together 'were able to maintain credit within their social networks'.[53]

McNabb's argument was not segmented according to social class, and none of her examples were associated explicitly with the gentry.[54] Nevertheless, it stands in interesting alignment with Claire Cross's important arguments about the continuing significance among the gentry of (and often court support for) present-tense consent in the face of frequent social pressures for marriages that reflected political priorities and careful arrangement,[55] and further her suggestions that gentry sexual morality was characterised by a constant tension with the discipline implied by church-controlled marriage, at the formation of the original contract and even more prominently in later attempts to escape from or vary it.[56]

McNabb and Cross's arguments, in suggesting that the church-court evidence from York and Chester might show us a traditional view of marriage as a privately contracted present-tense consent arrangement, both placed emphasis on the role played by support for this from neighbours of the couple. The York cause papers, in cases touching on the elite, do frequently include witnesses referring to 'the common voice and fame' in a parish, that a couple lived together as man and wife or had been known to commit adultery together. This was, however, generally deployed by the plaintiff, suggesting that any implication it might protect alleged offenders is misplaced in relation to gentry cases. Nicholas Bacon, for example, faced the accusation that 'it is the common opinion of the inhabitants of Long Cowton, Darneton, Yarme Northallerton and Bedall that you have beene and are an irreligious and profane person … a man publiquely defamed.'[57] Cross's assertion of the tendency to accept the unconventional relationships even of gentry women is still harder to support from the evidence. Reference was made in the testimonies to the effect of 'inordinate and lascivious' living upon the local communities in which the alleged adulterers and fornicators dwelt, particularly if they were women. Barbara Tetlam's behaviour (living apart from her husband and co-habiting with William Smith and then Robert Blintstone) was, for example, described as 'very offensive to the inhabitants of the said Parish of Brodesworth', near Doncaster.[58] Therefore, while there is some limited evidence for present-tense consent as a basis for marriage supported by kin and neighbours among the northern gentry, this form of relationship was not the predominant factor in 'illicit' relationships and the procreation of children of questionable legitimacy during the period.

All this evidence suggests the diversity of contexts within which relationships might be formed and maintained. It also suggests the frequency with which either party entered a relationship without the intention of forming some form of legitimate or alternative marriage. The matrimonial career of Rafe Holden was particularly complicated but illustrates something of what was possible in the accumulation of relationships. Based in Lancashire,

Holden's first marriage was to Gile Bilsbie, by whom he had at least one daughter, who married Simon Danbie, a merchant living in Hull. Bilsbie went (or was sent by Holden) in 1546 to live with the Danbies across the Pennines, where she was informed that her husband had taken a new wife, Isabel Haughton.[59] That Bilsbie's death in 1547 post-dated the marriage with Haughton was a key piece of evidence deposed in 1561 when Holden appeared before the Chester ecclesiastical court accused of bigamy and adultery. This was because at some time between 1547 and 1560 the Holden-Haughton marriage broke down and, bizarrely, he found himself in two courts simultaneously, defending himself against charges of adultery and bigamy with a woman whom he argued in another court he had never been lawfully married to. By 1560, Holden was involved in a relationship with Elizabeth Elston, who had previously contracted marriage with James Anderton. Elston sued Anderton for an annulment in the York Consistory, on the grounds that they had both been minors at the time of their wedding. In her evidence to the court, Elston described her belief

> that Rawfe Holdene sence the begynnyng of the said suyte between the said James Andertonne and hir had no wif nor yet hath any except this respondent, but before the suyte moved between … Andertonne and hir she beleveth he had a wif, but not a lawful wife because she beleveth she contracted with an other man and committed adultery.[60]

The outcome of Elston's case against Anderton is unknown, but at the same time Anderton sued Rafe Holden and Elizabeth Holden for their adultery. In describing his previous relationship, Holden argued simply that while his marriage to Haughton had been solemnised in the face of the church, it had been unlawful as she had been pre-contracted to another unnamed man.[61] Exactly where and when Holden and Elston exchanged vows and when their son Robert was born is unknown, but by 1563 High Commission ordered Holden to abstain from the company of Elizabeth on the basis of her relationship with Anderton, and the court seems to have met with some success in separating them. In 1567, Holden purchased lands in Chaigley near Clitheroe in 1567 for his 'bastard son Robert Elston, son of Elizabeth Elston.'[62] However, Robert Holden signed the 1613 visitation of Lancashire which suggests that he inherited his father's lands and that he presented himself as the legitimate son of Rafe and his wife Elizabeth, heiress of Richard Elston.[63]

Rafe Holden was not alone in having a marital life well out of line with the norms expected by the sixteenth-century church. His contemporary Ralph Rishton of Ponthalgh in Lancashire made a marriage with Helen Towneley when they were both under age, but evidence deposed in the York court suggests they were living together as man and wife by about 1540, when they were in their mid-to-late teens. Rishton repudiated Towneley and entered a relationship with Elizabeth Parker, whom he married in 1546 during the lifetime of his first wife. The Rishton-Parker relationship was solemnised in the parish church at Clitheroe by William Rishton who produced evidence of a Towneley-Rishton divorce at the request of Sir Thomas Talbot of Bashall. One witness testified that in approximately 1557, he saw Ralph Rishton pay £4 to the Commissary of the Bishop of Chester in lieu of penance and enter a bond 'to absteyne frome the company of Elizabeth Parker' (to whom he was supposedly married). The picture is complicated further by the involvement of Anne Stanley, daughter of Sir James and Lady Anne Stanley of Crosshall, and hence the granddaughter of the first earl of Derby. Henry Bowthman testified that also in about 1557 John Rishton, husband of Anne Stanley, told him that his daughter Jane Rishton 'is none of my doughter, she is Rauffe Rishtons'.[64] Witnesses testified that by 1562 Ralph Rishton had 'put away' Parker and married Anne Stanley at his house in Dunkenhalghe. Stanley's mother, Lady Anne, was almost certainly by this stage widowed, and in any case for many years before her husband's death lived as the mistress of William Venables of Kinderton. Her interest through her previous marriage in the Talbot of Bashall family manifested itself, since it was apparently in collaboration with her son Sir Thomas Talbot that she now acted. It was claimed that Anne Stanley, her daughter by her marriage to Sir James, was the mistress of Sir Thomas, her son by Edmund Talbot – and that together they manoeuvred Anne into this marriage with Rishton. Sir Thomas Talbot was undoubtedly influential and able to call on Stanley resources, as his election as senior knight of the shire in Lancashire in 1558 would suggest.[65] Parker launched a suit against Rishton and Stanley in 1562, the pair came to the attention of York High Commission shortly before Ralph Rishton's death in 1572, and the case was still live in 1577 when Archbishop Hutton ruled that Anne Stanley and John Rishton had been lawfully married.[66] Examples like this had implications for the status of children, such as John Rishton's son Harry and daughter Jane, theoretically born within wedlock, but regarded as illegitimate by sections of the east Lancashire community. The pattern of bastard-bearing therefore represents not the simple continuation of previous approaches to marriage, as McNabb would argue, but a range of attitudes to non-conventional sexual relationships, within which community-supported present-tense consent was not particularly significant.

There were other contexts for the production of illegitimate children, and court was notable among them. Paul Hammer has written of the spike in immorality at the Elizabethan court during the 1590s, in particular noting the sexual conduct of the queen's maids of honour resulting in marriages undertaken without royal permission.[67] The situations cited by Hammer to some extent parallel and contrast with extra-marital sexual liaisons among Henry VIII's courtiers during the 1540s, although the earlier cases all involve marriage breakdown leading to the bastardisation of children, while many of the later affairs focus upon illicit behaviour leading to marriage formation and the legitimation of subsequent issue. In 1543 alone, Margaret, Humfrey and Arthur, the three children of Elizabeth, Lady Burgh were declared to be bastards, and she confirmed that she had lived in adultery during the lifetime of her husband Sir Thomas; Anne, Lady Parr had left her husband and born an illegitimate child; and Lady Draycott, daughter and heir of John Fitzherbert, was reported to have left her husband Sir Philip twenty years previously and attempted to disinherit her children by him.[68]

Furthermore, Queen Elizabeth's death did not mean the end of extensive illicit behaviour. Writing after the accession of King James I and Queen Anne, Lady Anne Clifford noted in her diary: 'Now there was much talk of a Mask which the Queen had at Winchester, & how all the Ladies about the Court had gotten such ill names that it was grown a scandalous place, & the Queen herself was much fallen from her former greatness & reputation she had in the world.'[69] The Jacobean court was the setting for some notorious illicit affairs, in particular the relationship between Robert Carr, earl of Somerset, and Frances Howard, countess of Essex.[70] Frances Howard's brother, Sir Robert Howard, was the father of Frances Coke's son Robert, rather than her husband, John Villiers, Viscount Purbeck, and their sister Elizabeth, countess of Banbury was the mother of two sons considered to be fathered by Lord Vaux, but born during the lifetime of the earl.[71]

For some northern aristocratic and gentry families several of these contexts might be relevant. In many cases, through an amalgamation of a variety of different types of source material, it is possibly to piece together not just one or two isolated incidences of bastard-bearing, but a patchwork of kinship and familial connections of elite members of society among whom illegitimate members were important over a period of time. In the two centuries between c. 1450 and 1640, four out of the six Lords Clifford/earls of Cumberland produced at least one illegitimate child, while the seven generations of Stanley earls of Derby fathered at least five children through two of the heads of the family, and records also indicate the illicit but childless activities of Elizabeth de Vere, countess of Derby whose affair with the earl of Essex resulted in her rustication.[72] Some families demonstrated a prodigious capacity for bastard-bearing over the course of two or more generations. A variety of sources indicate that the Hesketh family produced four successive generations of base-born children between 1500 and 1620, including those possibly born to Jane Spenser in the lifetime of her first husband Richard Haresnape, prior to her marriage with Robert Hesketh and acknowledged by him.[73] Details of Robert Hesketh's will point to the three girls being fathered by Hesketh. He described them as 'my wife's daughters' yet granted them lands in 'Wrightington and Shevington', to 'them and their heirs forever.'

In addition to the Heskeths, the Halsall family, also from Lancashire, produced three successive generations of bastards between about 1525 and 1600. Sir Thomas Halsall fathered three illegitimate sons, Thomas, Gilbert and Cuthbert, as well as his legitimate son Henry, who in his turn was the father of base-born Silvester and Edward. By his wife Anne Molyneux, Henry Halsall also fathered a son Richard, the father of Cuthbert Halsall alias Norreys.[74] In Cheshire, Sir Ralph Egerton was the father of a legitimate son Richard as well as a number of base children, the daughters being so numerous (or he so careless) that he could not remember all their names.[75] Richard Egerton with Alice Sparke (rather than his wife Mary Grosvenor) begot Thomas, a bastard son who later became Lord Chancellor. Such descent within individual families suggests not just a culture of acceptance of adultery or fornication resulting in bastardy, but an active pursuit of alternative yet recognised families. Even where such extensive activity cannot be demonstrated, across the north, and throughout the period in question here, bastard children continued to be produced by members of the nobility and gentry at rates which meant that we must take more account of them and the cultures associated with them. Bastardy was widespread, and beyond the 1–2% of births usually assumed; and this level was sustained. The cultures of masculine honour and those around the formation of marriage continued to support the keeping of mistresses and the production of bastard children, whether a nobleman or

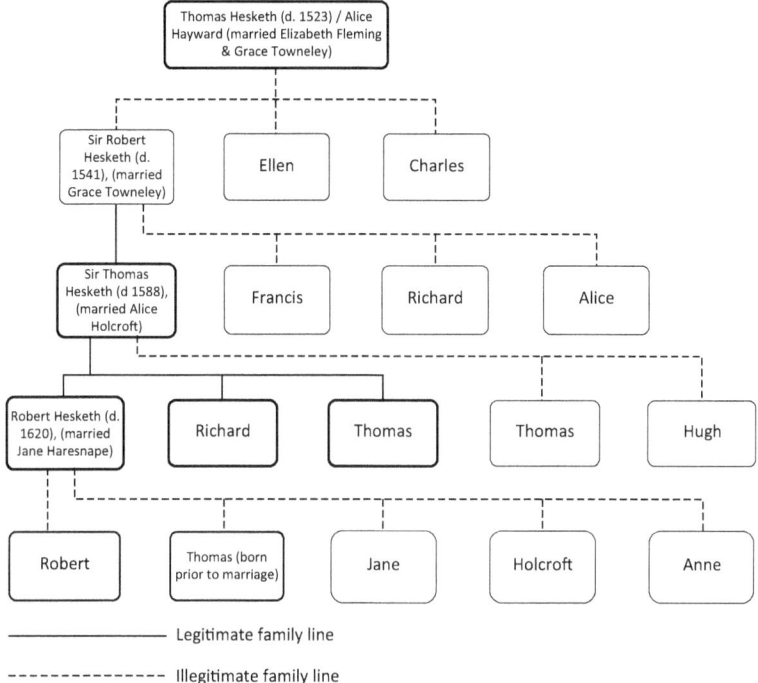

Figure 2   Simplified Hesketh family tree

gentleman was familiar with court and country and had wide social horizons, or was more limited in his spheres of activity. This has implications for the coherence of county society, especially when it is supposed to be built on traditionally defined family networks; alternative kin networks should be recognised, both for the connections they represented and the enmity they caused. Most immediately, we must consider the nature and significance of the relationships with the women who engaged in fornication or adultery with noblemen and gentlemen, and assess the role and status of the mistress.

Notes

1 T. H. Hollingsworth, *The Demography of the English Peerage*, supplement to *Population Studies*, 18 (1964), p. 49; Helen Sarah Matthews, 'Illegitimacy and English Landed Society c. 1285–c. 1500' (unpubl. Ph.D. diss., Royal Holloway University of London, 2013), ch. 2 and pp. 216–18.
2 Claire Cross, 'Sin and Society: The Northern High Commission and the Northern Gentry in the Reign of Elizabeth', in Claire Cross, David Loades and J. J. Scarisbrick (eds), *Law and Government under the Tudors: Essays Presented to Sir Geoffrey Elton ... on ... his Retirement* (Cambridge: Cambridge University Press, 1986). Other, limited, treatments of the subject include Ralph Houlbrooke, *Church Courts and the People during the English Reformation, 1520–1570* (Oxford: Oxford University Press, 1979), p. 79.

3 Cross, 'Sin and Society', pp. 195–209, at pp. 197, 202, 205.
4 For a breakdown of the figures by decade, see p. 36n.74 above.
5 BIA, HC.AB 6, fo. 84 (Ashton); HC.AB 12, fos. 120, 124v, 125v, 128v, 133v, 141v (Roos).
6 BIA, HC.AB 16, fos. 282, 282v, 284. Action against Shirburn did not progress in High Commission. See above, chapter 1, pp. 25–6 for a pardon granted to Shirburn & Gregson in 1621.
7 BIA, CP.G 1625. The simple statement that they had married is suspiciously sparse, in contrast with the elaborate details of marriage ceremonies in other cases, particularly marital validity cases.
8 BIA, HC.CP 1589/6.
9 BIA, CP.G 1096.
10 BIA, CP.H 1897.
11 Cheshire Arch., EDA 12/1; see above, chapter 1, pp. 21–2.
12 Cheshire Arch., EDA 12/2, fos. 19, 68; BIA, HC.AB 6, fo. 85.
13 Cheshire Arch., EDA 12; EDC 2; EDC 5; for the archdeaconry of Richmond, see LRO, ARR/2 and West Yorkshire Archive Service, RD/A/1–8.
14 DUL, DDR/EJ/CCA/1/8, fos. 165, 171, 172, 181, 189v, 190, 195, 196, 198, 202, 222, 224, 226, 230, 240, 242. See DUL, DCD/D/SJB/7, fo. 3 for a case in the Durham High Commission against Athie for incontinence with the wife of William Bankes.
15 DUL, DDR/A/ACN/1, fo. 145v.
16 See chapter 1, pp. 27–8, for Thomas Musgrave, Captain of Bewcastle and Thomas Carleton, Constable of Carlisle Castle; cf. *The Border Papers: Calendar of Letters and Papers Relating to the Affairs of the Borders of England and Scotland Preserved in Her Majesty's Public Record Office London*, ed. Joseph Bain (2 vols. Edinburgh: H. M. General Register House, 1894–96), i. 126, for details of 'a people that wilbe Scottishe when they will, and Englishe at theire pleasure'.
17 David Levine and Keith Wrightson, 'The Social Context of Illegitimacy in Early Modern England', in Peter Laslett, Karla Oosterveen and Richard M. Smith (eds), *Bastardy and Its Comparative History: Studies in the History of Illegitimacy and Marital Nonconformism in Britain, France, Germany, Sweden, North America, Jamaica and Japan* (London: E. Arnold, 1980), Part I: Britain, pp. 158–75.
18 *The Parish Registers of Saint Mary Stockport, Containing the Baptisms, Marriages and Burials from 1584–1620*, ed. E. W. Bulkeley (Stockport: Swain and Co., 1889).
19 *The Register of the Parish of Mirfield*, Part I: *Baptisms, Marriages & Burials 1559–1700*, ed. William Brigg, Yorkshire Parish Register Society, LXIV (1919), p. 61; *The Registers of the Parish Church of Croston in the County of Lancaster: Christenings 1543–1721; Weddings 1538–1685; Burials 1538–1684*, ed. Henry Fishwick, LPRS, 6 (1900), p. 12. Cf 'R[o]b[er]t Hesketh bastard' (1550) at p. 10, and 'An Molnax bast[ard]' (1578) at p. 16. Their legitimate peers are also listed without their parents' names.
20 *The Registers of the Parish of Burnley in the County of Lancaster: Christenings, Weddings, and Burials, 1562 to 1653*, ed. William Farrer, LPRS, 2 (1899), p. 25; *The Registers of the Parish Church of Colne in the County of Lancaster: Christenings, Weddings, and Burials, 1599–1653*, ed. Thomas Backhouse Ecroyd, LPRS, 17 (1904), pp. 16, 23, 26.
21 *The Court Rolls of the Honor of Clitheroe in the County of Lancaster*, vol. III, ed. William Farrer (Edinburgh: Ballantyne Press, 1913), pp. 186–7. Also note that the Court punished Ann Gryme for being a 'fornicatress' in 1555, in a rare immorality case: p. 368.
22 *Lancashire Inquisitions Returned into the Chancery of the Duchy of Lancaster and now Existing in the Public Record Office, London, Stuart Period Part III, 20 to 23 James I*, ed. J. P. Rylands, RSLC, XVII (1888), pp. 351–8.

23 *Pleadings and Depositions in the Duchy Court of Lancaster in the Time of Henry VII and Henry VIII*, ed. H. Fishwick, RSLC, XXXII (1896), pp. 27–31.

24 *Letters Written by John Chamberlain during the Reign of Queen Elizabeth*, ed. Sarah Williams, Camden Society, LXXIX (1861), p. 18; *The Letters of Lady Anne Bacon*, ed. Gemma Allen, Camden Society, 5th ser., 44 (2014), pp. 262–3. See also letters relating to the Cheshire-born Mary Fitton, in her notorious relationship with William Herbert – *Gossip from a Muniment-room, Being Passages in the Lives of Anne and Mary Fitton*, ed. Anne Emily Newdigate–Newdegate (London: Nutt, 1898), esp. pp. 40–6.

25 *The Plumpton Letters and Papers*, ed. Joan Kirby, Camden Society, 5th ser., 8 (1996), e.g. letters 17, 26, 44, 86–7, 150, 154, 173, 178, 182, 240–2.

26 *The Paston Letters*, ed. James Gairdner (6 vols. reprinted in 1; Gloucester: Alan Sutton, 1983), v. 271; *Paston Letters and Papers of the Fifteenth Century*, ed. Norman Davis (2 vols. Oxford: Oxford University Press, 2004–5), i. no. 230. There is also John II's possible bastard son 'little Tom': *ibid.*, i. 415. See Shannon McSheffrey, *Marriage, Sex, and Civic Culture in Late Medieval London* (Philadelphia: University of Pennsylvania Press, 2006), p. 183, for a likely reference in 1483 to William Paston II or III reportedly keeping a mistress in London.

27 *The Cely Letters, 1472–1488*, ed. A. Hanham, Early English Text Society, 273 (London: Oxford University Press, 1975), pp. 50, 81–2, 92–4, 107, 128–30, 156, 167, 173.

28 *Paston Letters*, ed. Davis, i. 127, 220; ii. 51; Anthony Smith, 'Heydon [*formerly* Baxter], John (d. 1479), lawyer', *ODNB* xxvi. 948–9; Roger Virgoe, 'The Divorce of Sir Thomas Tuddenham', *Norfolk Archaeology*, 34 (1969), 406–18.

29 *The Diaries of Lady Anne Clifford*, ed. D. J. H. Clifford (Stroud: Alan Sutton, 1990). It will be suggested by Jessica Malay in a forthcoming paper in the *Journal for Early Modern Cultural Studies* that Margaret Stanley (daughter of George Vernon of Haddon and Tong), wife of Sir Edward, was the mistress of Lady Anne's father, and therefore Venetia Stanley, later wife of Kenelm Digby, was Anne Clifford's illegitimate half-sister.

30 George Williamson, *Lady Anne Clifford, Countess of Dorset, Pembroke & Montgomery, 1590–1676: Her Life, Letters and Work, Extracted from all the Original Documents Available, Many of which are here Printed for the First Time* (Kendal: Titus Wilson and Son, 1922), p. 132.

31 *The Visitation of the County Palatine of Lancashire Made in the Year 1567 by William Flower Esq, Norroy King of Arms*, ed. F. R. Raines, Chetham Society, LXXXI (1870), pp. 78 (Stanley, earl of Derby), 89 (Scarisbrick); *The Visitation of Yorkshire in the Years 1563 and 1564 Made by William Flower, Norroy King of Arms*, ed. C. B. Norcliffe, Harleian Society, XVI (1881), pp. 62–3 (Clifford), 243 (Percy), 316 (Tempest).

32 TE; *North Country Wills, Being Abstracts of Wills Relating to the Counties of York, Nottingham, Northumberland, Cumberland and Westmorland at Somerset House and Lambeth Palace 1383 to 1550*, ed. J. W. Clay, Surtees Society, CXVI (1908); *Wills and Inventories from the Registry at Durham*, ed. W. Greenwell, J. C. Hodgson and H. M. Wood, Surtees Society, XXXVIII, CXII, CXLII (1860, 1906, 1929), ii–iv; *Wills and Inventories Illustrative of the History, Manners, Language, Statistics etc of the Northern Counties of England from the Eleventh-Century Downwards, Part One*, ed. J. Raine, Surtees Society, II (1835); *Wills and Inventories from the Registry of the Archdeaconry of Richmond, Extending Over Portions of the Counties of York, Westmorland, Cumberland and Lancaster*, ed. J. Raine, Surtees Society, XXVI (1853); *Lancashire and Cheshire Wills and Inventories from the Ecclesiastical Court, Chester*, ed. G. J. Piccope, Chetham Society, LI, LIV (1860–61), ii–iii; *Lancashire and Cheshire Wills and Inventories at Chester, With an Abstract of Wills now Lost or Destroyed Transcribed by the late G. J. Piccope, M.A.*, [hereafter *Lancashire and Cheshire Wills and Inventories at Chester*] ed.

J. P. Earwaker, Chetham Society, n.s., 3 (1884); *Lancashire and Cheshire Wills and Inventories 1572 to 1696 Now Preserved at Chester, With an Appendix of Lancashire and Cheshire Wills and Inventories Proved at York and Richmond 1542 to 1649*, [hereafter *Lancashire and Cheshire Wills and Inventories 1572 to 1696 now Preserved at Chester*] ed. J. P. Earwaker, Chetham Society, n.s., 28 (1893); *Lancashire and Cheshire Wills and Inventories 1563 to 1807 Now Preserved at Chester*, ed. J. P. Rylands, Chetham Society, n.s., 37 (1897).

33   In terms of identifying and defining illegitimacy, the guidelines in Peter Laslett, *Family Life and Illicit Love in Earlier Generations: Essays in Historical Sociology* (repr. with corrections, Cambridge: Cambridge University Press, 1980), and Richard Adair, *Courtship, Illegitimacy and Marriage in Early Modern England* (Manchester: Manchester University Press, 1996), have been followed. Beneficiaries described as illegitimate, bastard, base, base-born, spurious, where the father is described as 'reputed', or if the child is referred to as the son or daughter of the mother only, have been included. Adair does not use the term 'alias' as a term of illegitimacy itself, but accepts it with supporting evidence. This approach has been adopted for this study, which may exclude a number of other possibly relevant beneficiaries. The term 'natural' has been read with care, as in some cases testators referred to 'natural' children in their wills when there is no other evidence that these children were illegitimate; for example Isabel Plumpton made her will in 1547, mentioning her 'natural son' Robert (*TE*, vi. 260–2), but other sources (William Dugdale, *The Visitation of the County of Yorke, begun in Ao Dni MDCLXV and finished Ao Dni MDCLXVI*, ed. R. Davis, Surtees Society, XXXVI (1859), p. 191, and *The Plumpton Letters and Papers*, ed. Joan Kirby, Camden Society, 5th ser., 8 (1996), p. 15), suggest that he was legitimate.

34   *North Country Wills*, pp. 111–16 (Edward Stanley); *TE*, v. 50 (Elizabeth, Lady Scrope); *TE*, vi. 166–8 (Lady Northumberland); *Wills and Inventories from the Registry of the Archdeaconry of Richmond*, pp. 113–16 (Thomas Stanley). Hollingsworth, *Demography of the English Peerage*, pp. 47–9. We might compare this rate with the one in twelve testators mentioning bastard children in the late medieval period around Lyon: Philippe Contamine, *La noblesse au royaume de France de Philippe le Bel à Louis XII: essai de synthèse* (Paris: presses universitaires de France, 1997), pp. 60–1.

35   Adair, *Courtship, Illegitimacy and Marriage*, pp. 49–50; Hollingsworth, *Demography of the British Peerage*, p. 49.

36   Lewis Dibdin, *English Church Law and Divorce*: Part I, *Notes on the Reformatio legum ecclesiasticarum*; Part II: *Notes on the Divorce and Remarriage of Sir John Stawell* by Sir Charles E. H. Chadwyck Healey; with appendices (London: J. Murray, 1912), esp. 62–75, 83–92; Houlbrooke, *Church Courts*, pp. 70–1, 79; Lawrence Stone, *Road to Divorce: England, 1530–1987* (Oxford: Oxford University Press, 1990), pp. 302–8; Roderick Phillips, *Untying the Knot: A Short History of Divorce* (Cambridge: Cambridge University Press, 1991), pp. 22–4.

37   The wills have been allocated according to the main location of residence given; cross-county landholding means that they may be included even where this lies outside our immediate field of interest (e.g. Thomas Crewe of Denbigh, who bequeathed property in Cheshire, from where most of his executors were drawn; or Sir Godfrey Foljambe (Derbyshire) who also had property in Yorkshire around Tickhill).

38   *Somerset Medieval Wills (2nd Series), 1501–1530, with Some Somerset Wills Preserved at Lambeth*, ed. F. W. Weaver, Somerset Record Society 19 (Taunton, 1903); *Somerset Medieval Wills (3rd Series), 1531–1558*, ed. F. W. Weaver, Somerset Record Society 21 (Taunton, 1905); *Bedfordshire Wills,*

1480–1519, ed. Patricia Bell, Publications of the Bedfordshire Historical and Record Society XLV (Bedford, 1966); *Bedfordshire Wills Proved in the Prerogative Court of Canterbury, 1383–1548*, ed. Margaret McGregor, Publications of the Bedfordshire Historical and Record Society LVIII ([Bedford], 1979); *Bedfordshire Wills 1484–1533*, ed. Patricia Bell, Publications of the Bedfordshire Historical and Record Society vol. 76 (Bedford, 1997). *Lincoln Wills*, Volume. I, *A.D. 1271–1526*, ed. C. W. Foster, Lincoln Record Society 5 (Lincoln, 1914); *Lincoln Wills*, Volume. II, *A.D. 1505–May 1530*, ed. C. W. Foster, Lincoln Record Society 10 (Lincoln, 1918 for 1914); and *Lincoln Wills*, Volume. III, *A.D. 1530–1532*, ed. C. W. Foster, Lincoln Record Society 24 (Lincoln, 1930).

39 TNA, C 1/567/71; Matthews, 'Illegitimacy', pp. 148–9; H. Arthur Doubleday and William Page (eds), *The Victoria History of the County of Bedford* (4 vols. London: Constable, 1904–14), i. 366–70.

40 A survey of Chichester Diocese Court Act Books 1556–57, 1576–79 and 1582–88 (from Chichester, West Sussex Record Office, Ep/I/10), only produced one gentry fornication case and none related to elite bastardy; Houlbrooke, *Church Courts*, p. 79. Compare Ingram's identification of limited numbers of high-status defendants in adultery cases, e.g. *Carnal Knowledge: Regulating Sex in England, 1470–1600* (Cambridge: Cambridge University Press, 2017), pp. 105–6 (archdeaconry of Buckingham).

41 Martin Ingram, *Church Courts, Sex and Marriage in England, 1570–1640* (Cambridge: Cambridge University Press, 1987), pp. 327, 371.

42 *The Register of John Morton, Archbishop of Canterbury, 1486–1500*, ed. Christopher Harper-Bill, Canterbury and York Society, 75, 78, 89 (1987–2000), iii. 4–9, 168–239.

43 Philip Tyler, 'The Significance of the Ecclesiastical Commission at York', *Northern History*, 2 (1967), 27–44; C. A. Haigh, 'Slander and the Church Courts in the Sixteenth Century', *Transactions of the Historic Society of Lancashire and Cheshire*, 78 (1975), 1–13, at pp. 6–7; Ingram, *Church Courts*, p. 39.

44 Matthews, 'Illegitimacy', ch. 2 and pp. 216–18.

45 LRO, DDL 560. See also QDD/11, m. 21d.

46 Pilkington: *TE* iii. 23; Byron: *Lancashire and Cheshire Wills and Inventories 1572 to 1696 Now Preserved at Chester*, pp. 133–6.

47 See p. 40 for details of a child possibly born to Bridget Redman, who appeared before the York Courts in 1563 and 1573 charged with adultery with William Gascoigne. They married in Oct. 1586 and the child concerned, if theirs, would have been over twenty years old at the time of his or her parents' marriage: *The Parish Registers of Otley, Co. York*, Part I: *1562 to 1672*, ed. W. Brigg, Yorkshire Parish Record Society, 33 (1908), p. 141.

48 *North Country Wills*, p. 82. Pykerynge did not mention a wife in his will at all, but did refer to legitimate children William and Margaret. It is unclear whether the relationship with Jane began during or after Pykerynge's marriage.

49 BIA, HC.CP 1597/8. Fornication, adultery and deserting his wife were three of several charges levied against Middleton, who was also accused of Papistry and harbouring priests.

50 R. H. Helmholz, *Marriage Litigation in Medieval England* (Cambridge: Cambridge University Press, 1974), pp. 74–105; Ronald A. Marchant, *The Church under the Law: Justice, Administration and Discipline in the Diocese of York, 1560–1640* (Cambridge: Cambridge University Press, 1969), pp. 16, 20, 62, 68, 194, 219; Houlbrooke, *Church Courts*, pp. 55–7, 65–9 (although NB the exception at pp. 85–6, in mid-sixteenth-century London). E.g. Ingram has pointed

to the number of cases abandoned, as parties were made to understand the unlikelihood of their success before judges who were increasingly sceptical of poorly evidenced private marriage contracts: *Church Courts*, pp. 146–94; R. B. Outhwaite, *The Rise and Fall of the English ecclesiastical courts, 1500–1860* (Cambridge: Cambridge University Press, 2006), pp. 48–51. Other proposed explanations for the declining prominence of marital litigation relate to the process of litigation itself (lawyers profited more from cases related to tithes and wills) or other social factors, e.g. reduced opportunities for women in the labour market, resulting in women's economic disempowerment and the curtailment of those activities which had made for more protracted and sequential courtships, in favour of greater male and familial control: P. J. P. Goldberg, 'Gender and Matrimonial Litigation in the Church Courts in the Later Middle Ages: The Evidence of the Court of York', *Gender & History*, 19 (2007), 43–59. See above, pp. 18–21, for consideration of the context for this argument about *de praesenti* and *de futuro* marriage.

51 Helmholz, *Marriage Litigation*, pp. 100–5; Charles Donahue, *Law, Marriage, and Society in the Later Middle Ages: Arguments about Marriage in Five Courts* (Cambridge: Cambridge University Press, 2007), pp. 33, 64–7, 525–34; Andrew Finch, 'Repulsa uxore sua: Marital Difficulties and Separation in the Later Middle Ages', *Continuity and Change*, 8 (1993), 11–38; Sara M. Butler, 'Lies, Damn Lies and the Case of St Lucy: Cases of Judicial Separation from the Medieval Court of York', in Philippe Romanski and Aïssatou Sy-Wonyu (eds), *Trompe-l'oeil* (Rouen: C.É.L.C.L.A., Université de Rouen, 2002), pp. 1–16; Ingram, *Church Courts*, pp. 146–7, 181–2; McSheffrey, *Marriage, Sex, and Civic Culture*, p. 168.

52 Jennifer McNabb, 'Ceremony versus Consent: Courtship, Illegitimacy, and Reputation in Northwest England, 1560–1610', *Sixteenth Century Journal*, 37 (2006).

53 Adair, *Courtship, Illegitimacy and Marriage*; McNabb, 'Ceremony versus Consent', pp. 69–75, 78–9.

54 The exception is child-marriage, where she indicates that 'families of wealth and elevated social status in the northwest maintained the practice into the 1570s and 1580s and, to a lesser extent, even into the 1590s' and references Ingram, *Church Courts*, pp. 128–9, where such practices are noted in the north west of England: McNabb, 'Ceremony versus Consent', p. 66. She associates this with discussion of 'wealthy burgess' families, rather than gentry, however.

55 Cross, 'Sin and Society', pp. 197–9.

56 *Ibid.*, pp. 199–203.

57 BIA, CP.H 5200 (office v Nicholas Bacon). Of twelve instances of 'the common voice and fame' identified in our sample, ten were used against the defendant(s).

58 BIA, CP.G 2741.

59 F. J. Furnivall, *Child Marriages, Divorces and Ratifications etc in the Diocese of Chester, A.D. 1561–6*, Early English Text Society, 108 (1897), p. 72.

60 BIA, CP.G 774.

61 BIA, CP.G 774A.

62 LRO, Tatton of Cuerden MSS, DDTA 200. Hugh Anderton, father of James made a settlement with Rafe Holden and his wife Elizabeth concerning lands in Waddington in 1561, the same year Holden's marriage to Haughton was questioned in Chester. LRO, Parker of Browsholme MSS, DP/449/1/1/1.

63 *The Visitation of the County Palatine of Lancaster Made in the Year 1613 by Richard St George Esq, Norroy King of Arms*, ed. F. R. Raines, Chetham Society, o.s., LXXXII (1871), p. 82.

64 BIA, CP.G 1561.
65 See below, pp. 66–7, for further on the situation of Lady Anne as a mistress, and on the politics of the relationships, S. T. Bindoff, *The House of Commons, 1509–1558* (3 vols. London: Secker & Warburg for the History of Parliament Trust, 1982), iii. 421; Jack Brierley Watson, 'Lancashire Gentry 1529–58' (unpubl. M.A. diss., London Univ., 1959), pp. 492–4.
66 BIA, CP.G 1586, CP.G 1515, CP.G 1663; CP.G 1588; HC.AB 6, fos. 88, 134–5, 158–9, 160; LRO, DDF/989.
67 Paul E. J. Hammer, 'Sex and the Virgin Queen: Aristocratic Concupiscence and the Court of Elizabeth I', *Sixteenth Century Journal*, 31 (2000), 77–97.
68 *LP* xviii/1. 65–6 (caps. xl, xliii, xliv); see below, pp. 89–90, 102–3.
69 *Diaries of Lady Anne Clifford*, p. 27.
70 For the full story of the Carr-Howard relationship, see Anne Somerset, *Unnatural Murder: Poison at the Court of James I* (London: Weidenfeld & Nicolson, 1997).
71 For details of the Howard-Coke relationship, see Thomas de Longueville, *The Curious Case of Lady Purbeck: A Scandal of the XVIIth Century* (London: Longmans, Green and Co., 1909); *Calendar of State Papers: Domestic Series. The Reign of James I, 1623–25, with Addenda*, ed. Mary Anne Everett Green (London: Longman, Brown, Green, Longmans & Roberts, 1859), pp. 474, 476–8, 486, 497. For the Vaux-Howard affair: *CP*, i. 400–1; xii/2. 218–26.
72 The Stanley fathers were Thomas, the second earl, and Henry, the fourth earl.
73 *VCH Lancs.* vi. 122n4 suggests that the marriage of Thomas Hesketh and Elizabeth Fleming was dissolved in 1497 on the grounds of her adultery. The mother of Thomas Hesketh's children is identified as Alice Haward, rather than Fleming or Grace Towneley, a possible second wife who died in 1510 (and not to be confused with Robert Hesketh's wife also named Grace Towneley). *The Visitation of Lancashire and a Part of Cheshire Made in the Twenty Fourth Year of the Reign of King Henry the Eighth A. D. 1533*, ed. William Langton, Chetham Society, XCVIII, CX (1876–82), pp. 120–4, also suggests Haward as the mother; LRO, Parker Family of Browsholme MSS, 12/13 and *The Derby Household Books*, ed. F. R. Raines, Chetham Society, XXXI (1853), p. 125, for the will of Sir Thomas Hesketh dated 1560, in which he mentions 'bastard sister Alice', 'Richard and Francis Hesketh, my bastard brethren', his 'bastard son Hugh' and 'Thomas Hesketh, my bastard son'. LRO, DDB 8/2, is a bond dated 1618 between Thomas 'son and heir' of Robert Hesketh, and Robert, base son of Robert Hesketh; *Lancashire and Cheshire Wills and Inventories 1572 to 1696 Now Preserved at Chester, with an Appendix of Lancashire and Cheshire Wills and Inventories Proved at York and Richmond 1542 to 1649.*, ed. J. P. Earwaker, Chetham Society, n.s., 28 (1893), pp. 21–4 (for the will of Robert Hesketh, 1620).
74 *Visitation of Lancashire and a Part of Cheshire*, p. 166. For the will of Anne Molyneux, see *Lancashire and Cheshire Wills and Inventories from the Ecclesiastical Court, Chester*, ed. G. J. Piccope, Chetham Society, LIV (1861), ii. 143–6; *VCH Lancs.*, iii. 191–7.
75 E. W. Ives, 'Egerton, Sir Ralph (b. before 1476, d. 1528), *courtier and administrator*', *ODNB*, xvii. 1004–5.

3

The role and status of the mistress

'Butt as good naturks through humaine frailty are oftentimes misled: soe he fell to love a ladey of quality; which by degrees did draw and alienate his love and affection from soe verteous and well descerveing wife, it being the cause of many discontents betweene them for many yeares together'.[1] So wrote Lady Anne Clifford reflecting upon the state of the marriage of her father and mother, George Clifford, third earl of Cumberland (d. 1605) and Lady Margaret, daughter of Francis Russell, second earl of Bedford. Lady Anne did not divulge the identity of her father's mistress, which may have been well known to her contemporaries but, frustratingly, has been lost for certain to historians. Discretion was also to the fore in December 1596 when Lady Anne Bacon wrote to Robert Devereux, second earl of Essex condemning his 'dishonorable and dangerous … infaminge a noble mane's wyffe and so nere about her Majestie, with as yt were an incorrigible unshamfastnes'.[2] Essex's mistress has, however, been identified, as Lady Bacon's great niece Elizabeth de Vere, countess of Derby, wife since early 1595 of William, sixth earl of Derby, and who was rusticated to Knowsley in Lancashire by her husband in the wake of her affair.

The attitude of the two Lady Annes suggests a common theme around the identification of elite mistresses. In addition to contemporaneous personal correspondence and diary entries, which may have been read illicitly by servants and are therefore perhaps understandably obscure, official documentation such as wills can also be very discreet. In a survey of 876 noble or gentry wills from the north of England, 96 contain references to base-born children, yet only six mention the mothers of the children, and only three of these by name. The silence and ambiguity of so many of the sources has contributed to a partial and misleading view of the mistresses of the elite. Generally, they have been assumed to be drawn from the ranks of the lower orders and middling sort, to have been marginalised and disempowered, and to have played little role in the lives of their partners' families and wider society. This chapter explores these ideas and demonstrate that mistresses were not for the most part victimised servants, for example, however prevalent this pattern might have been, even in relatively closely neighbouring parts of the Midlands such as Leicestershire, for example.[3] The contexts for this discussion are rather to be found in the historiography of the female life cycle, especially the place within it of service, and of gender, especially where it questions the centrality of sexual conduct as the only pillar of female reputation in stark distinction from men's situation.[4] The backgrounds from which mistresses were drawn, the ways in which they were described, and their involvement with their children and wider families all demonstrate a significantly wider potential for their recognition and influence than has previously been allowed.

There is no doubt, however, that many of the sources provide challenges in idenitifying mistresses. Questions arise from wording that is ambiguous, but indicative of immorality, in some wills. In 1593 the Cheshire gentleman John Legh left 'to Ellen Stanley alias Baggily, wife unto Robert Stanley the younger four score pounds … which I do assign unto the said Ellenn S for her maintenance in regard of the fault I have made unto her, for which I entirely beg and crave at the hands of Almighty God to pardon and forgive my offence against her so committed as also for the rest of my offences the said Ellen shall keep with her a young daughter supposed to be mine which is called Margaret Leigh alias Downes'.[5] Legh did not state that Ellen Stanley was the mother of either of his putative daughters (he also provided for his illegitimate daughter Ellen Ogden alias Legh), but his willingness to provide a financial settlement and the language of repentance suggests that he had committed some kind of moral sin against her. Likewise, in 1543, another Cheshireman, John Dutton, bequeathed forty shillings to Katherine Wyrall 'in the way of charity to forgive me of such offences and trespasses as I have made her', but again did not specify whether or not she was the mother of his illegitimate offspring.[6] While Legh and Dutton may (or may not) have sought forgiveness for sexual misconduct, the language of repentance suggests suspicious behaviour with serious moral, financial and social consequences. Even more vague and open to misunderstanding are the hints provided by a very generous settlement for a servant or other female beneficiary. For example Richard Lassells of Sowerby in Yorkshire, gentleman, writing his will in 1472, indicated that his waiting maid Cecily should be supported for the term of her life from his goods: we can only speculate as to the reason for this generosity.[7]

Even when a mistress was associated with a child in a will, the identity of the woman might be left obscure. In 1538, for example, Sir Ingram Percy, brother of the sixth earl of Northumberland, left 'To my daughter £20' and 'to the mother of the said child, 20 nobles'.[8] In 1547 and 1620 respectively, the mistresses of Yorkshire esquire Edward Saltmarsh and Northumberland gentleman Thomas Burrell did not benefit directly from their lovers' wills, either having to administer bequests to their children or only benefitting in the event of the deaths of their illegitimate offspring.[9]

The apparent anonymity and discretion which surrounded the identities of gentlemen's mistresses renders attempts to quantify the extent of illicit relationships difficult, and makes consideration of the ways in which these women were treated harder. Yet it is possible to piece together evidence which provides a picture of the ways in which the experience of these mistresses, and of the situations from which they came and which they navigated in the course of their relationships with gentlemen and noblemen.

Surviving parish registers provide some limited information about women's experiences surrounding the births of their children. In earlier records, for example that of the baptism of 'Robert Blundell, nothus' in Croston in 1552, neither parent is named, in other cases only the father or mother, but most include both.[10] Even where one man fathered more than one base child, the records can be inconsistent. In May 1619, Edmond, base son of 'John Thornbrough, gent.' was baptised in Cartmel, yet the mother was unnamed. Seven years later, while Mary Taylor, the mother of his (half) sister is named, the words used suggest uncertainty over paternity.[11] Arguably, by naming Thornburgh in the parish records as possible father of her child, Taylor may have strengthened her case in the event of a maintenance claim, and the community its position in the face of a repeat offender. The wording stands in contrast to the more definite entry for 'Esther daughter of Margaret Kellett base begotten by Mr William Sands of Graithwaite in Fornes', in this instance a man from outside the immediate area, if a well-connected one.[12] These records occasionally illuminate wider issues faced by the mothers of base-born children. The parish registers of Mirfield in West Yorkshire record that in June 1595, Elizabeth Lyster gave birth to a son, Edmund, 'begotten by one Mr Ralf Holte of the Parishe of Ratchdale'. Three weeks later the registers record Edmund's burial. This case demonstrates that in addition to her pregnancy, Lyster travelled approximately thirty miles over difficult Pennine terrain from Rochdale to Mirfield, and then had to deal with the birth, illness and death of her child, presumably without the help and support of Holt while she was still recovering from labour.[13] Ten years earlier, Isabell Dobson faced a similar situation when she recorded the birth and death of her son John 'supposed to be begotten by Richard Thurgoland, gent.' in October / November 1585.[14] The high infant mortality rate is apparent in the parish registers, especially where baptisms and burials were recorded in the same volume. However, they remain silent upon the feelings of the mothers who were faced with the illness and deaths of their children. While a childbed mortality rate of 6–7% has been suggested for this period, as Patricia Crawford has pointed out, 'no pregnant woman could be sure that she would be among the fortunate survivors.'[15] A sampling of parish registers for each county has failed to uncover burial records in the name of the mother as given in the birth records. Neither are there more than a very few records of marriages made in the same name, and further investigation of those provides inconclusive results. In the Manchester registers, Katherine Marler is listed as the daughter of James Marler, baptised in 1579. A Katherine Marler's marriage to Edward Wyrall is recorded in September 1603, but in 1606 'Katheryn Marler' is listed as the mother of a base daughter Anne by Edward Rosthorne of Holcombe near Bury.[16]

Even within the judgemental sphere of the church courts, where fornicators and adulterers were punished for their moral laxity, anonymity abounds, since it was often the man who was the prime target of the action taken. In 1571, Maurice Ashton was presented before High Commission in York on the grounds that he kept 'a whore and hath done so for xiii or xiiii years and hath divers children with her.' Also before York High Commission in 1571–72 was Laurence Tetloe who 'hath kepte a Whore this xxtie yeres and hath had dyvers children by her'.[17] Despite such long-standing liaisons and the fact that the identities of these women must have been well known in Ashton-under-Lyne and Werneth (near Oldham) respectively, they remained unnamed in their partners' prosecutions. However, church court records do specify the names of some of the mistresses. Two mistresses of John Eden are identified in the Durham ecclesiastical court records. In 1570, Helen Maison was prosecuted in the Durham Consistory for her relationship with John Eden, who fathered her son.[18] Sibella Little followed in her footsteps in June 1580, and was probably the mother of Elizabeth Litle alias Eden, who received a bequest of £3 6s 8d in Eden's will, dated 1588.[19] Eden's grandson, also named John Eden, spent time in both Durham and York High Commissions explaining his relationship with one Mary Daniell.[20] Furthermore, during the course of the Eden / Daniell proceedings in York, it transpired that Margaret Dobbison 'late househould servant to the said John Eden fathered her base child on … John Eden'. Dobbison had performed penance in 'St Hellens Auckland Chappell' and Eden stood excommunicate for his adulterous lifestyle.

While discretion may be found in the cases dealing with immorality directly, a few names are available, and the sources provide us with a variety of insights into the ways in which the participants in illegitimate relationships were described and the gendered concepts implicit in those descriptions. While some were intrinsically condemnatory, such as 'whore', this was not always the case, and there is no straightforward relationship between the use of such language and the description of women in relationships with elite males. Even in the ecclesiastical courts, terminology might refer to pretensed marriage as often as to the keeping of whores or concubines. In Durham Consistory depositions, for example, the term 'whore' appears in four defamation cases, but not other pejorative terms such as 'harlot'. We find another use of the word 'hoore' in the Durham Deposition Book (Agnes Carr c Thomas Carr: he gave her 3d, telling her it was the price of 'a hoore'), and a 'fornicatrix' and a concubine in the Durham Act Book. The Durham Deposition Book also gives us examples of pretensed spouses, of which only one was a husband.[21] Defamation cases varied between those rooted in some element of truth in terms of sexual relationships and those which were simply highly gendered scandalmongering.[22] An example of the former would be a case from the archdeaconry of Richmond in 1635 which simply noted that Alexander Dauson had reported that Alice Skeldinge, the wife of the local vicar, had carnal dealings with Ferdinando Hudleston of Millom 'in a chare in the bodiestead of the fyrehouse'.[23] In 1619, the Durham Consistory court heard that when Alice Coleman called 'Barbara Errington whore the said Barbara said unto her I am sure thou wilt not call me whore but thou will name whose whore I am whereto the said Alice replied and said you are Andrew Clennells whore'.[24] Far more frequent, however, were more generalised slanderous disputes, in which sexual allegations were made and women felt obliged to defend their good names, but in which the substance of an irregular relationship is harder to identify or is unlikely. In a defamation suit brought in York in 1590, George Holden allegedly called Mary Grimston 'beggarlie whoore and beggarlie queane above a dozan tymes.'[25] The origin of the dispute centred upon Holden's access to water from a well rather than sexual misconduct on Grimston's part. Another neighbourly quarrel came to the courts in Durham in 1609–10, when the bad feeling between the Weighall and Todd families of Osmotherley reached a peak. Initially claiming that John Todd fathered 'a child that was begott of Alice Strangase' before their marriage, the two families actually turned out to be fighting over the lack of maintenance to a ditch between their properties. Nevertheless, the use of sexual slander meant that Alice Todd was described by Anna Weighall as 'whore and arrant whore'.[26] Further examples include Michael Constable in 1594 calling Alice Kirby 'whore, arrand whore, curtall knave, drabbe, scould, pockye queane and pockye whore'; if this was not sufficient he 'did further say she had the Frenche pockes'. William Newstead in 1557 called Agnes Fairfax 'noughty sparke And said openly that Thomas Helmsley and Walter Hewson did kepe her and were as consant with her as her husband'; John Coppindale in 1554 called Margaret Eldon 'drabbe queane and skacodinge queane'; and Alice Kay sued Agnes and Edmund Schofield for calling her 'houre, noughty queane, drabbe, noughtye scolde and noughtye harlott', the latter then countersuing her for describing Agnes as 'hoore & noughty hoore … She called the said Agnes hoor harlot noughty hoor noughty harlott'.[27]

As Garthine Walker suggests and the above cases illustrate, 'sexual insult could be a mundane response in every sort of local and personal conflict', highlighting the sexualised nature of female honour.[28] While the underlying conflicts may have been subsumed by the language of sexual impropriety, the responses themselves give the historian an extensive linguistic vernacular to consider in relation to those contemporaries engaged in illicit behaviour.[29] It is necessary, however, to go further in understanding how this language represented the situation of the mistress. Laura Gowing asserts that cases of sexual slander present a particular image of immoral behaviour, which also highlights the disruption of the flow of household capital, 'introducing different expenditures and consumptions through channels that are not part of the household economy', with money that rightfully should be used for wholesome domesticity spent on clothing, feeding and maintaining a 'whore'.[30] This is consonant with some historians' depictions of elite mistresses, for example Barry Coward describing the fourth earl of Derby's liaison with his mistress Joan Halsall in terms of his pecuniary problems and the diversion of increasingly scarce domestic funds to finance their relationship.[31] What was at stake here, however, was the support of the offspring of the relationship: the earl enfeoffed trustees to hold land in Childwall, Kirkby, Broughton and Ormskirk in 1581–82 in order to support his illegitimate family.[32] The extent to which Derby's mistress would benefit directly from the acquisition of these estates was severely curbed. Derby himself was the immediate beneficiary of the purchase; Halsall would only benefit personally in the event of Derby's death and if her sons were under the age of twenty-four years. In the event, the direct transfer of the landed settlement to Henry and Thomas Stanley in 1594 suggests that Jane predeceased the earl. It was possible for a man to allocate his mistress a personal landed endowment, as in the case of Sir Thomas Venables of Kinderton (Cheshire) in the mid-sixteenth century, in the form of a life interest in some of his properties: 'lands worth £4. 5. 10d. conveyed to Anne Bostock for life' were protected when arrangements were made for the marriage of his son Thomas and Elizabeth Brereton in 1552: but this was a very unusual situation.[33]

More morally damaging, but more typical of the type of support associated with the language of description and insult under discussion here, was the situation for which Sir Henry Savile's mistress Margery Barston was condemned in Henry VIII's reign. She was clearly linked with criminal activity when Star Chamber heard an allegation of the theft of valuable goods from Sir Thomas Tempest during the campaigning in France in the early 1520s.[34] One witness described how 'oon Margery Barston hadd and ware an image of gold and enamelyed with a stone abought her neckke of the gyfte of his Master unto her', completing the vivid account with a description of Savile's blood on the broken lock of Tempest's chest from which the jewel had been taken, his damaged knuckles concealed inside a glove. The clear inference is one of double moral outrage; that not only did Savile violently steal Tempest's valuables, he then compounded the crime by openly parading his mistress wearing them. Like many other mistresses, Margery Barston also held a position as a servant within the Savile household, and as such she would have been fed, clothed and sheltered as part of Sir Henry and Lady Savile's domiciliary arrangements.

Overall, therefore, the language used to describe mistresses varied. It was sometimes condemnatory and associated with specifical expectations of female sexual conduct, related to disruptions in the management of the household, but it was not always so straightforward, and therefore it permitted some space for these women's activity and definition. In fact, the openness of the language used to describe the majority of gentry mistresses who appear in the records and the obscurity of some of them means that their identities are not easily explored. The usual assumption that they were menial servants or came from other non-elite backgrounds, or were even victimised members of the families of the gentlemen themselves may in some instances be correct, but in others it is demonstrably true that they were themselves of independent gentry origin, or we may suspect gentry connections. Claire Cross has already identified the almost certainly incestuous relationship behind York High Commission prosecution of Anthony Hurleston of Millom esquire, who was persistent in his determination to live with his sister Anne Latows, wife of Ralph Latows, rather than his wife Mary, the daughter of the Oxfordshire knight and MP Sir William Barentyne of Little Haseley. Ralph was the son of Richard Latows, who had served as bailiff to Anne and Anthony's father Sir John. The case was first addressed in Chester, where High Commission considered 'suspition of incestuous demaynour … or at least not without suspition of breach of godly loue betwene' Anthony and Mary his lawful wife. Anthony's pleas that he might suffer great loss at Millom for lack of 'a trustie frende' to oversee his servants won Anne the right to reside there, but only if Anthony kept ten miles away. York High Commission intervened in 1572, restricting Anthony to his Durham and Yorkshire estates, suggesting their recognition of his determination to be with her in Cumberland, and only some years afterwards did the Privy Council itself allow him some greater freedom of movement.[35] More than half a century later, Edward Paylor, first baronet (created 1642), of Thoralby Hall not far to the east of York, in Bugthorpe parish, was involved with his sister's daughter, Elizabeth Sothaby alias Bulmer, wife of Francis Bulmer of Brampton in a case which ran through the 1630s.[36] Other mistresses might have been found among the widows of near relatives, with the relationships forged either before or after their kinsman's death: Thomas Daniell of Over Whitley, probably the son of Thomas of Tabley, Cheshire, recorded in the visitation of 1580, was under recognisance thanks to action in Chester High Commission in the 1560s because of his relationship with Elizabeth Daniell, widow. We cannot identify her with any certainty, but it seems likely that she was one of his kinswomen by marriage.[37] Then there was William Whittell, another gentleman, presented for his relationship with Alice Norres, his wife's sister, something which he did not contest and which resulted in his penance in Warrington market place on a scaffold, barefoot, barelegged, bareheaded, and clad in white sheet bearing a message declaring his offence.[38]

Servants are also specifically identified as mistresses in several cases, including that of John Eden of West Auckland, County Durham early in the seventeenth century, who appears to have been a serial or multiple adulterer, in the face of the objections of his wife Margaret. The two women identified with him were Mary Daniell and Margaret Dobbison, the second being specified as 'late househould servant'; both had borne him children.[39] In other cases, it was explicit that the mistress was a servant, although the commitment shown by each party to what was apparently a monogamous relationship was more striking. Chester High Commission considered the case of William Heiton esquire, suspected of breach of wedlock with Alice Eccles, whom he confessed to be his servant maid; he refused to bring her in to court for due order to be taken with her, and used what were considered very obstinate and wilful words in the face of the court to the evil example of others, with the result that he was committed to ward in Chester Castle without bail or mainprize.[40] In some cases, the perhaps expected pattern of abuse of a servant extended to the abuse of a servant's daughter, as in the case of Simon Wormley, who it was alleged had 'used the company of one Elizabeth Swallow a yong woman one of his servants doughters and not long since sent her furthe of the countrey where in hir absence she was delivered of a child and since hir reterne upon the feaste day of the epiphany last at night coming in place wher she and other yonge folks were in hir copany tooke hir in his arms and set hir upon his knee.'[41] The master–servant relationship was, however, more complicated in some cases than it might at first appear. For example, Roger Beckwith esquire was accused of breaking a previous injunction against associating with his mistress by keeping Alice Petty 'in his howse since the said iniuctyon as his servant and yet doth', the implication being that the role of servant was adopted to allow for their relationship to be maintained, not the initial basis for its establishment.[42] William Huddleston of Millom, son of the controversial Anthony, struck up a relationship with a woman called Elizabeth while he was resident with his mother Mary at her parental home in Oxfordshire; but although Elizabeth may have been described as a servant, it appears she came from gentle stock, for a 1595 settlement in favour, among others, of the children she had borne to William and would bear, shows that her father was one William Hartilpoole of St James', Clerkenwell, Middlesex, gentleman.[43]

Many of the mistresses we can identify were, in fact, very overtly the daughters and wives of gentry families, and not always from families of lower gentle status; some were illegitimate offspring of the elite themselves. For example, in a group of cases reported in the mid-1530s by Adam Beconsall from Cheshire, gentlewomen were prominent. Sir Peter Warburton kept the wife of Laurence Frenche of Budworth; William Venables, the baron of Kinderton, allegedly lived in adultery with the wife of Sir James Stanley but also kept a bastard daughter of Sir George Holford, by whom he had one or two children.[44] In the former case, the mistress was from the ranks of a family which at times spanned the unclear boundaries between the husbandmen, yeomen and lesser gentry; in the latter, a much more elevated background. Sir James Stanley was one of the five sons of George, Lord Strange, heir of Thomas, first earl of Derby; his wife was Anne, widow of Edmund Talbot of Bashall and daughter of Sir John Hart of Lullington (Kent), whose sister Elizabeth was the wife of Thomas Brooke, eighth Lord Cobham. Venables' mistress was therefore the sister-in-law and daughter-in-law of peers of the realm. Strikingly, by 1533 a marriage had taken place between William Venables' daughter Cecily and Anne's son by Edmund Talbot, Thomas, suggesting the wider intersection of the family interests through her. William Venables died in the summer of 1540, and the later machinations of Lady Stanley and her son Thomas Talbot, manoeuvring Lady Anne's daughter by Sir James, Anne Stanley, into a marriage with John Rishton of Dunkenhalgh, have already been covered in chapter 2 of this book.[45] The case of Margery Barston and Sir Henry Savile cited earlier indicates more of these issues: service in a greater gentry or noble household would naturally have involved younger kin and connections of gentle backgrounds, and so a relationship with a 'servant' might encompass the taking of a mistress who was herself a gentlewoman. Margery was probably related to Sir Henry's wife, Elizabeth Sothill, given that in 1509 Alice Sothill had made provision in her will for her son Thomas, the father of Lady Savile, and her daughter Margaret, wife of Peter Barston.[46] Higher up the social scale, service in a noble household involved fellow members of the aristocracy or gentry. In the case of the earl of Dorset (husband of Lady Anne Clifford), his mistress Lady Martha Penistone was the wife of Sir Thomas Peniston, a baronet associated with service in the earl's household.[47] Such connections of service were, however, inextricably linked with others of county government and estate management, especially in the complex and sometimes challenging economic environment of the period. Lady Martha's father, Sir Thomas Temple, was also connected to Dorset via a significant tripartite land transaction negotiated in 1617.[48] Exactly how, when and where the relationship between Lady Penistone and Dorset began is a matter of conjecture; Martha had been married since 1611 and was a noted beauty, described by John Chamberlain as 'a daintie fine young Lady'.[49] In mid-to-late 1619, Dorset's wife Lady Anne Clifford recorded the Penistones' visits, noting in particular the social censure directed at Dorset. As she put it, 'this coming hither of Lady Peniston's was much talked of abroad and my Lord was much condemned for it.'[50] Lady Anne also found Dorset's final visit to Lady Penistone in November 1619 significant enough to note in her diary, but whether the end of their relationship was caused by the critical opinion of society or other reasons, is unknown, and Lady Penistone's death from smallpox only weeks later in January 1620 parted them forever.[51]

Even in such social circumstances as those around a gentle-born mistress of a nobleman, conventional routes to financial security were unavailable, however, and so whether a mistress came from an elite or non-elite background, transactions involving money and resources remained a source of potential controversy. Giving money, possibly conceived as some form of annuity, and gifts of jewellery and other often highly symbolic goods did not constitute an absolutely secure independent income for the mistress, but provided a clear message to the community, especially to local women, about status and how a lower-status woman might have supported herself. One more than usually illuminating insight into how masculine and feminine culture perceived the financial value and broader status of a mistress is provided by a defamation case, when John Butler accused Alice Coniers of falsely naming him as the father of her child in 1588–89. Coniers worked as a servant in the household of John Rangell, a gentleman from Durham, and Francis Pearson described an evening in the house when 'certaine younge gentlemen to the number of six or thereabouts beinge drinkinge wyne in a high chamber in John Rangall his house beganne talke of the said Alice Coniers some of them said that they would give her an annuitie of x^s yerely some said they wold give her xx^s & called for paper to sett the same downe in writing & some of x^s yerely … of what intent they consented to give the said money yerely to hir this examinant cannot depose.'[52] Another servant in the Rangell household, Elizabeth Stele reported Alice's 'light behaviour' & that she 'did often tymes use the company of gentlemen … that resorted to the house … and that one gentleman had given her a gold ring & a handkerchief & another a purse.' Isabella Rennell and other women present at the birth of Coniers' child also mentioned that the ring, handkerchief and purse had been given to her by Butler. The testimony falls into highly gendered territory, the men noting the financial settlements to Alice, the women the material goods bestowed upon her. Although on one level gifts of a ring and handkerchief traditionally also indicated a close personal relationship and future intent to marry, those items could appear in wider combination as visible signs of profit from an illicit relationship and ones to which women may have been more sensitive.[53]

The idea of the greedy and rapacious mistress demanding fine clothes and expensive trinkets and involved in displays of conspicuous consumption does find traction in the case of Eleanor Britton, mistress of George Talbot, sixth earl of Shrewsbury, who initiated litigation against the new earl, Gilbert, immediately after her lover's death, claiming gold and jewellery had been given to her.[54] Gilbert Talbot admitted to William Cecil that while she had 'embezzled' a great deal from his father during his life time, the 'masses' were stolen as the earl lay on his deathbed.[55] The case reached the Council and was the talk of aristocratic society because of the tensions it revealed between the generations in the Talbot family. In June 1591, Sir Henry Lee reported that he was concerned at talk at court that the new earl had promised Eleanor Britton some 'harde meanes' at the time his father had been quarrelling with him. Interestingly given its implications for the continued standing of a mistress after an aristocrat's death, Lee's view was that the earl should now give her what his father would have done, but no more. The case was still ongoing in 1595 (five years after the sixth earl's death) having been fought through in two courts in addition to Chancery.[56]

Furthermore, the transactional nature of some relationships, and the active participation of a cuckolded husband, became apparent in one remarkable case from York High Commission. In 1598, Frances Nelson was prosecuted for her extra-marital relationship with Charles Barnby. However, this was no ordinary case of one couple's immorality; Nelson's husband William was complicit in drawing up a legal document which laid out the terms of Barnby's access to Frances' body. The court heard 'that the said William Nelson for and in consideracon of an annyty of xxli by yere for him made by Charles Barnby did covent and promise that the said Barnby shold have the use of the body of the said Ffrances Nelson his wief without contrement and suffered the said Barnby to have the use of her body'.[57] William then combined with Mary Readshaw to catch his wife and Barnby in bed together, theoretically enabling him to sue for a divorce on the grounds of Frances' adultery. While the issue of the legal agreement surrounding the annuity was left to the male protagonists in this case, the importance of material goods to Mary Readshaw was apparent from the testimony heard by the court. One witness testified that Readshaw 'received a some of money or some other stuff of the said William [Nelson]' for facilitating Frances and Barnby's adultery; another claimed 'William Nelson did promise to the said Mary Readshaw six yards of searge and an elne of lawne'. The whole scheme unravelled when Readshaw attempted to blackmail Barnby, who 'promised her a tuft taffety gowne and a kirtle of figured sattyn for her favor to conceale the said fallt'. However, after twelve days, she had not received the clothing and reported Barnby's conduct to the courts, implicating her own misconduct in the process. The potential benefits to William Nelson and Mary Readshaw ensured their prosecution for bawdry. For Frances Nelson, however, no material or financial benefits to her were mentioned in court, and any gifts or tokens given to her by Charles Barnby were unreported.

Writing about eighteenth-century Scotland, Leah Leneman has argued that for women taking legal action in order to prove the existence of a marriage denied by the groom, 'the economic aspect was undoubtedly very important'.[58] For the fifteenth to the mid-seventeenth centuries in England, historians lack the wealth of evidence available for those studying the demimonde of eighteenth-century Paris for example, where police reports and other sources provide a wealth of evidence for the financial system of patronage in operation there.[59] Concentrating upon the later seventeenth century, Mary Fissell has connected the mercantile and commercial activities of the period to the changing nature of the provision of sexual services for money, particularly referencing professional sex workers threatening a man's estate and wealth.[60] She identifies the later seventeenth or early eighteenth century as the point at which commentators viewed 'whores' as damaging to a man's financial position rather than his moral, spiritual or physical health. However, the cases outlined above connect the accumulation of material goods with the provision of sexual services as well as the withholding of property from legitimate kin, at least in the minds of contemporary, local witnesses. While not leading to the complete ruin of the family as suggested by Fissell's source material, it is clear that a century earlier the monetary and material aspects of pre- and extra-marital relationships were negotiated and constructed in various forms ranging from unofficial gifts, through quasi-legal arrangements to lawfully enforceable settlements. Women entering sexual relationships with men they were unlikely to marry considered the economic implications of their actions, and the wider community noticed the subsequent display of consumer goods.[61] It was a high-risk strategy; while an abandoned wife could sue for maintenance through the courts and a widow had dower or jointure provision, a mistress did not have any automatic legal right to an income from the estate of a dead lover. If the relationship terminated due to the death of the male partner, unless specific provision had been made in wills (which as we have seen was exceptionally rare) or by private landed settlement, the mistress could be left in a very vulnerable financial situation. Arguably, for those in more transient relationships, material goods formed capital which could be sold or exchanged at times of economic hardship.

More direct risks to a mistress than financial insecurity were perhaps surprisingly limited, however. As demonstrated by a case against Thomas Gerard in one of the earliest Chester High Commission actions, prosecution of 'dyvers concybines' themselves was not always forthcoming, even if their male gentry lovers did face trial.[62] Often the gentleman concerned was ordered to 'put his concubine from him' and pay a recognisance to ensure compliance, as Sir James Stanley discovered in 1543, with no specific attention paid to her identity or fate.[63] In cases of complete marital breakdown, parting from a lover was only one part of the courts' requirements, and the errant husband was also required to enter bond to live together with his wife in harmony. In 1566, Jeffrey Rishton was ordered to take his wife Alice 'unto his house and company', and it was only later, in 1567, and after several further disagreements, that he was required to receive her again and put 'furthe of his company all suspecte women'.[64] Very frequently, these other women are anonymous and their subsequent histories a mystery. Whether they returned to their families or were expelled from the household with no support is unknown. Where women were specifically punished, the penalties could vary and depended upon the financial position of the woman concerned. Alice Petty, the mistress of Roger Beckwith, was ordered to undergo penance in Selby and Cawood churches dressed in a white sheet.[65] Likewise, Beckwith's wife Elizabeth was punished for her relationship with an unnamed man and having a couple of children by him, by performing penance in Pickering and Thornton churches. It would appear in these cases that the transgressive women were treated in the same manner. However, a variety of other punishments were meted out to mistresses. Pascall Atkinson was carted through the streets of York and 'pute out of Walmegate Barr' (expelled from the city), to be treated as a vagabond in 1570; Alice Shuttleworth was imprisoned in the Kidcote and her diet restricted to bread and water on Wednesdays and Fridays in 1571; and Mary Gower, a widow with her own dower or jointure settlement, entered bond of 'CCli that she shall at all tymes hereafter forebeare to frequent use or kepe copany with John Milburne of Hindskelfe, gen. except it be openly in Church market or other open place … and not at any time hereafter to ly or lodge in the night season in the dwelling house of the said John Milburn or where he shall lodge neither suffer him to ly in any house of hers or where she shall then lodge or ly thereat.'[66] For those married women who faced prosecution, their husbands and families had to foot the legal bill and the financial implications could be substantial. Isabella Rhodes, wife of Robert Rhodes was brought before High Commission in 1629–31 for her adultery with Sir Richard Hawkesworth. After defying the court and refusing to perform penance in Otley church she was fined £10 in October 1630, and then had to provide 'sufficient suerties to be bounde of the some of CCli to his Majesties use that she should not kepe companye with Sir Richard Hawkesworth knighte' the following February. The Act Books record that Robert Rhodes undertook to enter bond with the assistance of his father, John.[67] If the initial identification and prosecution of mistresses was ambiguous and a mixture of punishments were applied to those who did make it into court, questions are raised about the courts' willingness and ability to command and control female immorality directly.

For the man, in purely economic terms the expense of a mistress was, for some, offset by the 'putting away' or disappearance of a wife. The surviving evidence from York High Commission, for example, suggests that Laurence Tetloe had lived with his mistress as man and wife for twenty years, and probably paid for her clothing, food and household requirements from his income. That the court ordered him to discover the whereabouts of his wife, and he had allegedly failed to locate her two years later, indicates that they had separated and Jane Tetloe had found an alternative source of income.[68] If the mistress was a married woman herself, her finances would have been managed by her husband, as was the case of Lady Everingham, who met her lover, Thomas Oglethorpe, in her servant's house.[69] For unmarried men, the costs associated with mistress-keeping and bastardy did not directly impact upon a wife; however, some of those deposing in court associated maintaining a mistress (or two) with other examples of personal excess or monetary mismanagement. George Burfitt fathered a child with Joan Ridley and another with Grace Flower but his immorality was exacerbated by 'the sin of drunkiness', allowing the miller to grind corn on Sundays, and permitting his property to fall into disrepair.[70]

Providing an income for a mistress therefore depended to a large extent upon the circumstances of those engaged in the relationship – whether either of them were married, if children had been born, whether the relationship was opportunistic or semi-permanent and if the relationship affected the balance of gender-related power within the household. The concept of squandering money upon another woman at the expense of a lawfully married wife and their legitimate children is one part of a complex picture; mistresses were dependent upon income derived from their own work, husbands, families and their lovers. A mistress was unable to claim maintenance or insist upon an equivalent of dower (if her partner died) as of right, although she might launch a suit in the courts if he failed to provide for his illegitimate children, thereby qualifying for financial entitlement (for the child) through motherhood. The moral and legal obligations to provide food, clothing and lodgings for a wife were not shared by a mistress, but in the cases of the long-standing relationships above (in particular the Tetloe case), there appears to have been a domestic framework of marriage underpinning their economic and sexual exchanges and, by extension, social standing.

The issue of marriage to a mistress was ultimately the most controversial issue raised by these illegitimate relationships. It was contingent upon the survival of the couple themselves as well as their husbands and wives. Referring to an earlier period, Helmholz suggested 'canons had once purported to disqualify all adulterers from marrying each other after the death of a first spouse', and there may have been some remaining sensitivity lingering around a marriage based upon immorality.[71] With the family at the centre of social, financial and political interest, the implications of translating a parallel relationship or one of 'customary concubinage' with no legal foundation (yet sanctioned by the local community) into one with official recognition challenged fundamental norms.

In some instances, it does seem that the mid-to-late sixteenth-century debate about divorce and remarriage had real resonances in cases in the north of England. In the case of Margaret Vawdrey of Riddings, daughter of Robert, a minor gentleman from the Timperley area of Cheshire, and Edward Legh of Baguley, it might have seemed unlikely that even their illicit relationship would be allowed to continue. When her father made his will in 1567 (and when it was proved in 1576), Margaret's inheritance was conditional upon her renouncing her immorality.[72] Edward Legh attracted the attention of York High Commission in 1571, with a bond of £200 being taken to ensure his attendance. Furthermore, Legh's wife Jane was well connected, as she was the daughter of Henry VIII's Privy Chamber groom Sir Urian Brereton of Handforth. But Urian had died some years previously, and the consequence of the action was in practice that Jane was divorced from her adulterous husband. It even seems possible that Margaret and Edward married and had children together who were recognised as his heirs.[73]

Marriage to a mistress might also be raised in the context of an even more destabilising context, that of physical threats to the life of a wife, especially given contemporary anxieties, although this was rare.[74] The York courts did, on one occasion, hear chilling testimony regarding the relationship between Sir Rowland Stanley of Hooton in the Wirral and Ellen Thomasyn, 'made to Lady Stanley' that included such threats. In 1560–61, Sir Rowland and his wife Lady Ursula both sought to annul their marriage. Lady Ursula sued Sir Rowland for a separation on the grounds of his adultery with Margery Cooke and Ellen Thomasyn and his cruelty, only to find him countersuing her for adultery with a near neighbour, Richard Hurleston, and this is a dispute which, through one aspect of its wider impacts, has gained prominence via the work of John Strype and his successors.[75] Sir Rowland Stanley owned substantial amounts of land and was the leading member of Cheshire society in Wirral hundred.[76] Related to the powerful Stanley earls of Derby, Rowland succeeded his brother William in 1546, shortly after the death of their father William,[77] and served as a Justice of the Peace from 1547.[78] The case was also, particularly in its later stages, prone to garner interest because of its religious aspects. Although from the distance of the twenty-first century his religious outlook is difficult to ascertain with certainty,[79] the careers of Sir Rowland's sons, particularly William, who surrendered Deventer to the Spanish in 1587 and then plotted against the queen, only added to other reasons for Protestants to look with suspicion on the loyalties of their father.[80] In the 1570s, with the case continuing to attract attention, one local participant, Robert Fletcher wrote to Archbishop Grindal, associating 'Sir Rowlands behavior towchinge his vnorderlye vsinge before your grace for his wief and that also even now the Sute he maynteyneth against your Grace your cowrt', with his 'prowd doinges and corrupt Religioon'.[81] Lady Ursula, by contrast, came from more notably Protestant stock, as the daughter of Sir Thomas Smith of Chester and brother of Sir Laurence, who enjoyed a distinguished career, serving as MP for Cheshire and mayor of Chester several times. The Smiths had resisted

Catholic restoration under Mary and were clearly identified with the Protestant cause early in Elizabeth's reign.[82] In 1560–61 this was largely in the future, however, and the case's significance in the current context is that the relationship portrayed in Lady Ursula's arguments had a more sinister aspect than an adulterous master–servant liaison, as a witness reported hearing Sir Rowland say 'thou shalt see me shortly devise away to be ryd of hir [Lady Ursula] or other lyke wordes' in order that he might marry Ellen Thomasyn. Still, in spite of the violence reportedly suffered by Lady Ursula, she survived to continue her role as a party in the cause for more than a dozen years and there was no marriage for Ellen Thomasyn or any other woman associated with Sir Rowland.[83]

More typical of the situations of mistresses in our study, as Bernard Capp has shown, was that 'a maid might even dream of marriage, if her master was single or had an ailing spouse', but such cases were still rare and often the patience required was extensive.[84] Only in a handful of cases from the northern courts has it been possible to trace a relationship from one of extra-marital adultery to marriage.[85] Bridget Redman and William Gascoigne of Caley in lower Wharfedale found themselves before the York courts in the mid-1560s, sometimes at the instigation of Bridget's husband Matthew.[86] Marriage was impossible until after the latter's death and thus did not take place until 1586.[87] That they were able to sustain an intimate relationship for so long and in the face of the church's suspicion of their adultery indicates a deep relationship and mutual compatibility. It is also worth noting that a further impediment (although of declining importance) to marrying an employer was the issue of social disparity,[88] but Bridget and William were of the same social background, which may have enhanced the likelihood of marriage.[89] York High Commission also prosecuted John Dickson for adultery with Anne Webster within the lifetime of William, her husband, in 1575. Their punishment for immorality, and the labelling of Anne by the court '[a]s an adulteresse (whose doings in and about have been verie offensive ungodlye and wickede)', were not impediments to their subsequent marriage.[90] For the courts, it was not so much the pre-marital adultery or even the speed of the marriage after William Webster's death that made them question the validity of the wedding ceremony, but that they were married 'in a morninge before fowre of the clocke the bannes not askede accordinge as is by Lawe appontede neither yet having any Licence from the Ordinarye of the Province in that behalf'. Some unhappily married wives and husbands understood that they had to wait until a spouse's death in order to remarry, but that was by no means the case for all. As demonstrated in chapter 2, the story of Anne Stanley and Ralph Rishton indicates how matters could be rather more complicated, and the conversion from mistress to wife problematic.[91] Rishton's marital career as a serial bridegroom came under the spotlight in both Chester and York, initially at the instigation of Rishton's second wife Elizabeth Parker. Her witnesses's insistence that banns had been read prior to solemnisation of their marriage in Clitheroe church indicates that her husband and Stanley were knowingly transgressing social norms when they began their sexual relationship and pushed that behaviour further when they exchanged vows privately at Rishton's house in Dunkenhalgh within Elizabeth's lifetime.[92] Both Parker and Stanley attempted to regularise their relationships with Rishton, which posed questions of dower or jointure entitlement after his death. While the mass of litigation surrounding both Rishton and also Rafe Holden (whose complex relationships with Gile Bilsbie, Isabel Haughton, and Elizabeth Elston were also discussed in chapter 2) obscures our view of their knowledge of divorce *a vinculo*, annulment and separation *mensa et thoro*, the fact remains that Rishton and Holden were able to form a series of sexual relationships, initially adulterous, later possibly bigamous, which left question marks over financial provision for the women concerned. Yet, despite the practical difficulties, marriage to an already-married lover was viewed as desirable by some mistresses.

In sum, evidence from across the north suggests the degree to which the mistresses of the northern gentry and nobility were far from a uniformly disempowered group. While their formal endowment and resourcing was almost always limited, it appears that in many cases the sustained commitment of both parties to their relationship supported these women and gave some prompts to the developing view of a mistress as a financial and economic charge on a male householder. It seems to have been possible for some to sustain the role without being fundamentally dishonoured, retaining an assured status in family and kinship networks – and hence they cause us to question the assumed pattern of society as built around legitimate marital relationships and suggest alternatives, both locally and through court more widely. Some mistresses might aspire, even, to eventual marriage. A significant proportion themselves came from gentle backgrounds, which is why it is necessary to turn next to the situation of gentle- and noblewomen who took lovers.

Notes

1 Richard T. Spence, *The Privateering Earl: George Clifford, 3rd Earl of Cumberland, 1558–1605* (Stroud: Alan Sutton Publishing, 1995), p. 211; G. C. Williamson, *George, Third Earl of Cumberland (1558–1605): His Life and Voyages* (Cambridge: Cambridge University Press, 1920), p. 264; *Anne Clifford's Great Books of Record*, ed. J. L. Malay (Manchester: Manchester University Press, 2015), p. 710. See above, p. 55n.29, for speculation as to the identity of this mistress.
2 *The Letters of Lady Anne Bacon*, ed. G. Allen, Camden Society, 5th ser., 44 (Cambridge, 2014), p. 263; P. J. Hammer, 'Sex and the Virgin Queen: Aristocratic Concupiscence and the Court of Elizabeth I', *Sixteenth Century Journal*, 31 (2000), 77–97, at p. 85.
3 R. C. Richardson, 'A Maidservant's Lot in Early Modern England', *History Today*, 60 (2) (Feb. 2010), 25–31; Martin Ingram, *Carnal Knowledge: Regulating Sex in England, 1470–1600* (Cambridge: Cambridge University Press, 2017), p. 95.
4 See above, pp. 3–7.
5 *Lancashire and Cheshire Wills and Inventories from the Ecclesiastical Court, Chester*, ed. G. J. Piccope, Chetham Society, LI (1860), ii. 241–3.
6 *Ibid.*, vol. I, XXXIII (1857), pp. 66–8.
7 *TE* iii. 198.
8 *North Country Wills, Being Abstracts of Wills Relating to the Counties of York, Nottingham, Northumberland, Cumberland, and Westmorland at Somerset House and Lambeth Palace 1383 to 1550*, ed. J. W. Clay, Surtees Society, CXVI (1908), pp. 156–8.
9 *TE* vi. 264–5 (Saltmarsh); *Wills and Inventories from the Registry at Durham*, vol. IV, ed. H. M. Woods, Surtees Society, CXLII (1929), iv. 141 (Burrell).

10 *The Registers of the Parish Church of Croston in the County of Lancaster: Christenings 1543–1721; Weddings 1538–1685; Burials 1538–1684*, ed. Henry Fishwick, LPRS, 6 (1900), p. 12.
11 *The Registers of the Parish Church of Cartmel in the County of Lancaster: Christenings, Burials and Weddings, 1559–1661*, ed. Henry Brierley, LPRS, 28 (1907), p. 60, for the baptism of Edmond; p. 169 for his burial only one month later; and p. 71 for the baptism of 'Mary, d. of Mary Taylor of Meethop supposed by Mr John Thornburgh' in Aug. 1626.
12 *Ibid.*, p. 69 (1625).
13 *The Parish Registers of Mirfield*, Part I: *Baptisms, Marriages & Burials 1559–1700*, ed. William Brigg, Yorkshire Parish Register Society, LXIV (1919), p. 49.
14 *Ibid.*, p. 35.
15 Patricia Crawford, 'The Construction and Experiences of Maternity in Seventeenth-Century England', in Valerie A. Fildes and Dorothy McLaren (eds), *Women as Mothers in Pre-industrial England* (London: Routledge, 1990), pp. 3–38, at p. 22.
16 *The Registers of the Cathedral Church of Manchester: Christenings, Burials and Weddings, 1573–1616*, ed. John Owen, Henry Brierley, Mrs. Brierley and Miss Wrigley, LPRS, 31 (1908), pp. 26, 456, 147 respectively.
17 BIA, HC.AB 6, fo. 82v (Ashton); BIA, HC.AB 6, fo. 81; HC.AB 7 fo. 78 (Tetloe).
18 DUL, DDR/EJ/CCA/1/2, fos. 212, 216, 219, 220, 224v, 257, 278; DDR/EJ/CCD/1/2, fos. 183v, 184; although she is not mentioned in his will of 1588, which names his children (p. 116 below).
19 DUL, DDR/EJ/CCA/2/1, fos. 71, 103.
20 See BIA, HC.AB 17, fos. 234, 241v, 254v, 266v, 273v, 277v, 281, 315, 325, 330v, 334v, 340, 347v, 355, for the prosecution of Eden, and HC.AB 17, fos. 234, 242, 249, 254v, 273, 278, 315, 325, 330v, 334v, 356v, for that of Daniell, in York High Commission 1629–30; DUL, Hunter MSS, vol. 16, fo. 71; Hunter MSS, vol. 17, fo. 70, for the prosecution of Daniell in Durham High Commission in 1633.
21 Cases from the York Act Books show use of the term 'whore' on four occasions (and a further one doubtful) and one mention of a supposed marriage. In the York Act Books, there are three 'concubynes'. On 'harlot', see Ingram, *Carnal Knowledge*, pp. 184–6.
22 See also J. A. Sharpe, *Defamation and Sexual Slander in Early Modern England: The Church Courts at York*, Borthwick Publications, 58 (York: Borthwick Institute of Historical Research, 1980); David Hewitt, 'Some Cases from the Defamation Jurisdiction of the Archdeaconry Court of Richmond', *The Journal of Legal History*, 19 (1998), 251–69.
23 LRO, ARR/2/4/4/148.
24 DUL, DDR/EJ/CCD/1/11, fo. 152. Barbara Errington was the wife of Thomas Errington but later married Clennell clandestinely; see DUL, DDR/EJ/CCA/1/12, fos. 20, 22v, office c Andrew Clennell & Barbara Errington als Clennell in 1633.
25 BIA, CP.G 2573.
26 DUL, DDR/EJ/CCD/1/9, fos. 185v, 187, 188, 233.
27 BIA, CP.G 2883; CP.G 696; CP.G 3486; CP.G 539A; CP.G 539.
28 Garthine Walker, 'Expanding the Boundaries of Female Honour in Early Modern England', *Transactions of the Royal Historical Society*, 6th ser., VI (1996), 235–45, at p. 236.
29 Note also the use of the word 'harlot' against men, e.g. BIA, CP.G 3061, Thomas Ellwood c Alice Kirby, who called him 'a shytten harlott both of thy tonge and thy tayle' in response to which he called her 'slutt'; CP.G 253, Robert Thorpe c Robert Dickinson, 'thow noghty false harlot'. See Ingram, *Carnal Knowledge*, pp. 184–6.

30 Laura Gowing, 'Gender and the Language of Insult in Early Modern London', *History Workshop*, 35 (1993), 1–21.
31 Barry Coward, *The Stanleys, Lords Stanley and Earls of Derby, 1385–1672: The Origins, Wealth and Power of a Landowning Family*, Chetham Society, 3rd ser., XXX (1983), p. 32.
32 LRO, DDM/35/31 (Childwall & Kirkby), DDK/6/16a (Ormskirk); *VCH Lancs.*, iv. 217–22.
33 Cheshire Arch., DVE/1/M/4.
34 TNA, STAC 2/22/270 (*Yorkshire Star Chamber Proceedings*, ed. William Brown, H. B. McCall and John Lister, YASRS, 41, 45, 51, 70 (1909–27), iii. 32–7, at pp. 32–3). These events are conventionally dated to 1513–14, but the identification of Henry Saville's active role, given his likely birth date of 1498–99, either makes a point in the 1520s more likely. Savile's behaviour with Barston may have been perceived as the worse for taking place in a military context: see the concerns expressed in 1513, in *Tudor Royal Proclamations*, ed. Paul L. Hughes and James F. Larkin (3 vols. New Haven CT: Yale University Press, 1964–69), i. 113.
35 Cheshire Arch., EDA 12/2, fols. 124v–125 (1564); BIA, HC.AB 6, fos. 147, 161–2, 184; HC.AB 7, fos. 92–3, 169, 183–4; HC.CP 1572/2; *APC*, vii. 114, 146. Claire Cross, 'Sin and Society: The Northern High Commission and the Northern Gentry in the Reign of Elizabeth', in Claire Cross, David Loades and J. J. Scarisbrick (eds), *Law and Government under the Tudors: Essays Presented to Sir Geoffrey Elton ... on ... his Retirement* (Cambridge: Cambridge University Press, 1986), pp. 195–209, at pp. 206–7. S. T. Bindoff, *The House of Commons, 1509–1558* (3 vols. London: Secker & Warburg for the History of Parliament Trust, 1982), i. 378–9.
36 BIA, HC.AB 17, fos. 462, 465, 471, HC.AB 18, fos. 2v, 8v–9, 10–10v, 13–14v, 17, 19, 24, 24v, 28, 31, 34, 49, 59, 73, HC.AB 19, fos. 69v, 71v; Cross, 'Sin and Society', p. 207; BIA, HC.AB 17, fos. 462, 465, 465v, 471; HC.AB 18, fos. 2v, 6, 8v–9, 10–10v, 13–14v, 17, 19, 24, 24v, 28, 31, 33, 34, 49, 52, 59, 60, 73; HC.AB 19, fos. 69v, 71v, 80v, 84. Bulmer owned lands adjacent to Paylor's estate at Thoralby: Edward married Elizabeth to him because of the proximity of their lands: HC.CP 1631/1.
37 *The Visitation of Cheshire in the Year 1580, Made by Robert Glover for William Flower with Numerous Additions and Continuations Including those from The Visitation of Cheshire made in the Year 1566; With an Appendix Containing the Visitation of a Part of Cheshire in the Year 1533 made by William Fellows for Thomas Benolte and a Fragment of The Visitation of the City of Chester in the Year 1591 made by Thomas Chaloner*, ed. J. P. Rylands, Harleian Society, XVIII (1882), p. 71; Cheshire Arch., EDA 12/2, fo. 116.
38 Cheshire Arch., EDA 12/2, fo. 126.
39 BIA, HC.AB 17, fos. 234, 254v, 266v, 273v, 277v, 281, 315, 325, 330v, 334v, 340, 347v, 355.
40 Cheshire Arch., EDA 12/2, fos. 19, 68–v.
41 BIA, HC.AB 11, fo. 217.
42 BIA, HC.AB 9, fos. 161, 190.
43 Leicestershire, Leicester and Rutland Record Office, Braunstone Estate Documents, 16 D 66 / 461, confirms that Elizabeth Hartilpoole gave birth to William junior, George, Barantine and Elizabeth by Huddleston. *Oxford Church Courts: Depositions, 1592–1596*, ed. Jack Howard Drake (Oxford: Oxfordshire County Council, 1998), no. 71: curate Thomas Jones had been summoned by Huddleston to baptise a child in his house; Jones had since been told that it was now commonly reported that the child had been unlawfully begotten by Hudleston on Elizabeth a single woman who had had other children by him. William was elected to parliament in 1601: P. W. Hasler, *The House of Commons, 1558–1603* (3 vols. London: HMSO for the History

of Parliament Trust, 1981), ii. 350–1. For William's father's complex relationship with his sister, see above, p. 17, and for William's mother's response, below, p. 104.
44 *LP* viii. 496.
45 See above, pp. 28, 50–1; John Venn and J. A. Venn, *Alumni Cantabrigiensis: A Biographical List of all Known Students, Graduates and Holders of Office at the University of Cambridge, from the Earliest Times to 1900* (2 parts in 10 vols. Cambridge: Cambridge University Press, 1922–54), ii. 178; Marjorie Cox with L. A. Hopkins, *A History of Sir John Deane's Grammar School, Northwich, 1557–1908* (Manchester: Manchester University Press, 1975), p. 86; Bindoff, *House of Commons, 1509–1558*, iii. 421, 522–3. Sir James himself also kept a mistress: Cheshire Arch., EDA 12/1, p. 12.
46 *TE* v. 6.
47 R. T. Spence, *Lady Anne Clifford: Countess of Pembroke, Dorset and Montgomery (1590–1676)* (Stroud: Sutton, 1997), p. 60.
48 Brighton, East Sussex Record Office, SAS/D/125; /128; AMS 315. This involved the large sum of £800 rent charge. For the increasingly difficult financial position of the Temples during the seventeenth century, see also E. F. Gay, 'The Temples of Stowe and Their Debts: Sir Thomas Temple and Sir Peter Temple, 1603–1653', *Huntington Library Quarterly*, 2 (1939), 399–438.
49 *Letters of John Chamberlain*, ed. Norman Egbert McClure, Memoirs of the American Philosophical Society, XII, pts. 1–2 (2 vols. Philadelphia: The American Philosophical Society 1939), ii. 284.
50 *The Diaries of Lady Anne Clifford*, ed. D.J.H. Clifford (Stroud: Alan Sutton, 1990), pp. 78–9.
51 *Ibid.*, p. 81; Lady Anne was pregnant at the time and her diary records bouts of ill health, see also p. 246, where on 2 Feb. 1676 she noted that her 'little son Thomas' was born exactly fifty-six years previously, placing his birth in 1620.
52 DUL, DDR/EJ/CCD/1/5, fos. 80–81v.
53 Cf. BIA, CP.G 924 Matthew Usher c Katherine Hamerton, who exchanged gifts of a handkerchief, purse, silk and 'an old rial' prior to promising each other marriage.
54 David N. Durant, *Bess of Hardwick: Portrait of an Elizabethan Dynast* (revised paperback edn, London: Peter Owen, 1999), p. 147.
55 *Calendar of the Manuscripts of the Most Hon. The Marquis of Salisbury K.G. ... Preserved at Hatfield House, Hertfordshire*, ed. R. A. Roberts, M. S. Giuseppi, and G. Dyfnallt Owen, Historical Manuscripts Commission, 9 (24 vols. London: HMSO, 1883–1973), iv. 114–15.
56 Lambeth, Lambeth Palace Library, Talbot Papers, MS 3199, fo. 299; Shrewsbury Papers, MS 701, fo. 87.
57 BIA, HC.AB 13, fos. 208, 210v, 212, 214, 225, 233, 237, 239, 240, 242v, 243v, 248v, 252, 254, 272v, 274v, 276v, 277v; HC.AB 14, fo. 56v.
58 Leah Leneman, 'Wives and Mistresses in Eighteenth-Century Scotland', *Women's History Review*, 8 (1999), 671–92.
59 Nina Kushner, *Erotic Exchanges: The World of Elite Prostitution in Eighteenth-Century Paris* (Ithaca NY: Cornell University Press, 2013), especially ch. 5 'Contracts and Elite Prostitution as Work', pp. 129–62.
60 Mary Fissell, 'Remaking the Maternal Body in England, 1680–1730', *Journal of the History of Sexuality*, 26 (2017), 114–39.
61 Although from the evidence available, Frances Nelson's agency in the contract with Barnby seems minimal.
62 Cheshire Arch., EDA 12/1, p. 2.

63 Cheshire Arch., EDA 12/1, p. 12.
64 BIA, HC.AB 3, fos. 11, 144.
65 BIA, HC.AB 10, fos. 129–v. Beckwith was ordered to pay. The Court heard that Beckwith had performed his penance and declaration in Selby but commuted the penances in Cawood and Brayton into a payment of £50 (£6 13s 4d to the poor of Cawood; £6 13s 4d to the poor of Brayton; 20 nobles to the poor of Selby; £5 to be spent on books [the *Acts & Monuments*] for the 3 churches; £5 to the officers of the Court; and £20 towards making a causeway between Cawood and Shereburn).
66 BIA, HC.AB 5, fo. 189v (Atkinson); HC.AB 6, fos. 10v–11 (Shuttleworth); HC.AB 13, fo. 78 (Gower).
67 BIA, HC.AB 17, fos. 305, 308, 354, 360, 366, 372, 414, 439.
68 BIA, HC.AB 6, fo. 81; HC.AB 7, fo. 78.
69 BIA, CP.G 331.
70 BIA, CP.H 1870.
71 R. H. Helmholz, *The Oxford History of the Laws of England*, vol. 1: *The Canon Law and Ecclesiastical Jurisdiction from 597 to the 1640s* (Oxford: Oxford University Press, 2004), pp. 552–3.
72 *Lancashire and Cheshire Wills and Inventories from the Ecclesiastical Court at Chester, the Second Portion*, ed. G. J. Piccope, Chetham Society, LI (1860), p. 80.
73 BIA, HC.AB 6, fos. 36v, 75, 110, 112–112v, 148, 150, 153, 154v, 157. The marriage to Vawdrey does not appear in *Visitation of Cheshire in the Year 1580*, p. 149, or Richard St. George and Henry St. George, *Pedigrees Made at the Visitation of Chester, 1613*, ed. George J. Armytage and J. Paul Rylands, RSLC, LVIII (1909), p. 153; it is referred to in Peter Leycester, *Historical Antiquities in Two Books the First Treating in General of Great-Brettain and Ireland: The Second Containing Particular Remarks Concerning Cheshire* (London: printed by W. L. for Robert Clavell,1673), p. 219 (George Ormerod, *The History of the County Palatine and City of Chester*, 2nd edn, revised and enlarged by Thomas Helsby (3 vols. London: Routledge, 1882), i. 552).
74 Anxieties perhaps most prominently exhibited around the death in 1560 of Amy Robsart, wife of Robert Dudley earl of Leicester: Chris Skidmore, *Death and the Virgin: Elizabeth, Dudley and the Mysterious Fate of Amy Robsart* (London: Weidenfeld & Nicolson, 2010), esp. pp. 203–372.
75 BIA, CP.G 975A (Lady Ursula Stanley c Sir Rowland Stanley) and CP.G 1042 (Sir Rowland Stanley c Lady Ursula Stanley). Lady Ursula was Sir Rowland Stanley's second wife and the mother of two daughters by him, Margaret and Mary; Sir Rowland's first wife, Margaret Aldersey, was the mother of his legitimate sons: St. George and St. George, *Pedigrees Made at the Visitation of Chester, 1613*, p. 222. John Strype, *The History of the Life and Acts of the Most Reverend Father in God, Edmund Grindal* (London: printed for John Wyat and John Hartley, 1710), pp. 183–4, and the subsequent Oxford, Clarendon Press edition of 1821. Patrick Collinson, *Archbishop Grindal 1519–1583: The Struggle for a Reformed Church* (London: Jonathan Cape, 1979).
76 'A List of the Freeholders in Cheshire in the Year 1578', ed. William Fergusson Irvine, in *Miscellanies, IV*, RSLC, XLIII (1902), p. 20.
77 Ormerod, *Chester*, ii. 416; Cheshire Arch., ZDCAS/3.
78 JP: 26 May 1547: *Calendar of Patent Rolls … Edward VI* (London: HMSO, 1924–9), i. 81; 1550: TNA, CHES 24/92/9; 1551: TNA, CHES 24/92/7; 1554: 'Commission of the Peace for Cheshire in 1554', *Cheshire Sheaf*, 3rd ser., 17 (Sept. 1920), 86–7; 1555, Apr. x May: *Calendar of State Papers: Domestic Series of the Reign of Mary I, 1553–1558*, ed. C. S. Knighton (London: Public Record Office, 1998), p. 160. All as 'armiger'.

79 Ormerod, *Chester*, ii. 229–31.
80 K. R. Wark, *Elizabethan Recusancy*, p. 182. William's brothers Edward and John became Jesuits.
81 BL, Lansdowne MS 17 fols. 112–14 (printed in *The Cheshire Sheaf*, 3rd ser., IV (1902): 111–13, 121; Strype, *Life and Acts of the Most Reverend Father in God, Edmund Grindal* (1821), pp. 265–7). Collinson, *Archbishop Grindal*, p. 209.
82 Bindoff, *House of Commons, 1509–1558*, iii. 334–5; Hasler, *House of Commons, 1558–1603*, iii. 398; Ormerod, *Chester*, iii. 503; Tim Thornton, *Cheshire and the Tudor State, 1480–1560* (Woodbridge: Boydell, 2000), p. 236.
83 The method Sir Rowland might have used to be rid of Lady Ursula is unspecified, but we might remind ourselves that even if the Stanleys separated, remarriage was impossible until the death of one of the spouses. See further on this case below, pp. 82, 106–10, 136–9.
84 Bernard Capp, *When Gossips Meet: Women, Family, and Neighbourhood in Early Modern England* (Oxford: Oxford University Press, 2003), p. 159.
85 It is not intended to detail here breach of contract cases where marriage was allegedly initially promised prior to intercourse or those of pre-marital fornication.
86 BIA, CP.G 1096 (1563, Matthew Redman c Bridget Redman); CP.G 1670 (1573, Bridget Redman c Matthew Redman); HC.AB 7, fos. 18v, 23, 23v, 32v, 43, 46v, 57, 65, 67, 67v, 69, 76, 89, 112v, 113, 120, 130, 152, 153, 155, 167–167v, 168, 170–171, 174–175, 176v, 177, 179v, 180v, 182, 183, 185, 198, 202–203, 203v (1572, Office / Matthew Redman c Bridget Redman / William Gascoigne); HC.AB 8, fo. 27 (1574); HC.AB 11, fo. 69v (1586, Office c William Gascoigne & Bridget Redman).
87 *The Parish Registers of Otley, Co.York*, ed. W. Brigg, Yorkshire Parish Record Society, 33, 44 (1908–12), i. 141 (Gascoigne marriage), 196 (Bridget's burial in 1608).
88 Helmholz, *Oxford History of the Laws of England*, p. 552. The evidence from the York courts suggests that this was a rare problem for higher-status women defending themselves against restitution actions from servile men. BIA, CPG. 3084 Thomas Kighley c Jane Ponsonby; CP.H 208, CP.H 156 Gervase Steel c Margaret Savile. Both women won their cases.
89 *The Visitation of Yorkshire, made in the Years 1584/5, by Robert Glover, Somerset Herald; to Which is Added the Subsequent Visitation made in 1612, by Richard St. George, Norroy King of Arms*, ed. Joseph Foster (London: Privately printed for the editor, 1875), p. 285; *The Visitation of Yorkshire in 1563 & 1564, Made by William Flower, Esquire, Norroy King of Arms*, ed. C. B. Norcliffe, Harleian Society, XVI (1881), pp. 136 (Gascoign), 262 (Redman); William Greenwood, *The Redmans of Levens and Harewood: A Contribution to the History of the Levens Family of Redman and Redmayn in Many of its Branches* (Kendal: Titus Wilson, 1905), pp. 113–14 (which includes a discussion of Matthew Redman's financial problems).
90 BIA, HC.AB 8, fos. 160v, 161, 168. William Webster's death in the middle of his divorce suit against Anne enabled her rapid remarriage to Dickson.
91 See above, pp. 28, 50–1.
92 Whilst not forgetting the validity of the Parker-Rishton marriage was called into question by the Towneley-Rishton union.

4

Gentlewomen and their lovers

IN A PREPARATIVE TO *Marriage*, first published in 1591, Henry Smith drew his readers' attention to female immorality and its association with vanity, claiming 'a woman may have too many ornaments: frisseled locks, naked breasts, painting, perfume and especially a rolling eye are the forerunners of adultery, and he which hath such a wife hath a fine plague.'[1] Smith also identified adultery as 'the disease of marriage', the only cure for which is 'divorcement' for the benefit of the chaste partner 'least they should be tied to a plague while they live'. In addition, by identifying extra-marital sexual activity as a contagion, which originated with Eve in the Garden of Eden, Smith seems to have identified women as the instigators of such immorality, which could only be cured by divorce for the benefit of the innocent party. A survey of the surviving York ecclesiastical court records suggests that gentry women were three times less likely to appear as defendants in immorality or adultery cases than gentlemen.[2] A more detailed reading of witness testimonies, however, indicates a more complex picture, and that female elite immorality was more extensive than this record would suggest, but that the ecclesiastical courts were unwilling or unable to directly challenge it. This chapter will explore this more elusive evidence for an understanding of the ways in which noble- and gentry women were involved in illicit relationships. It will explore the limited role which the ecclesiastical courts played in their affairs, and consider the implications for them of the life cycle and family control of property and financial resources. That context provides explanations for the networks which in some cases constrained, but in others opened up, opportunities for illegitimate relationships in ways which traditional views of gender, and especially the double standard, might make very surprising. Rather than seeing female honour as almost entirely defined in terms of sexuality, and of potential or actual transgression, the evidence seems to suggest a wider scope for action.[3]

In 1520, when Lady Florence Clifford sued her husband Henry, Lord Clifford for restitution of conjugal rights, she did not perhaps expect her own conduct to be brought into question. But, under examination by Dr Machell, her lover Roger Wharton admitted, 'I will never denye ffor a man may be in bedd wth a woman and yett do noo hurte'.[4] In one simple statement, Wharton shed light upon the sexual mores of the Clifford household and summed up one of the major issues for women involved in illicit sexual conduct, that of pregnancy. The absence of any evidence from the church courts suggests that Lady Florence was, however, not expected to answer a charge of adultery herself. She was not unique in this respect. The servants in the Everingham household were prosecuted for enabling Lady Agnes Everingham's adultery with Thomas Oglethorpe in 1545. One of those accused, Robert Langdale, admitted that Oglethorpe had previously been 'comanded to absteyn' from Lady Agnes' company, but did not refer to any such order pertaining to the conduct of the gentlewoman herself.[5]

It was possible for aristocratic or knightly women to find themselves defendants in adultery cases in the ecclesiastical court records, but it was rare. Lady Ursula Stanley and Lady Elizabeth Foljambe faced litigation initiated either by their husbands, Sir Rowland and Sir Francis, or on their behalf, in 1560 and 1629 respectively. In the case of Elizabeth Foljambe, accusations against her were made into York High Commission. Lady Elizabeth was the daughter of Sir William Wray of Glentworth in Lincolnshire, who was a major supporter of godly religion in the county, and recipient of the dedication of Simon Patrick's translation of Jean de Hainault's Calvinist work *L'état de l'église*.[6] By contrast, Sir Francis was notorious for his extreme profligacy and the destruction of his inheritance, but this did not prevent him challenging his wife's behaviour. She was accused of adultery with 'Johanne Courtrapp' of the City of London, gentleman, probably John Courthope, second son of John Courthope of Wileigh in Sussex and brother of Sir George. If the identification is correct, then this relationship is suggestive of connections and relationships forged at court, given the Courthopes' strong associations with Sussex, Kent and especially the City of London, which Lady Elizabeth presumably accessed through the court and London season.[7] Sir Francis had thrown her out of his house about ten weeks beforehand when the court decreed that she should be paid £4 a week maintenance, on pain of £100 if he did not swiftly comply.[8] Whether there was any direct connection or not is unclear, but it appears that the expulsion occurred directly after a visit to one Mr Webster, a near neighbour, at Carhouse in Rotherham parish

> the said Ladie Elizabeth Ffouliambe walkeing abrode to take the fresh ayre & in goeing in to one Mr Websters house of Carhouse within the Parish of Rotheram about a mile distant from Aldwarke Hall beinge the house of Sirr Ffrancis Ffouleambe upon Tuesday the foweth day of August last (as this deponent hath heard) was shutt out & excluded from Aldwarke Hall aforesaid at her returne home the same day by the said Sir Ffrancis (or some others by his direction) he beinge then present in the said house at Aldwarke since which tyme she the said Ladie hath not being [sic] admitted into his said house or any of his houses nor had any mayntenance from the said Sir Ffrancis otherwise then the Courte hath ordered & decreed unto her.[9]

The court was relatively supportive to her. It appears that at some point during the process, and when Sir Francis was failing to pay alimony, Richard Brooke, a notary public, began to make more specific allegations against Lady Foljambe, we might assume with some support from Sir Francis, but the court acted to prevent him, sanctioning him when she complained by suspending his right to act as a proctor of the court.[10] What began as an adultery case against Lady Elizabeth in July 1629, had turned, by October, into an alimony dispute with Sir Francis as the defendant. That the court sanctioned the couple's separation suggests a serious problem with the marriage (which presumably originated with Lady Elizabeth's relationship with Courthope), but with no accusations of extreme violence or adultery / fornication against Sir Francis, and a failure to deal with Lady Elizabeth's immorality, the court ended up spending four years policing the Foljambes' financial settlement.

In the case of Lady Ursula Stanley and her husband Sir Rowland, whom we have already encountered because of his unconventional relationships, more detail is available of Lady Ursula's alleged activities. It was in the course of action in relation to Sir Rowland's relationships that he orchestrated specific allegations about his wife's behaviour. They centred on two overnight visits supposedly made to Hooton by Richard Hurleston, a neighbour of the Stanleys, resident at Picton to the south-east, the previous April and September/October. Sir Rowland's trusted servants Robert Pitts, Henry Lloyd, Hugh ap William, and William ap Howell allegedly combined to take a number of witnesses to see 'such a sight as thou never saw sence thou was borne' – Hurleston wandering the corridors of Hooton in his nightgown. It was Lady Ursula's alleged lover, Hurleston, who initiated a suit in Star Chamber, probably soon after March 1560, claiming that Sir Rowland Stanley tried to murder him, as well as referencing Sir Rowland's 'greate outrage towardes Dame Vrsula Stanley his wief', affirming 'that she had abused her self with your seid soibiecte … and therevpon in the night tyme did put [her] from hym out of his saied howse', suggesting that there was an immediate connection between the discovery of the alleged adultery, whether staged or not, and Lady Stanley's ejection from his house.[11] The case involving the couple in the church courts continued across more than a decade; there is no further specific reference to Hurleston, but while Sir Rowland expressed himself willing to take Lady Ursula back as his wife, she notably refused to engage with the process, shielded by her influential family, the Smiths of Chester, whose early commitment to the Protestant cause distinguished them clearly from the emerging suspicions around Sir Rowland's religious conservatism.[12]

Other cases do refer less directly to gentlewomen's adultery, even if it is not the prime point at issue. Each tends to show the prominence of the women involved, suggesting the extensive opportunities available to them in certain circumstances, and extensive influence that might be exerted through those relationships. In 1617, it seems to have been the widow Dorothy Heywood of Laverton who was the prime target of High Commission's pursuivant, although the violent reaction of her alleged lover, the gentleman William Dawson of Azerley, who happened to be at her house and who emerged threatening murder unless she was released, meant that attention was soon switched to him. She was prominent perhaps thanks to her late husband's influential role in local and regional society: Fabian Heywood and a companion had, in 1607, led followers to the number of 400, organised in troops, onto land involved in the disputed enclosure of Thorpe Moor near Kirkby Malzeard, resulting in action in Star Chamber.[13]

In some other cases, while it was the male gentry participant in an illicit relationship that was the prime target of the action in the church courts, a gentlewoman was caught up in the taking of bonds which followed. This was the case with a relationship between a prominent widow, Mrs Mary Gower of Stittenham, Yorkshire, and John Milburn of nearby Henderskelfe, or Hinderskelfe (the location of the present Castle Howard), gentleman. Mary was the widow of Thomas Gower and the daughter of Gabriel Fairfax of Steeton. Thomas had been a well-known military figure, having served as Marshal of Berwick and governor of Aymouth Fort, and he had died in 1592. Their eldest son Sir Thomas, born in 1584, was in 1620 to be created a baronet and serve as High Sheriff of Yorkshire. But by early 1597, Mary was being questioned over her conduct with her neighbour John. John was the subject of action in York High Commission, but unlike so many female participants in such relationships, she was bound to forbear his company, except in specified respectable circumstances. The amount in which she was bound, £200, suggests a reason for the action, given that she was of higher social status than her lover.[14]

In another case, the issue of adultery was evidently suspected but hard to prove and subordinate to more pressing concerns about one gentlewoman's religious opinions. Anne Woodruff of Woolley in the West Riding, wife of George, was examined in 1587 for her possible illicit relationship with an unfortunately vaguely identified Mr Lee, 'but no matter fell out against hir which was touching adultery or fornicacon' and she denied the matter. Still, she was bound in a recognisance to abstain from all suspicious company with him. The size of this bond, £500, probably had as much to do with the current concern with her recusancy and her influence on her husband, for in the same year Edwin Sandys, archbishop of York reported, in commenting on her husband among other magistrates, that she was 'an obstinate recusant; and of long time hath been. One that doth very much hurt. An argument that he is not well affected himself. Such men as have such wives are thought very unfit to serve in these our times.'[15] This was a remarkable recognisance to take from a woman in respect of such a claim of adultery and most likely arose from the associated concerns over her religious influence on her husband – whatever the possible state of their marriage.

The cases involving Alice Dockray provide greater details than most about how extramarital relationships operated and were detected, suggesting above all the resources, ingenuity and opportunities at the disposal of an elite woman intent on keeping a lover, given the involvement of neighbours, servants and children. She first appears in the Chester court records in 1593, when her husband Robert Bindloss divorced her for adultery, although later proceedings suggest that they had obtained a separation from the York Consistory a year or two before.[16] Alice now believed herself free to remarry and was back in the York Consistory in 1599 when the legality of her marriage to William Carr of Giggleswick came under scrutiny.[17] The crux of this was the nature of her separation from Bindloss; her divorce from him was from 'cohabitacon from bedd and bord and not frome the bond of matrimony by reason of a fault or crime of Adultery by the said Alice comittyd confessyd and adiudged.' Bindloss reportedly at that point 'was and yet is lyving'. The court heard that during an adulterous relationship with James Potter in 1587, 'she did kepe the said James secrett in a greate chamber there dureing the tyme of his aboade there and that always he came by night and was kepte close in the day.' On occasions, Alice had to trust her maid Margaret Milner to leave the great chamber door open and hide Potter in an outhouse at the Bindloss house at Helsington, until the household were asleep 'whereatt when all were att their rest he might come in but wyshed him when he came to her bed to be ware in anye wise of waykinge the chylde that laye wth her.'[18] Meanwhile Bindloss had grown suspicious of his wife's conduct, and hid himself in the outhouse where 'Margaret did suppose she had likewise spoken the said words to the said James yet in truith the words were spoken to … Robet Byndlose who having iustly conceived suspecon of … Alice her lewd life had secretly conceihled himselfe into the said house to watch what was her behaviour in his absence.' Approximately four years later 'Robert Byndlose upon suspecion of lewde behaviour betwene … Alice and Richard Warriner had forbidden them boothe to kepe any company or societye togeather.' Bindloss' demand fell upon deaf ears as the couple were caught in bed together,

> where … Alice did lye att the Towne End Hall neere Kendall … beinge att that tyme the dwelling house of one James Midgley … for the said James Midgley and his wife lying in bedd heare in the night tyme such rumblings and cracking of the bed where the said Alice did lye as seemed soe strange unto them that … James Midgley arising somewhat early in the morninge to knowe the cause thereof did mete … Alice coming furthe of her chamber and found Richard Warriner naked in the said bed in the chamber and wrapped in the bed cloathes.

Alice also claimed that she and Warriner had wanted to marry, but would not 'for feare of Robert Byndlose', they lay together every week, he lay between her and her maid 'and never offere to stir her maide.'

In contrast, while defending her marriage to Carr, Alice was keen to stress the ages at which she and Robert wed, fifteen and thirteen years of age respectively, and that the ceremony had taken place 'in a chamber within the dwelling house of Robert Bindelose father of Robert Bindelose at Helston' (Helsington, near Kendal), suggesting that her emphasis was upon the bridegroom being underage and the clandestine nature of the ceremony.[19] Initial evidence to the York Consistory in 1599 could not pinpoint when the marriage had taken place – any time between ten and eighteen years previously, although Alice herself claimed that it was about 'thirtene yeres since [i.e. in 1586] this respondent being then fiftene yeres of age or thereabouts & Robert Bindelose being then about thirtene yeres old'. By trying to shift the focus of proceedings in such a way, Alice Dockray was trying to validate her marriage to Carr, which had been celebrated in the church at Gisburn, albeit without banns. However, when asked whether she had been divorced on the basis of her adultery Alice said 'she knoweth not.' Nevertheless, Alice went to a great deal of trouble to pursue sexual relationships with both Potter and Warriner, involving servants, tenants and co-sleeping arrangements. The relationship with Warriner seems to have been particularly serious, although it did not result in their marriage.

Despite such detailed examples as this, few women of gentry backgrounds found themselves prosecuted for immorality, therefore, although they were more likely than noblewomen to be found as defendants before the church courts.[20] Viewed within a wider context, this relative absence of elite female defendants in adultery cases in the ecclesiastical courts of the north of England during our period is not unusual. Sara McDougall's study of the medieval courts in northern France also points to an absence of formal punishment for transgressive women and suggests that this may be because women did not have the economic ability to pay fines and legal fees, the women could not be traced or because a wife's adultery was a private matter, dealt with within the home.[21] The effect of these attitudes is also evident in parish registers, where the challenges posed by the recording of elite bastards already noted are understandably even more acute in the case of suspected offspring of elite female fornicators and adulterers. Katherine Holland, the mother of a bastard daughter Alis baptised in Ormskirk, may have shared her surname with a local gentry family, but whether she was the daughter of William Holland of Sutton near Wigan is unclear.[22] Extra caution is also required when considering Jane Halsall (not to be confused with the mistress of the 4th earl of Derby), whose son by Thomas Worthington was baptised in Manchester in 1593. She may have been a member of the extensive Lancashire gentry family and/or be the same Jane Halsall buried in Manchester in 1610, where she was identified as 'servant to Sir John Radcliffe'.[23] While Adair does not find the geographical clustering of popular surnames to be particularly problematic in linking birth records to those of marriages and burials, subtle social nuances of status are not always reflected in the Registers, making positive identification of gentlewomen particularly challenging.[24]

The fact that a wife or daughter's adultery or fornication was primarily dealt with as a private matter, handled within the family, can be seen in its treatment through privately negotiated settlements – and interpersonal disputes – at knightly and gentry levels of society. Jane Foljambe, the wife of Sir John Leke, received lands in Kirk Hallam (Derbyshire) and Collingham (Nottinghamshire) after 'the said Dame Jane eloped and went away from the company of the said John Leke.' Sir John's death in 1523 precipitated legal difficulties as Jane's son by Sir John Leke, Francis, had to sue his mother for the lands at Kirk Hallam and Collingham after his father's death, which suggests Jane's arrangements had been effective and they did not form part of any financial settlement after the death of Leke.[25] In a case which has already been seen to have possibly eventually ended in marriage, during the 1560s and 1570s, Margaret Vawdrey, a member of the branch of the minor Cheshire gentry recently established at Riddings in Timperley, was initially the target of considerable pressure from her family over her relationship with Edward Legh. She was prosecuted in York and Chester alongside Edward in 1572, but it was previously, in 1567, that her father Robert had attempted to use his will to resolve the situation, in terms which indicated his firm disapproval: 'To Margaret V at suche tyme as she shall leave her dishonest and uncleane lyvynge, for and durynge all suche tyme as she shall lyve honestlye Vli by yeare'. The will was proved in these terms in 1576 which suggests that, in her father's eyes, she had still not by then amended her ways, despite the attention of the courts.[26] The financial implications of Anne de la Riviere's extra-marital relationship were at the forefront of her husband Thomas's mind when he sued John Barton in Star Chamber in 1520.[27] While noting that during his absence serving the king on the Anglo-Scottish border, John Barton 'of hys evyll and unlawfull disposicion … sterred, procured, and moved Anne, then and yett wif of your sayd besecher, to accomplysshe his unlawfull, voluptuous and carnall appetite and desier with her', de la Riviere also complained that the adulterous pair 'spoyled the goods and cattalls' belonging to him. His evidence suggests there had been an attempt to resolve the issue privately, as he indicated he had warned Barton and Anne to 'use ne company togethere', but Anne remained in a house Barton built for her with their children. The charge of adultery then became part of a wider complaint against Barton, who was also accused of approaching de la Riviere with a gang of 'ryotouse and mysruled persons, in ryotous manner arrayed' with intent to kill him, wounding and killing William Wyldon and indicting two of de la Riviere's servants before the coroner to answer for the death. In his testimony, Barton claimed de la Riviere owed him £10, his servants had been attacked and that, far from being guilty of adultery, 'the same compleynant was discontentid with the said Anne bycause she hadd fownde the same Delaryver ageyne the lawis of God abhomynably usyng hymselffe with one Jane Wildon'; Anne had been put out of her marital home and her only refuge was Sinningthwaite nunnery.[28]

For most elite wives and widows in the north, it was these economic considerations (in the form of the prospect of financial forfeiture or maintenance in the event of separation), rather than the strictures of the ecclesiastical court, that were the key issues in their conduct. One contemporary treatise pointed out the legal position of an eloping wife in relation to dower: 'A woman in her frenzy may cut her husbands throat, and it is no forfeiture of Dower; but if she make an elopement (which is a mad tricke) Dower is forfeited.'[29] A later edition of Sir William Blackstone's *Commentaries on the Laws of England* commented on the situation in the eighteenth century and drew a distinction between dower and jointure. 'A jointure is not forfeited by the adultery of a wife as dower is … but by express stipulation, jointure and separate maintenance may be forfeited by any prohibited intercourse with a third person.'[30] In 1604, William Wentworth advised his eldest son Thomas (the future earl of Strafford) 'for her jointure let it be not too large, lest your heir feel the smart and a second husband the sweet of that gross oversight … Ever remembering that after your death, yea though she may be wise and well given, she is most like to be wife to a stranger and peradventure no friend to your house.'[31] Ferdinando Stanley, fifth earl of Derby specified in his will, 'if my said wife shall fortune to marrye after my decease then it is my will that her estate and interest in the full moytie of the said manners Lordshippes landes tenementes and hereditaments with all and everie theire appurtenences soe bequeathed unto her as aforesaid shall cease and noe further have continuance.'[32] Neither Wentworth nor Stanley were concerned with immorality as such, but the diversion of resources into another family unit upon the remarriage of a wife. Still, the transition from wife to widow (and in some cases to remarriage) came under some level of scrutiny from contemporaries as it was perceived as one of the clearest points at which infidelity might manifest itself. Sir Thomas Overbury identified two types of widow in his book *The Wife*, published in 1614. The 'virtuous widow' honoured the memory of her late husband and refused to remarry (never mind engage in an illicit relationship), but in comparison, the 'ordinary widow' took 'chiefest pride in the multitude of her suitors'.[33] *The Lawes Resolutions of Womens Rights*, referring to Roman Law described 'women which within the yeare of mourning for their husbands betake them of wedlocke again, should be reputed infamous and defamed.' Furthermore, 'if a man promise to a woman which he hath adulterously polluted that he will marry her when his wife dyeth etc … then these villanies are such perpetuall cankers in marriage, that they doe not only hinder it to be made but also rend it asunder when it is made.'[34] The position of widows, especially young widows of child-bearing age, was subject to intense scrutiny. In 1587, Lady Elizabeth Booth, widow of Sir William Booth of Dunham Massey in Cheshire who had died in 1579, faced allegations related to her conduct with one William Boult and a bastard child. She evidently believed they were a serious enough threat to her reputation to take a case against him in the Chester court. The interrogatories in the case highlight the intense interest that might be directed towards the conduct of a relatively young widow in these circumstances, with witnesses being asked to dwell on the question of whether the two were ever together in her chamber, and Elizabeth's attitude if anyone tried to close the door to the chamber at that time. Elizabeth's cause depended on a tight-knit group of kinsfolk and servants, who united to protect her character: not only was she able to rely on her Booth family, but as the daughter of Sir John Warburton of Arley she also had Warburtons to call upon as well.[35] Lady Elizabeth remained unmarried through her long widowhood, but despite the advice so widely circulated, rapid remarriage to someone of lower social standing, perhaps to a younger household servant of significantly lower social rank, did sometimes take place, even though it might at least raise eyebrows and at worst prompt gossip that the intimate relationship predated the decease of the husband. Frances Brandon, duchess of Suffolk married Adrian Stokes, her Master of the Horse, in 1554, only a year after her husband Henry Grey's execution, and her step-mother Katherine Willoughby had married her gentleman usher Richard Bertie in 1552 (although that was a slightly more dignified seven years after her first husband Charles Brandon's death).[36] Salacious scandal followed Alice Barnham, widow of Francis Bacon, Viscount St Alban, after his death in 1626. She married her gentleman usher, John Underhill, less than a month after Bacon's demise, which prompted John Aubrey to comment 'she made [Underhill] deafe and blind with too much of Venus'.[37] Kimberley Schutte makes the point that in many cases (and others such as those of Anne Stanhope and Frances de Vere), despite the differences in age and social status, widows remarried trusted supporters during or after times of political crisis for the whole family.[38] This may have been the issue in one prominent northern case, with Lady Anne Markham presented by the churchwardens of Arnold to the archdeaconry court in Nottingham in 1616 for her adulterous relationship with 'Jervis Sandforth', a servant.[39] Lady Anne's husband, Sir Griffin Markham, had been imprisoned and exiled for his role in a plot against James I in 1603, and it seems he never returned to England.[40] Her position was legally that of a married woman; however, the reality of her circumstances demanded that she step outside convention. In 1606, a correspondent of the earl of Shrewsbury described her appointing the 'bowberer at Bestwood', despite the fact that her husband was a 'banished traitor' and she 'femme couvert'.[41] It is possible that, by 1613, she was consolidating her financial position including dower and jointure lands which would have been granted to her upon the death of Sir Griffin and thus regarded herself as a widow.[42] The actions of the churchwardens of Arnold culminated in Lady Anne performing penance at St Paul's Cross in November 1617 'for marrying one of her servants, her husband still being alive; she will have to do the same elsewhere and was fined 100 0l'.[43]

The sexual voracity of widows was a feature of the Jacobean theatre, with the older, sexually experienced widow standing in contrast with the young, male gallant who pursued her, usually for her money.[44] Four centuries after it was first performed, debate still surrounds the most famous remarrying fictional widow, the duchess of Malfi. Positing her as a widow with agency to marry her choice of husband, Elizabeth Oakes argues that her financial independence 'empowered her' with regard to marriage and the duchess was acting 'within the [real-life] bounds of custom, law and decorum'.[45] Limited evidence and some isolated examples illuminate an imperfect basis for the stage interpretations of the remarrying widow. Thomas Dekker's play *Keep the Widow Waking* was based on the real case of Anne Elsdon, a sixty-two-year-old widow abused and dispossessed by Tobias Audley.[46] The final 'diabolical' fourth marriage of Katherine Neville, duchess of Norfolk took place when she was over sixty years of age and her bridegroom, John Woodville, nineteen. That marriage might notoriously have been for the groom's financial benefit as much if not more than it was for hers, but her second and third marriages, which followed in quick succession after the death of her first husband, the duke, in 1432, appear more clearly to reflect the power this gave her to choose marriage partners from those she already knew well among his followers.[47] In 1535, with an eye to parliamentary action, Thomas Cromwell noted the question of 'some way to be devised betwixt this and next session by which young men should be restrained from marriage till they be of potent age, and tall and puissant persons stayed from marriage of old widows.'[48] This indicates some significant level of official concern regarding the marriages of widows, but parliament did not in the event progress the issue further. Arguably the examples of socially prominent widows marrying household staff, and comparatively rare cases of exceptional abuse, fuelled popular dramatic tropes, giving contemporary credence to the idea of the insatiable widow. As Ira Clark has pointed out, the work of Barbara Todd and Amy Louise Erickson underscores the apparent dichotomy between fictional depiction of remarrying widows and scholarly research which suggests that remarriages formed only 25 per cent of all marriages during this time.[49]

While widows were affected directly by dower and jointure provision at the end of their marriages, financial pressure could also be brought to bear upon gentry daughters in order to make a suitable marriage, and thereby not to elope with anyone unacceptable. In 1578, Thomas Brooke of Norton, esquire directed a settlement 'that if any of his daughters Anne, Frances, Dorothie and Clare Brooke, shall marry during his lifetime without his consent or, after his death, without the consent of Sir Richard Brooke, Knt., and/or Thomas Marbury, esq., and/or Thomas Marbury, gentleman, his uncle (during their three lives), then their marriage portions of Mks. 400 each chargeable upon his messuages, lands, tenements and hereditaments with appurtenances in Thelwall, Over Walton and Matton shall not be paid to her or them so marrying.'[50] It is tempting to speculate that one, if not all, of the sisters had previously formed an attachment to an unacceptable suitor and that it was as a result of this that their father felt the need to control his daughters' portion and dower provision after his death. Control of portion money in order to prevent an unsuitable match did not always work. At her death in 1642, Elizabeth Boughton dowager countess of Devonshire left her granddaughter Elizabeth Crofts £4000 towards her marriage as long as she married with the consent of her father, Sir Henry.[51] Elizabeth married Frederick Cornwallis, but did so without Sir Henry's permission and thus her portion was reduced to £2000, her sisters Katherine and Hester sharing the reserve.[52]

Ultimately, of course, the sanction of the courts might be used against gentlewomen involved in fornication and adultery; the role in this of fathers, husbands and other kinsfolk varied. For those women who did find themselves in court, cases were initiated by both the office of the court or the plaintiff, most often the husband of the adulterous spouse, such as William Pennington, who promoted a case against his wife Anne and her lover John Hall of Millom in 1607.[53] The death of a husband did not prevent prosecution; in 1577–78 York High Commission heard Mr Rasing had promoted 'an infamous libell' against his wife Elizabeth, and she was still punished for her adultery with John Mason after her husband's death.[54] As indicated earlier, Mary Gower, a widow with her own jointure income was prosecuted and fined heavily in 1596 for her relationship with John Milburn.[55] There was inconsistency in the court's approach; Elizabeth Leigh 'late wief of Thomas Leigh gen' deceased' was not called before High Commission to explain her pregnancy by Edward Middleton only a couple of years later in 1598.[56]

The use of landed, propertied and financial power to govern the behaviour, and on some occasions punish, adulterous wives stands at the intersection between the jurisdiction of the church and common law courts. While ecclesiastical jurisdiction held sway over divorce *a mensa et thoro* and alimony for valid marriages, the common law courts settled property disputes, meaning that although church courts might sanction a separation between spouses, any inheritance devised to a married heiress became the property of her husband under common law practice of coverture.[57] Where a couple were mismatched within a valid marriage, an inheritance dispute exacerbated existing domestic tensions; adding an extra-marital relationship and illegitimate children born to the heiress could prompt legal action and even efforts to use parliament.[58] The 1540s saw a number of noble marriages break down in the face of mutual incompatibility and consequent adultery involving the estranged wife, with impacts upon estate ownership. William Parr, brother of future Queen Katherine, married Anne Bourchier in 1527, when she was ten and he thirteen years old; as Anne was the only child of Henry Bourchier, earl of Essex, Parr had hopes of acquiring a landed inheritance and the earldom. It was not until after Anne Bourchier had eloped with John Lyngfield (alias Hunter) and given birth to their children in 1542–43 that Parr sued for divorce, with the process secured through parliament: noting that Lady Anne was 'most shamefully carnally taken in Aduowtrye', continuing despite being 'monysshed therof by dyuerse of her fryndes to leaue the same', and, finally, two years past, leaving Parr's company and having a child begotten in adultery, it was enacted that the child and all future children she might have should be regarded as bastards. The birth of children potentially affected Parr's position in relation to the Bourchier inheritance, which he eventually managed to secure for himself.[59] Anne Bourchier was not the only adulterous noblewoman to have her behaviour brought into question in parliament in 1543. Elizabeth, wife of Sir Thomas Burgh, the eldest son of Thomas Lord Burgh (d. 1550) was accused by her father-in-law of having lived in adultery during her husband's lifetime, and had children 'that is to wit Margaret Humphrey & Arthure gotten by other persons then by her seid husband duryng the espouselles bytwene the seid sir Thomas Burgh & the seid Elizabeth as it is notoriously & openly knowen & by the seid Elizabeth hertofore partely confessed & recognised, [on the basis of which it was ruled in a parliamentary act they were to be] demyd adiugged accepted reputed & taken to be basterd & basterds'. Elizabeth Draycott, wife of Sir Philip, of Paynsley in Draycott (Staffs.), was the subject of another act, her estranged husband being himself a member of the same parliament; on this occasion it was she that was accused of having conceived 'suche mortall and vnnaturall hate' towards her children with him, that she attempted to disinherit them, and parliament was successfully asked to protect in particular the interests of John Draycott, Sir Philip's grandson by his deceased eldest son Richard.[60]

That said, we should not assume the pattern of reactions among kin by blood and marriage which adultery or fornication might provoke. In one rare case, a husband colluded with his wife's adultery, although his motives for doing so remain obscure. Margery Awde appeared before the courts in Durham and York in 1579–80 accused of adultery with Peter Maddyson. Her husband Edward was also prosecuted for permitting the relationship: he had argued 'that neither Bishop nor Chancellor should nor coulde call or have anything to doe with his wif so longe as he himself is not displeased therewithe and shall permit the same'.[61] That might have been an extreme case, but the evidence provided so far suggests other contexts in which male (and female) kinsfolk might have found reason to be more supportive (or at least permissive) of their kinswomen's behaviour. There is a consistent theme, for example, to the disapproval of the behaviour of the husbands of Ladies Elizabeth Foljambe and Ursula Stanley shown by so many of their neighbours. A broken marriage in which the husband was a notorious waster of his inheritance might provide greater scope for his wife's conduct.[62]

In fact, it was not unusual for the mechanisms of landed, propertied and financial power to produce an outcome which was relatively favourable to an adulterous woman. Alice Dockray fared well financially after her adultery with two men was revealed. Robert Bindloss divorced her in 1593 at Chester on the grounds of her relationships with James Potter and Richard Warriner.[63] An agreement dated 1594 settled Townend Hall in Kendal upon 'Thomas Dockrey of Giggleswick' (presumably a trusted relative of Alice) and references 'Alice Byndclose als Dockrey lately divorced from Robert'.[64] Legally, Alice and Robert had separated, with Alice suitably accommodated in one of Bindloss' properties in Westmorland. Townend Hall was an interesting choice of residence on the part of Bindloss, as documents from York Consistory reveal that it was her noisy nocturnal activities with Warriner there that alerted the householders to her immorality. Possibly, she was already living there as part of an informal separation and it made sense for her to continue her residence when maintenance was formalised. Her use of the hall and lands was limited, as she claimed to have married William Carr of Giggleswick, some thirty miles from Kendal in 1597, and by 1603 Robert Bindloss was free to marry Mary Eltofts and had fathered a son with her.[65]

For single gentry women, legal action often took place against a wider background than simply their own immorality. Mary Rossell's pregnancy was the catalyst for her marriage to John Alred, the rector of Clifton church, Nottinghamshire, but there was clearly ill-feeling between the bridegroom and his in-laws. Rossell's father John sued Alred in York High Commission 'for such offensive woordes as hee hath spoken and uttred', one witness reporting he 'hathe harde the said John Alred reporte that the wief of the said John Rossell Esquier shoulde saie that shee thought shee had founde an other father than the said Alred for her daughters child', and the commissioners' attention was drawn to the clandestine nature of their marriage.[66] Alred was sentenced to penance in the church at Radcliffe-on-Trent, but Mary Rossell was not prosecuted by High Commission for her pre-marital pregnancy. Patterns of wider relationships affected a gentlewoman's capacity, for example, to conceal a birth. In the mid-1620s Katherine Parker, daughter of Edward Parker, gentleman of Gressingham, on the River Lune in north Lancashire, gave birth to a bastard child. At the Easter Quarter Sessions in 1625, Laurence Croft was charged with fathering her child, and by November her father was ordered to appear before the Justices with Katherine.[67] The conduct of Katherine Parker and the birth of her child took place amidst very localised tensions in Gressingham. Again in 1625, Agnes and William Wilkinson were both ordered to keep the peace to Edward Parker and at the same session that Parker was ordered to present his daughter, Edward Carter of Gressingham sought to prosecute Katherine Parker for stealing two of his geese.[68] By October 1629, James Harries, a carpenter from the neighbouring parish of Melling, was compelled to appeal to the Justices of the Peace. He claimed 'that (about the middle of Januarie last past) one Mrs Parker the wyffe of Edward Parker … did bringe a child (being basse begotten of Katherin Parker daughter of Edward Parker) to your peticoners wyffe to nurssinge and upon an agrement then made, your peticoner tooke the child for a quarter of a yeare at thend of which quarter your peticoner brought the childe to the said Mrs Parker, but shee utterly refused to take the said child or to Allowe Anie further maintenance for the same. Whereupon your poore peticoner not knoweing howe to be lawfully discharged of the said child hath bene forced ever since thend of the said qtr to keepe the child … he beinge a verie poore man'.[69] The Justices ordered the churchwardens and overseers of the poor of Gressingham, the Parkers' native parish, to 'mainteyne' the child until the parents could take responsibility for their offspring. Katherine Parker came to the attention of the Justices again in 1629–30 when they had to enquire into the maintenance arrangements of her child by George Kellett.[70] The Justices were not concerned with the morality or otherwise of Parker's conduct so much as who would bear the cost of feeding, clothing and maintaining the child when what might otherwise have been expected to be well-resourced private arrangements broke down.

The Rossell and Parker cases indicate a role for the mothers of single gentlewomen; in the one finding a suitable marriage partner for her daughter or father for her grandchild and in the other finding adoptive parents for the child. As far as the daughters are concerned, the two cases posit deep questions around the treatment of single women in both the church and secular courts. The voices of Mary and Katherine are unheard. The scribes did not record whether Rossell wished to marry Alred (or vice versa) or whether Parker wanted to keep her child. The two cases also illustrate another aspect of immorality affecting single gentlewomen – the capacity for concealing births was only compromised when the relevant transactional relationships broke down and the details emerged in court.

As with male aristocrats and gentlemen, we might suggest that certain households and the networks around them were more supportive of unconventional relationships involving gentlewomen than others. Margery Brandling features in the records of the Durham courts as both an illegitimate daughter of William Brandling and Isabell Carlell in 1561 and for fornication and fleeing to Humphrey Blaxton's house in her own right in 1579.[71] There seems to have been a culture of illegitimacy and extra-marital relationships within the Brandling family, as Sir Robert Brandling was renowned in the north east for his behaviour – in an argument over his will, one of the witnesses claimed 'they saye in this town if you had not so many bastardes you would have maid your will or no', to which Sir Robert answered 'if I have any I am hable to fynd them.'[72] It is also perhaps significant that when Thomas Brandlyng applied for denisation for his sons William and Cornelius in order for them to gain admission to the Fellowship of English Merchants at Antwerp, their mother was referred to as 'a woman of that country', and not by name or by marital status.[73]

Similarly, as the daughter of Sir Henry Savile, Dorothy Savile can only have been too aware of her father's controversial relationship with Margery Barston, especially given the prominence in family and county affairs of the offspring of that liaison, in the form of Robert Savile of Howley. Whether this had a bearing upon her own relationship with John Kaye of Oakenshaw is unknown, but she and John came to the attention of the archbishop through a visitation and subsequent presentation in York before High Commission.[74] Katherine Savile, another member of the extensive Yorkshire family, was presented to York High Commission in 1581 for bearing two children by two different fathers, one of whom was known only by his surname, Watson.[75]

The experiences of gentry women identified as engaging in fornication or adultery are interpreted and formulated around the fulcrum of marriage. Conventional sixteenth- and early seventeenth-century thinking articulated the need for sexual relations to be a function of marriage for the procreation of children. Yet the extent to which women had agency to accept or reject elements of matrimony and motherhood remains a matter of conjecture and their motives variable. These experiences also need to be considered within the shifting context of women's legal status. In the introduction to *The Lavves Resolutions of Womens*

Rights several legal identities for women were identified, depending upon their ages and life experience – 'children in government or nurture of their Parents or Gardians, Mayds, Wives, and Widowes'.[76] For a single gentlewoman such as Dorothy Savile (whose father died in 1558), marriage to the father of her children seems to have been a desirable outcome for both parties, even though York High Commissioners had 'enioyned the said Dorothea Savell to abstein from all suspicious company with the said Mr Keye hereafter'. Mary Rossell, seemingly faced with family pressure to marry a man who would accept her child, appears less well placed to have exerted any independent influence of her own in the matter of marriage.

That official branches of the church and state had the legal right to challenge female adultery and fornication is not in any doubt. In practice, however, the relatively small numbers of female defendants identified in a study of church court records suggests that there was an inability or reluctance to prosecute. Yet such official apparatus was not the only mechanism for controlling female sexuality. Wills, marriage settlements, portion arrangements, dower and jointure could all be constructed by relatives, in-laws and husbands in order to maintain the chastities of unmarried women, wives and widows, and as a result control with whom they networked and allied themselves. The effectiveness of these private measures is, however, highly questionable, and these mechanisms might be used in parallel by women to enable their relationships. So while the separation and maintenance of an adulterous wife by her husband, representing the most extreme form of the managed failure of these measures, might be scarce in the documentary record, there are nonetheless repeated signs of the diversity and scope of unconventional relationships of northern gentlewomen.

Notes

1 Henry Smith, *A Preparatiue to Marriage: The Summe Whereof was Spoken at a Contract, and Inlarged After. Whereunto is Annexed a Treatise of the Lords Supper: And Another of Vsurie* (London: printed by R. Field for Thomas Man, 1591), p. 68.

2 An examination of the High Commission Act Books and the Cause Papers indicates a total of thirty female gentry defendants and ninety-four male. Not all defendants were convicted; for example, having launched a successful validity suit in 1508 (BIA, CP.G 32), Katherine Gascoign faced litigation in 1514 on the grounds of her adultery (CP.G 864). She proved her innocence, won the case and was also successful when she subsequently sued her husband William for Restitution of Conjugal Rights in 1515 (CP.G 110).

3 Claire Cross, 'Sin and Society: The Northern High Commission and the Northern Gentry in the Reign of Elizabeth', in Claire Cross, David Loades and J. J. Scarisbrick (eds), *Law and Government under the Tudors: Essays Presented to Sir Geoffrey Elton … on … his Retirement* (Cambridge: Cambridge University Press, 1986), pp. 195–209, in particular, has suggested there was more potential for elite women to take lovers than the strictures of the double standard, particularly in its most extensive form, might suggest. See above, esp. the work referenced in notes 19 & 29 of the Introduction and discussion on pp. 5–7.

4   BIA, CP.G 159; Richard T. Spence, *The Shepherd Lord of Skipton Castle: Henry Clifford, 10th Lord Clifford 1454–1523* (Skipton: Skipton Castle, 1994), p. 56. Wharton also spoke of Clifford's relationship with Jane Browne.
5   BIA, CP.G 331. Langdale did not specify where or when Oglethorpe had been prosecuted.
6   Thomas S. Freeman, 'Darcy [née Wray; other married names Foljambe, Bowes], Isabel, Lady Darcy (d. 1622), patron of clergymen', *ODNB*, xv. 126–7; Jean de Hainault, *The Estate of the Church: with the Discourse of Times, from the Apostles Vntill this Present: Also of the Liues of all the Emperours, Popes of Rome, and Turkes: As Also of the Kings of Fraunce, England, Scotland, Spaine, Portugall, Denmarke, &c. With all the Memorable Accidents of their Times*, trans Simon Patrick (London: printed by Thomas Creede, 1602).
7   John senior died in 1615; John junior's date of birth is not clear, but his elder brother Sir George's son, also George (who was the author of a memoir), was born in 1616: 'The Memoirs of Sir George Courthop, 1616–1685', ed. S. C. Lomas, in *Camden Miscellany*, XI, Camden Society, 3rd ser., 13 (1907), p. 103; William Berry, *County Genealogies: Pedigrees of the Families in the County of Sussex* (London: Sherwood, Gilbert, and Piper, 1830), p. 216. For the use of 'Courtrapp' as an equivalent for the surname, see e.g. the report of the Aug. 1679 parliamentary election in *The Protestant [Domestick] Intelligence: Or, News Both from City & Country*, no. 18; Friday, 5 Sept. 1679; Basil Duke Henning, *The House of Commons, 1660–1690* (3 vols. London: Secker & Warburg for the History of Parliament Trust, 1983), i. 427.
8   BIA, HC.AB 17, fos. 205, 248.
9   *Ibid.*, fo. 269. The role of Lady Foljambe in the case is even more invisible than that of her husband in Nathaniel Johnston, 'History of the Family of Foljambe', *Collectanea Topographica et Genealogica*, i (1834), 91–111, 333–61; ii (1835), 68–90, at p. 87. His profligacy is, however, evident, as it is in e.g. G. E. C[okayne], *The Complete Baronetage* (5 vols. Exeter: William Pollard, 1900–9), i. 205.
10 BIA, HC.AB 18, fos. 23, 26.
11 TNA, STAC 7/3/10.
12 S. T. Bindoff, *The House of Commons, 1509–1558* (3 vols. London: Secker & Warburg for the History of Parliament Trust, 1982), iii. 334–5; P. W. Hasler, *The House of Commons, 1558–1603* (HMSO for the History of Parliament Trust, 1981), iii. 398; George Ormerod, *The History of the County Palatine and City of Chester*, 2nd edn, revised and enlarged by Thomas Helsby (3 vols. London: Routledge, 1882), ii. 229–31, iii. 503; Tim Thornton, *Cheshire and the Tudor State, 1480–1560* (Woodbridge: Boydell, 2000), p. 236. See above, pp. 72–3, 78, and below pp.106–8, 136–8.
13 TNA, STAC 7/1/7; STAC 8/4/3.2,8,18; /5/D23/3; Andy Wood, 'Social Drama and Rituals of Rebellion', in Stuart Carroll (ed.), *Cultures of Violence: Interpersonal Violence in Historical Perspective* (Basingstoke: Palgrave Macmillan 2007), pp. 99–116, at p. 102; Andy Wood, 'Subordination, Solidarity, and the Limits of Popular Agency in a Yorkshire Valley, c. 1596–1615', *Past & Present*, 93 (2007), 41–72; *Feet of Fines of the Tudor Period*, ed. Francis Collins, YASRS, 2, 5, 7–8 (1887–90), iii. 115.
14 BIA, HC.AB 13, fos. 77, 78, 92v–93, 235v; M. W. Barley, 'Castle Howard and the Village of Hinderskelfe, N. Yorkshire', *Antiquaries Journal*, 58 (1978), 358–60; William Page (ed.), *The Victoria History of the County of York: North Riding* (3 vols. London: Constable and Co., 1914–25), ii. 183.
15 BIA, HC.AB 11, fo. 107; John Strype, *Annals of the Reformation and Establishment of Religion* (4 vols. in 7; Oxford: Clarendon Press, 1824), iii/2. 465.

16 Chesh. Archives, EDC 5/1593/36.
17 BIA, CP.G 3082.
18 Presumably one of her daughters by Bindloss, Anne or Alice, neither of whom were presumed to be illegitimate.
19 See William Farrer, *Records Relating to the Barony of Kendale*, ed. J. F. Curwen, Cumberland and Westmorland Antiquarian and Archaeological Society, Record Series, 4–6 (1923–6), i. 334–6. Note that in his father's Inquisition *post mortem* taken in 1596, Robert's age was given as 34, placing his date of birth in 1561–62. Even if the marriage had taken place at the earliest year suggested in 1581, Robert would have been about nineteen at the time.
20 Other examples include Anna Staveley, wife of William Staveley, gent., in York High Commission in 1571, for her affair with John Gill, an offence 'notorious and famous' in and around Ripon: BIA, HC.AB 6, fos. 32, 32v, 34v–35.
21 Sara McDougall, 'The Opposite of the Double Standard: Gender, Marriage, and Adultery Prosecution in Late Medieval France', *Journal of the History of Sexuality*, 23 (2014), 206–25. See also James A. Brundage, *Law, Sex, and Christian Society in Medieval Europe* (Chicago: University of Chicago Press, 2014), p. 519.
22 *The Registers of the Parish Church of Ormskirk in the County of Lancaster*, Part 1: *Christenings, Burials and Weddings 1557–1626*, ed. Josiah Arrowsmith, LPRS, 13 (1902), p. 55; *The Visitation of the County Palatine of Lancaster Made in the Year 1567 by Wm Flower Esq.*, ed. F. R. Raines, Chetham Society, LXXXI (1870), p. 115.
23 *Registers of the Cathedral Church of Manchester*, pp. 82, 391. Although note the discussion in ch. 3, at pp. 66–7, of women from gentry backgrounds performing service in household positions with other noble and gentry families.
24 Richard Adair, *Courtship, Illegitimacy and Marriage in Early Modern England* (Manchester: Manchester University Press, 1996), p. 30.
25 TNA, STAC 2/24/36; *Yorkshire Star Chamber Proceedings*, ed. William Brown, H. B. McCall and John Lister, YASRS, 41, 45, 51, 70 (1909–27), iii. 95; Sir John Leke was far from innocent, as he sired three illegitimate daughters with Anne Mainwaring.
26 BIA, HC.AB 6, fos. 112, 148, 150, 152, 153, 154, 156–7; *Lancashire and Cheshire Wills and Inventories from the Ecclesiastical Court at Chester, the Second Portion*, ed. G. J. Piccope, Chetham Society, o.s., LI (1860), p. 80; Ormerod, *Chester*, i. 548–9. For the case, see above, p. 72. Vawdrey also refers in his will to 'my disobedyent sonne Thomas' who attracted drunken evil company.
27 *Yorkshire Star Chamber Proceedings*, i. 68–73; TNA, STAC 2/18/284.
28 Whatever the truth of this case, all the voices heard are male. The protagonists were both keen to stress the damage to their reputations and property; both themselves fathered illegitimate children, Barton an illegitimate son Henry (the mother's identity unknown), de la Riviere three illegitimate daughters, Thomasine, Eleanor and Elizabeth. TNA, C 78/28/17.
29 Thomas Edgar, *The Lavves Resolutions of Womens Rights: Or, The Lavves Prouision for Woemen A Methodicall Collection of Such Statutes and Customes, with the Cases, Opinions, Arguments and Points of Learning in the Lavv, as Doe Properly Concerne Women. Together with a Compendious Table, Whereby the Chiefe Matters in this Booke Contained, May be the More Readily Found* (London: printed by [Miles Flesher for] the assignes of Iohn More Esq. and are to be sold by Iohn Groue, 1632), p. 144.
30 William Blackstone, *Commentaries on the Laws of England, Book the Second. By Sir William Blackstone, Knt. one of His Majesty's Justices of the Common Pleas. 12th Edition with the last corrections of the author; and with notes and additions by Edward Christian, Esq. Barrister at Law, and Professor of the*

Laws of England in the University of Cambridge (London: printed by A. Strahan and W. Woodfall, Law-Printers to the King's Most Excellent Majesty, for T. Cadell, in The Strand, 1794), p. 139.
31 *The Wentworth Papers, 1705–1739: Selected from the Private and Family Correspondence of Thomas Wentworth, Lord Raby, Created in 1711 Earl of Strafford,* ed. James Joel Cartwright (London: Wyman and Sons, 1883), p. 20.
32 TNA, PROB 11/84.
33 Thomas Overbury, *New and Choise Characters, of Seuerall Authors Together with that Exquisite and Unmatcht Poeme, The Wife / Written by Syr Thomas Ouerburie; With the Former Characters and Conceited Newes, all in one Volume* (London: T. Creede for L. L'isle, 1615), unpaginated.
34 Edgar, *Lavves Resolutions*, pp. 59, 61.
35 Cheshire Arch., EDC 5/1587/26; Ormerod, *Chester*, i. 525.
36 Retha M. Warnicke, 'Grey [other married name Stokes], Frances [née Lady Frances Brandon], duchess of Suffolk (1517–1559), noblewoman', *ODNB*, xxiii. 836–7; Susan Wabuda, 'Bertie [*née* Willoughby; *other married name* Brandon], Katherine, duchess of Suffolk (1519–1580), *noblewoman and protestant patron*', *ODNB*, v. 486–8.
37 John Aubrey, *Brief Lives, Chiefly of Contemporaries*, ed. Andrew Clark (2 vols. Oxford: Clarendon Press, 1898), i. 71; *CP* xi. 285.
38 Kimberly Schutte, 'Marrying Out in the Sixteenth Century: Subsequent Marriages of Aristocratic Women in the Tudor Era', *Journal of Family History*, 38 (2013), 3–16. See Barbara J. Harris, *English Aristocratic Women, 1450–1550: Marriage and Family, Property and Careers* (Oxford: Oxford University Press, 2002), pp. 160–7, for other examples of widows marrying for love.
39 Nottingham, University of Nottingham Manuscripts and Special Collections, AN/PB 295/6/67. Lady Anne had previously been in trouble for her failure to attend the parish church in 1607, 1609 and 1610: AN/PB 293/7/5; /8/105; /295/1/157.
40 Mark Nicholls, 'Markham, Sir Griffin (b. c. 1565, d. in or after 1644), *army officer and conspirator*', *ODNB*, xxxvi. 690–1.
41 Lambeth, Lambeth Palace Library, MS 705, fo. 12.
42 Nottingham, University of Nottingham Manuscripts and Special Collections, Ne D1802: Sebastian Harvie, alderman of London, Bryan Broughton, esquire, and Anthony Latham promised to transfer the manor of Arnold to Sir John Holles in the event of a jointure claim by Lady Anne Markham (1 July 1613).
43 *Calendar of State Papers: Domestic Series. The Reign of James I.*, ed. Mary Anne Everett Green (5 vols. London: Longman, Brown, Green, Longmans & Roberts, 1857–72), vol. ii: *1611–18*, p. 516.
44 See, for example, Ira Clark, 'The Widow Hunt on the Tudor-Stuart Stage', *Studies in English Literature, 1500–1900*, 41 (2001), 399–416. Clark cites numerous works of fiction which focus on widowhood.
45 Elizabeth Oakes, '"The Duchess of Malfi" as a Tragedy of Identity', *Studies in Philology*, 96 (1999), 51–67.
46 Charles Carlton, 'The Widow's Tale: Male Myths and Female Reality in 16th and 17th Century England', *Albion*, 10 (1978), 118–29.
47 Rowena E. Archer, 'Neville [*married names* Mowbray, Strangways, Beaumont, Woodville], Katherine, duchess of Norfolk (c. 1400–83), *noblewoman*', *ODNB*, xl. 512–13. Woodville was a brother of Edward IV's Queen Elizabeth, and whilst it may be speculated that his wife's wealth would be

the foundation of his fortune, Woodville's execution in 1469 meant that Katherine Neville outlived him by at least fourteen years.
48 *LP* ix. 725ii, discussed in Carlton, 'Widow's Tale', p. 121.
49 Clark, 'Widow Hunt', p. 400.
50 Cheshire Arch., DBN/B/1/7.
51 TNA, PROB 11/190/122.
52 *Calendar of the Proceedings of the Committee for Advance of Money, 1642–1656*, ed. Mary Anne Everett Green (3 vols. (paginated through); London: HMSO, 1888), ii. 696.
53 BIA, HC.AB 15, fos. 94v, 107, 122v, 154, 179.
54 BIA, HC.AB 9, fos. 122, 123, 124, 125, 127.
55 See above, pp. 70, 87.
56 See above, p. 48; BIA, HC.CP1597/8.
57 Tim Stretton, 'Marriage, Separation and the Common Law in England, 1540–1660', in Helen Berry and Elizabeth Foyster (eds), *The Family in Early Modern England* (Cambridge: Cambridge University Press, 2007), pp. 18–39.
58 See also Harris, *English Aristocratic Women*, p. 81.
59 Westminster, Parliamentary Archives, HL/PO/PB/1/1542/34&35H8n39 (c. 43: Parr); *LP* xviii/1. 66III. Susan E. James, 'A Tudor Divorce: The Marital History of William Parr, Marquess of Northampton', *Transactions of the Cumberland and Westmorland Antiquarian and Archaeological Society*, 90 (1990), 199–204; James concedes 'neither had been particularly faithful during the strained years of their marriage', but it was Anne Bourchier's immorality that was the catalyst for legal action.
60 Parliamentary Archives, HL/PO/PB/1/1542/34&35H8n32 (c. 40: Burgh), HL/PO/PB/1/1542/34&35H8n40 (c. 44: Draycott); *LP* xviii/1. 66III; Bindoff, *House of Commons, 1509–1558*, ii. 55–6. There may have been as much if not more of an issue with Burgh senior's mental health than Lady Burgh's relationships: Susan E. James, *Kateryn Parr: The Making of a Queen* (Aldershot: Ashgate, 1999), pp. 53–4.
61 *The Injunctions and Other Ecclesiastical Proceedings of Richard Barnes Bishop of Durham from 1575 to 1587*, ed. James Raine, Surtees Society, XXII (1850), pp. 117, 119, 123; BIA, CP.G 2001, 2008.
62 See above, pp. 81–2.
63 Cheshire Arch., EDC 5/1593/36.
64 Hereford Record Office, F8/11/466.
65 Joseph Nicholson and Richard Burn, *The History and Antiquities of the Counties of Westmorland and Cumberland* (2 vols. London: printed for W. Strahan; and T. Cadell, 1777), i. 86; Andrew Thrush and John P. Ferris (eds), *The House of Commons, 1604–29* (6 vols. Cambridge: Cambridge University Press, 2010), iii. 232.
66 BIA, HC.AB 9, fos. 249v, 250; for Alred see theclergydatabase.org.uk/jsp/search/index.jsp.
67 LRO, QSB/1/4/10, QSB/1/16/18. Both Parker and Croft are described as 'gent'.
68 LRO, QSB/1/3/9, QSB/1/3/10 (Wilkinson); QSB/1/16/17. (At the same time, Carter also accused his neighbour William Walton of stealing more geese: QSB/1/17/27.)
69 LRO, QSB/1/60/22.
70 LRO, QSB/1/64/37.
71 DUL, DDR/EJ/CCA/3/2, fos. 8, 21 Carlell c Brandling; *Injunctions and Other Ecclesiastical Proceedings of Richard Barnes*, pp. 114, 117.

72 DUL, DDR/EJ/CCA/1/2, fos. 88, 96, 97, 141 (*Depositions and Other Ecclesiastical Proceedings from the Courts of Durham: Extending from 1311 to the Reign of Elizabeth*, ed. James Raine, Surtees Society, XXI (1845), p. 121).
73 *LP* xviii/1. 66II.
74 W. J. Sheils, *Archbishop Grindal's Visitation 1575 Comperta et Acta Book*, Borthwick Texts & Calendars: Records of the Northern Province (York: Borthwick Institute of Historical Research, University of York, 1977), p. 22; BIA, HC.AB 8, fo. 146v. In an interesting historiographical note, J. W. Clay in the 1920s ('The Savile Family', *Yorkshire Archaeological Journal*, 25 (1920), 1–47, at p. 15), saw Dorothy as highly distinctive: 'The daughter is almost the only lady of the great Yorkshire houses of the sixteenth century who has been handed down as having sullied the honour of her family', selecting a phrase earlier used by Joseph Hunter, *Antiquarian Notices of Lupset, the Heath, Sharlston, and Ackton, in the County of York* (London: printed by J. B. Nichols and Son, 1851), p. 22. Dorothy is said to have had seven illegitimate children.
75 BIA, HC.AB 10, fo. 145. Christopher Warren and Mr Watson were not prosecuted alongside her.
76 Edgar, *Lavves Resolutions*, unpaginated 'Epistle to the Reader'; Tim Stretton, *Women Waging Law in Elizabethan England* (Cambridge: Cambridge University Press, 2005), p. 103.

5

The 'wronged' partner

An honest man that had but one eie and a quean to his wife, entring vpon the sudden into his bed chamber by night, a knaue chanced to be then a bed with her, who hearing her husbands voice, shifted him suddenlie behind the doore, and thus she said vnto her Goodman: What husband, is't you euen welcome my good husband: I hope in God my dreame is come to passe: I was eue now adream'd that you could see with either of your eyes, in so much as I waked for joy, and I hope to find it true: And with that she arose from out her bed, & comming toward him: Good husband (she said) let me lay my finger on your seeing eie, and then tell me whether you discerne anie thing with the other: He answered: No, not anie thing. In this mean time she beckened to the Adulterer to be gone: who straight slipped from behind the doore downe the staires, and so scap'd quite away.[1]

In the late 1590s, Anthony Copley devoted a chapter to the description 'of cuckolds', depicting the unfortunate men as figures of fun. Despite the centrality of wifely adultery to the situation, cuckoldry has been identified as a transaction between men, particularly in Renaissance drama.[2] Frequently depicted as wearing a pair of horns, the cuckold was judged by an act in which he did not participate, and the legitimacy and inheritance of his children might be brought into question. In contemporary terms, he was unable to control the sexual activity of his wife; however throughout Europe the idea developed that the adulterous wife transmitted the cuckold's horns from her lover to her husband.[3] Mary Fissell has noted that 'ballads about cuckolds dating from the 1620s and 1630s often place the blame for extra-marital sexual activity on the man's shoulders even when it is the wife who errs.'[4] She also tracks the changing nature of interest in cuckold literature, increasing during the Restoration period, intensifying a crisis of paternity and transferring the blame for adultery onto the wife.[5] Faramerz Dabhiowala has observed of the same period in the late seventeenth century how attributes such as wealth and social position could insulate against immorality, and he identifies the state of cuckoldry as being overpowered by the force of the man's status or rank.[6] Certainly, gentlemen, esquires, knights and noblemen were rarely described as cuckolds in the evidence we have from the northern ecclesiastical courts. In one rare case the concept was addressed, but it was a gentleman who sued for the allegation of making, not of being made, a cuckold: John Vaisey, gentleman, sued Mary Shepherd for sexual slander claiming she had said to a number of witnesses, 'Hang Thee Thomson for thou art a cuckold and a wittold too … for John Vessies went in and fucked thy wife.'[7] There is no surviving evidence to suggest that Hugh Thomson tried to sue Shepherd either for the implication of his wife's adultery or for calling him a cuckold. One objective of this chapter is therefore to explore the experience of elite males whose wives engaged in illicit relationships, for whose experience the ecclesiastical courts only provide limited evidence. For these men, gendered expectations of masculinity, given recent emphasis on the importance of household control centred on male sexual potency, might suggest shame would have a powerful impact in driving their behaviour and shaping its limited public exposure.[8]

The cuckqueane, in contrast, rarely features as such in sixteenth-century literature. Eleanor of Aquitaine appears in William Warner's 1597 version of *Albion's England* and Samuel Daniel's *The Complaint of Rosamund* as a jealous rival who poisoned Rosamund Clifford, mistress of her husband Henry II. 'Came I from France as Queene Dowager, quoth shee to pay so deare, For bringing him so great a wealth as to be Cuckquean'd here … The French King once, himselfe euen now, for faire preferred me.' Daniel commented upon her motive, suggesting there was 'no beast fearcer then a iealous woman.'[9] There is no evidence to suggest that the real queen murdered her husband's mistress, but the authors chose to depict her as a monstrous murderess seeking revenge upon a younger victim.[10] This is, however, just one of a range of gendered stereotypes available to authors describing the 'wronged' woman, at the other end of which might sit Fulke Greville's 'Honourable Lady' (who remains anonymous), addressed in a letter which draws similarities between the governance of a husband and that of a monarch, in which constancy is interpreted as a conscious and deliberate act of self will rather than simply passive obedience.[11] In this chapter we will consider the experience of elite wives whose responses to their situation might range across a spectrum from acceptance, which might include active support for illegitimate offspring even long after the death of their wayward husband, to powerful rejection and refusal to accept their treatment. For both men and women, it will be important to understand the interactions of the individual experience of 'betrayal' with the roles of father and mother, master or mistress of a household, and wider authority in family and political networks, and of the ways those networks helped shape and determine experiences, actions and reactions. The newly constituted institutions which might intervene in such matters, especially the ecclesiastical commissions, provided additional opportunities for spouses or those acting on their behalf to address their situation. The degree to which they chose to do so will illuminate questions not just of elite masculinity and femininity, but also the role of what might be seen as an expanding state in moral questions and of the willingness of the northern gentry and nobility to accept or even lead it there.[12]

It is important to begin by recognising that those writing about contemporary figures could adopt a more sympathetic view of the wife dealing with her husband's adultery than the extreme portrayal of Eleanor of Aquitaine and perhaps more subtle than Greville's constant 'Honourable Lady'. Samuel Daniel was also the recipient of patronage from

Margaret Russell, countess of Cumberland and he dedicated his *Letter from Octavia to her Husband Marcus Antonius* to her in 1599. Octavia was characterised as the long-suffering, virtuous wife of the philanderer Mark Anthony and the virtues she espoused were ascribed to the countess in Daniel's dedication.[13] Mark Anthony's service in Egypt and his relationship with Cleopatra may parallel Earl George's voyages abroad, in particular his voyage to Puerto Rico in 1598. However, the earl's biographers have not identified a foreign mistress and the focus of the poem is Octavia / Countess Margaret.[14] Certainly George Clifford's mistress acted as hostess to King James I, when Cumberland hosted him at Grafton Regis a few years later in 1603. Countess Margaret was actually present and in attendance upon Queen Anne, and her position in society was therefore directly undercut. Daniel's work poses questions around the countess's self-representation; to other members of courtly society, she chose to depict herself as a stoic in a way which also drew explicit attention to the earl's adultery.[15] The themes running through the fifty-one verses may provide some insight into the feelings and thoughts of a high-profile aristocrat, forced to accept the public demonstration of her husband's love for another woman.

Daniel indicates that innocent Octavia also carries the shame of Anthony's guilt:

> Yet why should I bearing no part of sinne
> Beare such a mightie part of his disgrace?
> Yes though it be not mine, it is of mine;
> And his renowne being clips'd, mine cannot shine.

Later, Octavia asks Anthony if she is the cause of his philandering:

> What fault haue I committed that should make
> So great dislike of me and of my loue?

The poem also references Anthony's mistress, suggesting a battle between matrimonial love and illicit love:

> Th'Inchantres straight steps twixt thy hart & thee
> And intercepts all thoughts that came of mee.
> She armes her teares, the ingins of deceit
> And all her batterie, to oppose my loue.

Daniel also suggests that Octavia's brother interceded on her behalf in order to negotiate a separation, but as she explains it is impossible to part company from someone who has already departed.

> And yet my brother *Caesar* laboured
> To haue me leaue thy house, and liue more free,
> But God forbid, *Octauia* should be led,
> To leaue to liue in thine, though left by thee.[16]

It is clear from Lady Anne Clifford's diary for 1603 that Countess Margaret and her daughter spent much time at court and in the countryside with their extensive network of Russell relatives at that time, only occasionally meeting Earl George.[17] While Daniel touched upon the emotional aspects of blame, shame, innocence and deceit, he therefore referenced the support offered to women by their birth families, a factor which also played out in the courtroom.

While Countess Margaret sought solace in stoic philosophy and more concrete support from her kinsfolk, however, William Stanley, sixth earl of Derby vented his frustration violently upon discovering his wife Elizabeth de Vere's affair with Robert Devereux, second earl of Essex. After a 'violent course', Derby removed his wife 'from the eye of the world', meaning court, to Lancashire where his wrath continued.[18] 'He is in such a jealous frame as we have had such a storm as is wonderful', wrote Edward Mylar to Sir Robert Cecil from Knowsley.[19] Derby's household officers, 'seeing my Lord's madness and my ladyship's patience … all went to my lord when he was looked to go to Court and leave my lady to shift for herself, and told him that as they had served him and his father … if he held his jealousy in that force as he did, themselves seeing my lady's carriage of herself … if he would hate her and [not] desist from this humour they must all hate him and follow her in those honourable courses she professeth and performeth.' Mylar signed off by saying 'my lady wanteth not friends, friends firm to our purpose, wise and experienced in this humorous house.' Despite being an injured party, Derby's conduct did not generate any sympathy from those around him; the gravity of the countess's offence was diminished by her husband's violent conduct and her patient behaviour while in the midst of it.[20] The tempest soon abated as two days later, on 11 August 1587, Mylar wrote to Cecil, 'I formerly writ of a storm … but now I write of a calm', the catalyst for which seems to have been the presence of Derby's philandering uncle, George Clifford (husband of Countess Margaret).[21] This involved a landed or financial settlement negotiated by Earl George, who may well have realised that Derby would need the help of Countess Elizabeth's powerful Cecil kindred in his dispute with his sister-in-law dowager Countess Alice and her daughters.[22] Life for the Derbys gradually became less turbulent, and their eldest son James was born ten years later in 1607. Stanley even gave his wife responsibility for administering the Isle of Man once he had regained it from his nieces, a position she maintained until her death in 1627.[23] The incident served to demonstrate that, however severe the initial reaction, competing and clashing social, financial and household factors served to moderate the performance and experience of cuckoldry by the earl, to the extent of permitting the restoration of relations between them and her being entrusted with a key element of the family's inheritance.

While the church courts dealt with the moral side of adultery or fornication (and the financial aspect of separation), the wider implications of dower, jointure and inheritance as they affected the 'wronged' party could be dealt with in a variety of legal formats. An unusual marriage settlement negotiated by the South Lancashire gentlemen William Norres of Speke and Laurence Ireland late in the fifteenth century provided for the end of the marriage in the event of adultery by the bride, Beatrice Norres, although there was no indication that she would be provided for in the event of a separation due to her bridegroom's incontinence.[24] In the cases where wealthy men such as William Parr, marquess of Northampton and Thomas Lord Burgh were dealing with the consequences of wives' explicit adultery, private acts of Parliament bastardised and disinherited 'their' children. In these cases action was taken against the children of the wife in order to prevent another man's child from inheriting rather than to punish immorality.[25] By contrast, a formal relationship with a husband's illegitimate children was, on occasion, required when wives acted as executors of their husband's wills. In a survey of ninety-six wills mentioning base-born beneficiaries, seventeen male testators appointed their wives as executors, and these women were therefore expected to administer bequests to their spouse's illegitimate children. Of these, for the unnamed wife of John Dutton, Eleanor Percy (wife of Sir Richard Holland), Katherine Langley (wife of Thomas Legh) and the unnamed wife of Marmaduke Elwick involvement went as far as being given responsibility for bringing up their husband's illegitimate children.[26] While Sir Ralph Bigod did not say explicitly that Arthur Bigod 'basterd' was his child, he did instruct his wife Agnes and Sir Ralph Eure to 'put and bounden prentesse at a crafte in London & then to have v l to make him a stoke of the encrease to remayne to his awne use.'[27] This reinforces some limited hints in church court records that elite wives might sometimes help arrange the fostering and care of their husbands' illegitimate offspring. Thomas Cooke of Houghton-le-Spring told Durham High Commission that his wife had, for the past five years, nursed and brought up Robert Ayton's child by Elizabeth Page; the arrangements had been made by Ayton's wife and she had paid them 12d per week.[28] And some 'wronged' gentry wives themselves chose to recognise their husband's illegitimate offspring: when Dorothy Booth came to write her will in 1553, she made provision for her late husband's base children Richard and Mary Booth, and his legitimate daughter by his first wife Cecily Warren. There was, however, an important caveat:

> all ye residue of my sayd goods and cattels which shall happen to remene over my funerall debts and legacies payd shalbe wholly ymployed by my executors for ye helpe and releafe of Alis Bothe daughter [of] my sayd late husband John Bothe deceased in such wise as by my sayd exectres shalbe thought most mete and convenient. It is my will yt my said executres shall not be bunden to deliver to ye sayd Alis Bothe Richard Bothe or Marie Bothe or to any of the any parte or parcell of my goods until ye terme of ten yeres next ensuying my deceasse shalbe fully past duryng all which terme my executres shall kepe ye residue of my said goods in ye hands for defence of all such sutes as shall happen towching ye exhibicion of my said daughter Dorithie.[29]

In other words, the legal and financial interests of her daughter Dorothy took precedence over any potential inheritance of her half-brother and -sisters. There is no room in the wills for the women to reflect explicitly upon the responsibility of bringing up, feeding and clothing another woman's children fathered by her husband. There are, however, hints in the nature and timings of the bequests. In 1479, Isabell Grymston left money, goods and a green gown to 'Thomas, that was my husband's son'.[30] And it is hard to doubt the genuine support and affection for their charges shown in instances such as that of Katherine Langley: outliving her husband Thomas Legh by over twenty years, she still provided for his base-born children in her own will.[31]

Wider acceptance of illegitimate children can be found in the involvement of the wife's kinship circle in their upbringing and financial settlements. John Hurleston of Idenshaw in Cheshire did not expect his wife to bring up his base son John, but he did entrust him (and his £100 inheritance) to the care of his father-in-law, George Massey, and his brother-in-law Richard Brereton.[32] This suggests some level of acceptance of the children within the wife's family and an attempt on the part of Hurleston senior to avoid conflict after his death. Furthermore, these attitudes may reflect that the birth of the children might have preceded the husband's relationship with his wife and the latter may have known the nature of the familial structure she was marrying into. For example, Dorothy Booth, née Butler, was John Booth's second wife.[33]

At the opposite end of the spectrum from these examples of more or less willing acceptance and engagement with an illegitimate family lay exit, and there are examples of spouses who risked sanction in removing themselves from situations in which betrayal had apparently left their position in their eyes unsustainable. As a result of the contentious relationship of Anthony Huddlestone with his sister, Anthony's wife Mary moved to her parental home at Great Haseley in Oxfordshire, and it seems that her children by him lived with her there too. This included their son William, along with his wife Mary, and it was only when Anthony died in 1598 that William and the others moved back to Millom. Mary is commemorated by a monumental brass at Great Haseley, and represented alone as a single female figure. Although the inscription refers to her husband (and to her father), it is mainly concerned with her own personal qualities of 'wisedome & godlynes'.[34] Other women who notably removed themselves from households where their husbands were involved in illicit relationships included Mary, the wife of Henry Mallom in 1595–96.[35] More mysteriously, the whereabouts of Robert Jackson's wife Agnes were much discussed in an immorality case from Driffield in December 1563.[36] It was William Edrington and not Agnes Jackson who brought a suit against Robert and Ellen Barker when witnesses confirmed that 'Robert Jackson and his wife have not accompanied together of long time', and that they had not dwelt together 'this quarter of a year' or 'since Lammas'. No-one seemed to know where Agnes Jackson had gone or why and whether her absence was a catalyst for the extra-marital relationship or the result of it. By the time the case was referred to High Commission in February 1563–64, Agnes and Robert had not reconciled, nor apparently had he stopped his association with Barker.[37]

It is clear that some husbands of adulterous wives attempted to deal with the matter privately. The earl of Derby removed Countess Elizabeth from Court: other husbands sought to separate their wives from lovers, or themselves from their wives. Richard Thornton deliberately went to live 'in the South parts', only taking legal action after his wife Dorothy fell pregnant by another man.[38] John Ridley also 'lived in the South partes, and hath not repaired to his said wife nor doth nor will cohabit with her, by reason of her very lewd behaviour'; Ridley's wife Agnes was prosecuted by Durham High Commission after the birth of her illegitimate child.[39]

The opportunities for objecting to a spouse's immorality (beyond a basic mutual separation) were provided by the courts. In particular, church courts in Carlisle, Durham, York and Chester provided forums for husbands and wives to initiate litigation against wayward spouses. Richard Thornton sued his wife twice in the York court for her long-term adultery, particularly with Timothy Askwith. The first case in 1631 heard that Dorothy had borne two children in adultery; 'the child wherewith her said husband had been charged for was none of his' and she would not name the father of the second 'except her husband Richard Thornton would give her xxx li and for that she would reveal the whole truth.'[40] Five years later Thornton sued his wife successfully for her immorality with 'diverse persons and especiallie of the said Timothie Askwith.'[41] Thornton's divorce however was conditional upon him living 'chaistely and continently' during Dorothy's lifetime. It was perhaps because of the limited resolutions available that for many wronged spouses the church courts were not a choice actively taken. Durham provides a partial exception. Notably, women make up seven of the nine plaintiffs in the relevant High Commission instance cases there, although this includes Janet Dixon, who sued Christopher Athie for filiation and to enforce matrimony in 1611.[42] However, in 1614, it was the office which was responsible for prosecuting Athie in High Commission for adultery with one Mrs Bankes.[43] In 1629 it was again the office (and not a Mrs Athie) which proceeded in High Commission against Elizabeth Dixon 'for notorious incontinency' with Athie.[44] Further, Anne Ridley sued both her husband William and his mistress Anne Moralee in 1635. After objecting to Moralee's initial compurgators as 'unfitteing', Moralee was ordered to pay Anne Ridley's expenses from 'the begineing of the suite'.[45] Elsewhere, in practice, office cases were by far the most frequent mechanism by which immorality was prosecuted, with no litigation directly instigated by wronged partners in the evidence we have from Carlisle, for example. Precise figures are difficult to specify, given the nature of the documentary record, and given that it is possible for one and the same case to be recorded variously across its life as involving both the office and a 'wronged' spouse, and again simply the office. At other times, plaintiffs may appear whose connection to the 'wronged' party may not be clear, but who may be a blood relative or other close connection – or may just as well have been linked to one of the targets of the litigation, as in the case in the Chester Consistory when Thomas Leigh prosecuted Elizabeth Hope and William Sotherne in an adultery case.[46]

Other wives were seemingly less willing to prosecute immorality, but did resort to the courts to enforce financial settlements agreed in the aftermath of adultery or fornication. Mary Hawkesworth, for example, ensured her income, a house, cattle and firewood while limiting her husband's access to 'his usuall chamber and study' in the property identified for her use.[47] Meanwhile, Hawkesworth's mistress, Isabella Rhodes had been ordered to pay a £200 bond 'that she shold absteyne and forbeare to use the company of Sir Richard Hawkesworth knight'. The financial commitment was met by her husband Richard Rhodes and father-in-law John.[48]

Most frequently, therefore, the evidence suggests that wronged partners preferred informal or semi-informal routes to resolution of their situations. They did so to navigate the complications of their own priorities in the context of their family and wider networks, and the expectations of contemporary masculinity and femininity. Another case which illustrates the less-than-straightforward involvement of a spouse in the responses to their husband's adulteries is that of Matilda Venables, long-suffering wife of Sir Thomas Venables of Kinderton. This case has been referred to on more than one occasion already. A dispensation for the marriage of Matilda Needham and Thomas Venables, at a very young age, had been issued in 1518; by 1558 she was attempting to assert her conjugal rights, and we know Sir Thomas had bastard sons by at least two different women by late 1562.[49] During the 1560s, when Sir Thomas was conducting a relationship with Anne Broke, who was described as his pretensed wife and who, from her surname, may have been connected to a well-established gentry family from just over a dozen miles away at Mere, Matilda provides a very distinctive example of a gentlewoman who would not abide the efforts of High Commission, in her case in Chester, to reconcile her with her errant husband. The efforts of the court to force her husband to put away his mistress have already been described, but here it is relevant that when they eventually seemed to have borne fruit Lady Matilda failed to appear on two occasions and on the second a messenger, John Mynshull reported she was not at home in Nantwich and was reported to have left the diocese of Chester.[50] Matilda later provides another less straightforward area of involvement for a spouse in cases of their partner's adultery, in relation to bonds taken to secure future good conduct. In this case it was Sir Thomas's later relationship with Jane Varnam which was in question. Lady Matilda was the daughter of Sir Robert Needham of Shavington Hall, just over the county boundary in Shropshire, and in 1571 she and some of her Needham kin, along with Sir Andrew Corbet, wife of her sister Jane, were the subjects of an attempt to compel them to appear before High Commission, as the court attempted to bring in Sir Thomas's bond. The necessity to use compulsion suggests reluctance: whatever the possible advantage of having High Commission's support in bringing Sir Thomas's behaviour under control, it appears Lady Matilda, or at least Lady Matilda with her kinsfolk, preferred not to involve them in her marital troubles.[51]

Some of the most prolonged matrimonial litigation triggered by complaints about a husband's adultery centred upon the dispute between Sir Rowland Stanley and his wife Lady Ursula in the late sixteenth century, already mentioned in connection with the apparent threats made by Sir Rowland to his wife, and her own apparently adulterous relationship. The case is rich in detail which allows us to explore Lady Ursula's position as a wife in a marriage where each partner accused the other of immorality, where domestic disorder was extrapolated into wider society, and where the ambiguities of her situation were laid bare, in particular by her attempts to impose discipline upon the household (including her husband's mistress). At the same time, and in the aftermath of Sir Rowland's commission to lead 200 troops from Cheshire as part of the English invasion of Scotland in 1560, one of his neighbours (and Lady Ursula's suspected lover), Richard Hurleston, initiated a suit claiming that Stanley tried to murder him.[52] Hurleston claimed that Sir Rowland had also embezzled government funds in relation to the expedition, refused to ride to Scotland with the English army, failed to give evidence in a murder trial in Chester, and engaged in illegal dealings relating to the manor of Ince (Cheshire), as well as referencing Sir Rowland's 'greate outrage towards Dame Vrsula Stanley his wief', in the form of an allegation 'that she had abused her self with your seid soibiecte … and therevpon in the night tyme did put [her] from hym out of his saied howse'. Meanwhile, Lady Ursula launched an annulment suit, on the grounds of her husband's adultery and cruelty, in the ecclesiastical court in York, a move that was countered in July 1561 when Sir Rowland sued his wife on the grounds of her adultery with Hurleston.[53] The immediate outcomes of these cases are unknown (although it is likely that Sir Rowland was considered to be chiefly at fault), but the witnesses called by each party in the matrimonial disputes provide significant testimony concerning the events at Hooton and what Sir Rowland and Lady Ursula deemed to be acceptable proof of the virtue of their cause.

At first sight the Stanley cases present a classic example of 'double standard' engendered politics, the husband having carte blanche to behave in an adulterous fashion, while the wife was expected to maintain a good reputation; in the meantime, both husband and wife had to retain their honour and be able to enforce authority over the household. Lady Ursula's case hinged upon Sir Rowland's adultery with Margery Cooke and Ellyn Thomasyn and his aggressive behaviour towards her. Lady Ursula's attempts to enforce good governance of her household were met with violence from her husband, compromising her authority over the domestic servants at Hooton. Upon discovering that one of the maids, Elizabeth Pendleton, was pregnant, allegedly by another servant, Robert Pitts, Lady Ursula dismissed her and 'laboured her husband to put the said Pitts away … for his lewd demeanour'. It was for the attempted removal of Pitts rather than Pendleton that Lady Ursula received a violent beating by Sir Rowland. Pitts was also accused of having stolen 'two dosen pairs of wymens hose att London' and openly bragged 'sence my Lady hath been beaten for my cause I wilbe gone upon Monday next for I am sure not to have hir favour. But by Gods word before I go I will mayke suche a storie as was never hearde in Hoton.'[54] Pendleton's removal from Hooton reinforces Shannon McSheffrey's point about ideas of female disruption of the proper social order within the household and suggests connivance in those ideas by contemporary women.[55] However, the social aspect of status also needs consideration: Lady Stanley was trying to exclude a male servant on the basis of his 'lewd demeanour'. As the lady of the house, she could demand his dismissal; however, she ran into the patriarchal authority of Sir Rowland as she was overruled by him in his position as head of the household. Lady Stanley also 'put away' her husband's lover Ellen Thomasyn, but, again, he flexed his patriarchal muscles by swearing he would not 'take her [Lady Ursula] as his wife' unless Ellen was reinstated.

As Frances Dolan has pointed out, the married mistress of the household occupied a double position encompassing both authority over servants, yet also subordination to her husband, which enabled him to discipline her.[56] While noting that sixteenth-century reformers did not question the right of a husband to beat his wife, Dolan indicates the ambivalence surrounding domestic violence, as slightly later authors such as Gouge, Whateley, Heale and Smith counselled that restraint was more 'dignified, authoritative and expedient.' In highlighting Sir Rowland's violent conduct, Lady Ursula may also have been raising wider questions in the minds of the judges, as (again admittedly later) conduct books such as *The Married Woman's Case* (1634) and *The Court of Good Counsell* equated the use of violence against women with 'unmanly cowardice' and an unwillingness to enter combat with other men. There is a striking coincidence, in any event, with Hurleston's charge of Sir Rowland's failing to lead Cheshire troops to Scotland.[57] Lady Ursula mounted a vigorous defence of her conduct as she must have realised that the stakes for her were potentially ruinous. If she were found guilty of adultery, not only would her case against Sir Rowland be defeated, but her right to jointure and dower in the event of his death might be compromised.[58] By contrast, as accepted interpretations might lead us to expect, the surviving evidence suggests that Sir Rowland was unconcerned with the accusations against him of adultery with Cooke and Thomasyn as he did not appear to refute the allegations. One examinant deposed that Sir Rowland had promised 'that he should have a lyving of hime whyle he lived, yf he wold say that my Lady were a hore with Hurleston [despite the fact that] … this examinant never knew nor suspected any suche evell conduct between my Lady and the said Hurleston'; another testified that one Henry Lloyd became the keeper of one of Stanley's parks, a servant was put from the house and lost his livery, and others suffered from physical violence or were threatened with a dagger in the pursuit of the case. Yet, for Sir Rowland, bribery and intimidation do not seem to have been an effective strategy: in addition to the violence used by their master against them, deponents testified that his witnesses 'are falce and corrupted by their said Master to say against the said Lady Stanley', and several witnesses testified that she was of good character and they could not believe she had slept with Hurleston. By removing his wife from the marital home, theoretically Sir Rowland restored balance to the domestic environment. However, several witnesses asserted that she was not guilty, and those who testified to her guilt were charged with doing so out of malice towards her. By initiating suit, therefore, Lady Ursula opened up the possibility that her own household would be shown to be corrupt and misgoverned, giving a poor reflection of her husband at the head. The domestic scene portrayed by Lady Ursula in the courtroom at York showed a house in disorder, with the head of the household committing adultery with two women, intimidating or bribing witnesses, and defending the actions of an alleged thief. Following the earlier efforts to deal with the case in York, and then subsequently in the middle of the decade in Chester,[59] in October 1571, York High Commission, energised by the presence of Archbishop Grindal, proceeded against both husband and wife for their failure to cohabit. Sir Rowland indicated he was 'for his parte willinge to take his said wief', provided his bonds were brought in and cancelled; but Lady Ursula would not come in to court, and it seems that her brother, Sir Lawrence Smith was influential in shielding her from its censure. Smith was summoned by special messenger to appear, bringing with him Lady Ursula and the bonds. Yet it was soon recognised that action in York was unlikely to bring success, and by the early part of 1572 there were attempts to transfer the case to Chester, the ineffectiveness of which saw the issue roll on into 1573.[60]

The Stanley case emphasises the collision between contrasting social mores expected of elite women, particularly with regard to the wife's authority over the husband's mistress. Although the officials of the church courts did not pass comment upon the implications of the status or roles of Sir Rowland's mistresses, the presence of a husband's lover within the household must have provided an emotionally difficult atmosphere. Thomasyn was Lady Ursula's maid, and as such, in intimate attendance upon her. As indicated in chapter 3, Sir Henry Savile's mistress Margery Barston was a member of the Savile household and may have been a distant relative of Lady Savile, exacerbating a challenging situation for her. In both the Stanley and Savile cases, however, Smith and Sothill familial support was forthcoming throughout the long-running legal processes, and the vigour with which the 'wronged' wife in each instance pursued her case fluctuated according to the extent to which backing might be obtained from her husband's opponents. Lady Savile seems to have initiated a suit in 1525, seven years after her marriage. In September 1526, the dean of York, Brian Higdon wrote to the all-powerful Cardinal Wolsey commenting 'she has good reason', but had nonetheless 'deferred the matter' as Sir Henry Savile was the latter's servant. Wolsey and Sir Henry had their enemies, however, and potentially powerful ones too: Lady Savile's father, Thomas Sothill, was listed as one of Thomas, Lord Darcy's retinue in 1523, and in an indenture of 1531 Sothill was bound not to alienate any of his lands or to end his legal arguments with Savile without the consent of Darcy. In the same year, he also referred to Darcy's administration of a payment of £20 to a notary in relation to the divorce, suggesting that the Sothill-Savile litigation was still ongoing.[61] In 1530, Savile admitted to Lord Hussey 'the effect of my business is caused by my lord Darcy', and (his own patron the Cardinal now having fallen) requested 'I beseech you to show him, if it please him to remember, I am his kinsman … and I am of his blood, and it is no honor to him for malice to put me to trouble that would be glad to do him pleasure'.[62] Sir Henry Savile's kinship with Darcy was not enough to override the connection with Sothill, however. That Lord Darcy was acquainted with the Sothill affairs and finances was perhaps pivotal for them; his execution in 1537, in the aftermath of the Pilgrimage of Grace, marked the end of any record of a separation between the Saviles, and the birth of Sir Henry and Lady Elizabeth's son Edward in 1538 points towards reconciliation at that time. This was a process of acceptance and adaptation on both sides: not only did Lady Elizabeth have to submit to a husband she had fought so hard to resist, but Sir Henry had to reconcile himself to the fact that his beloved son by Barston, Robert, would not inherit, and so began building up an estate for him, especially around Kirkstall.[63]

The presence of illegitimate children was a factor for both Ladies Ursula and Elizabeth to consider. The mother of Sir Rowland's illegitimate children, Edward Stanley alias Pendleton and Anne, is identified in an enfeoffment of 1576 as Sibyl daughter of William Thomason.[64] Whether Thomason had any relationship or interaction with Lady Ursula is unknown but the birth of her son did not displace Sir Rowland's legitimate male heirs William and John (born to his first wife Margaret Aldersey) or his two daughters, Margaret and Mary (born to Lady Ursula). For Lady Elizabeth, the possible birth of Robert some years before that of her son Edward may have made her position difficult in relation to her husband, but in his letter to Hussey, Sir Henry Savile asserted that 'whilst I live I may take her as my wife, and never agree to the contrary, and ever follow the law as I may to attain her.' Clearly Savile either could not or did not undertake marriage to Barston, the mother of Robert, a consideration which may have been influenced by Lady Elizabeth's Fitzwilliam inheritance.[65]

Ursula Stanley and Elizabeth Savile between them sum up many aspects of the position of betrayed spouse: far from uncomplicated, and most importantly not one held in isolation. Cuckoldry did not simply affect men, nor a set of expectations of disempowerment associated with the double standard universally afflicting women. Responses ranged from acceptance to violent resistance and exit, in the case of both men and women, and these responses were ones which were navigated and experienced not simply as wives and husbands but as parents, heirs or heiresses, and authority and political figures, and in the context of ideas about proper male and female conduct. Relationships with spouses's lovers and associated social or kinship networks had to be negotiated in personal, legal and financial terms and triangulated within these frameworks. These were not significantly overridden during the period in question here by new state mechanisms of discipline or other types of dispute resolution being imposed on the north. Nor were those who might have had something to gain by an appeal to those mechanisms, as the 'wronged' partners in a marriage, as prominent in building those new mechanisms as might be imagined.

Notes

1 Anthony Copley, *Wits fittes and fancies Fronted and entermedled with presidentes of honour and wisdome. Also: Loves Ovvl. An idle conceited dialogue betwene loue, and an olde man* (London: by Richard Iohnes, at the sign of the rose and crowne nexxt aboue S. Andrews, 1595), p. 95.

2 Michael Neill, '"In Everything Illegitimate": Imagining the Bastard in Renaissance Drama', *The Yearbook of English Studies*, 23 (1993), 270–92, at p. 272, and 'Bastardy, Counterfeiting, and Misogyny in The Revenger's Tragedy', *Studies in English Literature, 1500–1900*, 36 (1996), 397–416, at p. 398.

3 See Francisco Vaz Da Silva, 'Sexual Horns: The Anatomy and Metaphysics of Cuckoldry in European Folklore', *Comparative Studies in Society and History*, 48 (2006), 396–418.

4 Mary E. Fissell, *Vernacular Bodies* (Oxford: Oxford University Press, 2006), p. 216.

5 Fissell discusses the example of the circumstances surrounding Charles II's paternity of the duke of Monmouth and the potential for the latter to transform from a bastard to a legitimate heir, in which blame is placed upon Monmouth's mother, Lucy Walter: *ibid.*, pp. 225–7.

6 Faramerz Dabhoiwala, 'The Construction of Honour, Reputation and Status in Late Seventeenth- and Early Eighteenth-Century England', *Transactions of the Royal Historical Society*, 6th ser., 6 (1996), 201–13.

7 BIA, CP.H 2076.

8 Esp. in the context of the ideas initially developed by Elizabeth A. Foyster, *Manhood in Early Modern England: Honour, Sex and Marriage* (London, Harlow: Longman, 1999).

9 William Warner, *Albions England a Continued Historie of the same Kingdome, from the Originals of the First Inhabitants thereof: and most the Chiefe Alterations and Accidents there Hapning:Vnto, and in, the Happie Raigne of our now most Gracious Soueraigne Queene Elizabeth. VVith Varietie of Inuentiue and Historicall Intermixtures. First Penned and Published by VVilliam VVarner: and now Reuised, and newly Inlarged by the same Author* (London: printed by the widow Orwin, for I[oan] B[roome], 1597),

p. 200; Samuel Daniel, *Delia. Containing Certaine Sonnets:With the Complaint of Rosamond* (London: printed by I[ohn] C[harlewood] for S. Watersonne, 1592) (unpaginated).
10 Jane Martindale, 'Eleanor, suo jure duchess of Aquitaine (c. 1122–1204)', *ODNB* xviii. 12–22.
11 *The Prose Works of Fulke Greville, Lord Brooke*, ed. John Gouws (Oxford: Clarendon Press, 1986), pp. 137–76, esp. 167–70, 254. See Julie Crawford, *Mediatrix:Women, Politics, and Literary Production in Early Modern England* (Oxford: Oxford University Press, 2014), p. 40, for a discussion of the political and personal aspects of female stoicism and constancy.
12 NB Tyler's view of High Commission, which might now be read in the context of Hindle's understanding of state-formation: Philip Tyler, 'The Ecclesiastical Commission for the Province of York 1561–1641' (unpubl. D.Phil. diss., Oxford University, 1965); Steve Hindle, *The State and Social Change in Early Modern England, c. 1550–1640* (Basingstoke: Palgrave, 2000).
13 See, for example, Yvonne Bruce, '"That Which Marreth All": Constancy and Gender in The Virtuous Octavia', *Medieval & Renaissance Drama in England*, 22 (2009), 42–59; John Pitcher, 'Daniel, Samuel (1562/3–1619)', *ODNB*, xv. 71–8.
14 For Cumberland's Puerto Rican venture, see Richard T. Spence, *The Privateering Earl: George Clifford, 3rd Earl of Cumberland, 1558–1605* (Stroud: Alan Sutton Publishing, 1995), pp. 141–75, esp. p. 148, where the author suggests 'coolness in his letters to his wife already presaged their separation.'
15 Other issues surrounding the marriage in the late 1590s included the earl's debts (exacerbated by his foreign ventures, gambling and maintaining a courtly lifestyle) and the disposal of his property in the wills made before each voyage; however, Daniel, presumably working under guidance from Countess Margaret, focused upon the earl's philandering and personal relationship with his wife. See also a portrait miniature of Countess Margaret painted by Laurence Hilliard after Earl George's death inscribed with 'Constant in the Midst of Inconstancey': https://collections.vam.ac.uk/item/O1067940/miniature-portrait-of-a-lady-portrait-miniature-hilliard-laurence/.
16 Samuel Daniel, *The Poeticall Essayes of Sam. Danyel* (London: printed by P. Short for Simon Waterson, 1599), pp. B3, [B3v], [C3v].
17 *The Diaries of Lady Anne Clifford*, ed. D. J. H. Clifford (Stroud: Alan Sutton, 1990), pp. 21–7. Countess Margaret's sisters Anne and Elizabeth Russell were married to the earls of Warwick and Bath. They and their children feature more strongly in Clifford's earliest diaries than does her father.
18 *Calendar of the Manuscripts of the Most Hon. The Marquis of Salisbury K.G. ... Preserved at Hatfield House, Hertfordshire*, ed. R. A. Roberts, M. S. Giuseppi, and G. Dyfnallt Owen, Historical Manuscripts Commission, 9 (24 vols. London: HMSO, 1883–1973), vii. 339. Discussed in Johanna Rickman, *Love, Lust, and License in Early Modern England: Illicit Sex and the Nobility* (Aldershot: Ashgate, 2008), pp. 64–6, who also makes the point that the Cecils were interested in defending their own family honour and reputation.
19 *Calendar of the Manuscripts of the Most Hon. The Marquis of Salisbury*, vii. 339. Cecil was Countess Elizabeth's uncle.
20 *Ibid.*; Mylar commented 'she hath by courtesy and virtue got the love of all here.'
21 *Ibid.*, p. 344.
22 Barry Coward, *The Stanleys, Lords Stanley and Earls of Derby, 1385–1672:The Origins,Wealth and Power of a Landowning Family*, Chetham Society, 3rd ser., XXX (1983), details the long-running inheritance dispute after the death of Earl Ferdinando.

23 Roger J. Dickinson, *The Lordship of Man Under the Stanleys: Government and Economy in the Isle of Man, 1580–1704*, Chetham Society, 3rd ser., XLI (1996). She was succeeded in that role by her eldest son, James Stanley.
24 LRO, DDIN 64/33. The settlement appears undated, but *VCH Lancs.*, iii. 203 indicates John Ireland died in 1514, his son by Beatrice being 47 years old.
25 E.g., Westminster, Parliamentary Archives, HL/PO/PB/1/1543/35H8 (*LP* xviii/1. 66 iii (cap. xl)) for Thomas Lord Burgh; for these cases more generally, see above pp. 51, 89–90, 102–3, although note Parr's appropriation of his *wife's* inheritance, which he was also able to keep from her children.
26 For Dutton, *Lancashire and Cheshire Wills & Inventories from the Ecclesiastical Court, Chester*, vol. I, ed. G. J. Piccope, Chetham Society, XXXIII (1857), pp. 66–8; Percy, *TE*, vi. 192–3; Langley: *Lancashire and Cheshire Wills and Inventories at Chester, with an Appendix of Abstracts of Wills now Lost or Destroyed* [1477–1746], transcribed by G. J. Piccope, ed. John Parsons Earwaker, Chetham Society, n.s., 3 (1884), pp. 126–30; Elwick, *TE*, vi. 295–6.
27 *TE*, v. 55. John Bigod, 'basterd', was to be treated in the same manner.
28 DUL, Hunter MSS, vol. 17, fo. 66 (*The Acts of the High Commission Court Within the Diocese of Durham*, ed. W. Hylton Dyer Longstaffe, Surtees Society, XXIV (1858), p. 43).
29 *Lancashire and Cheshire Wills and Inventories from the Ecclesiastical Court, Chester*, ed. G. J. Piccope, Chetham Society, LIV (1861), iii. 54–7.
30 *TE* iii. 251.
31 *Lancashire and Cheshire Wills and Inventories at Chester, with an Appendix of Abstracts of Wills now Lost or Destroyed* [1477–1746], pp. 126–30.
32 *Lancashire and Cheshire Wills and Inventories at Chester* [1477–1746], ed. Earwaker, Chetham Society, n.s., 3, pp. 120–3. Massey and Brereton were also responsible for the upbringing of Hurleston's legitimate children. Brereton was likely to be the husband of Hurleston's sister Maude.
33 *The Visitation of Lancashire and a Part of Cheshire Made in the Twenty Fourth Year of the Reign of King Henry the Eighth A. D. 1533*, ed. William Langton, Chetham Society, XCVIII, CX (1876–82), p. 78.
34 Illustrated in Herbert Druitt and Sydney Smith, *A Manual of Costume as Illustrated by Monumental Brasses* (London: Alexander Moring Ltd, The De la More Press, 1906), opposite p. 287; *Oxford Church Courts: Depositions, 1592–1596*, ed. Jack Howard Drake (Oxford: Oxfordshire County Council, 1998), no. 71. For other aspects of this case, see above, pp. 17, 64–5.
35 BIA, HC.AB 12, fo. 207v.
36 BIA, CP.G 1097.
37 BIA, HC.CP 1563/1; HC.AB 1, fos. 95v, 104, 104v, 108, 108v, 110, 110v, 119, 146, 174, 186.
38 BIA, CP.H 1897.
39 DUL, Hunter MSS, vol. 17, fo. 8 (*Acts of the High Commission Court Within the Diocese of Durham*, ed. Dyer Longstaffe, p. 6).
40 BIA, CP.H 1897.
41 BIA, CP.H 2097.
42 DUL, DDR/EJ/CCA/1/8, fos. 165, 171, 172, 181, 189v, 190, 195, 196, 198, 202, 222, 224, 226, 230, 240, 242.
43 DUL, DCD/D/SJB/7, fo. 3.
44 DUL, Hunter MSS, vol. 16, fo. 11.
45 *Acts of the High Commission Court Within the Diocese of Durham*, ed. Dyer Longstaffe, pp. 135–9.

46 Cheshire Arch., EDC5/1608/92.
47 BIA, HC.AB 17, fos. 112, 117, 139.
48 BIA, HC.AB 17, fo. 439.
49 Cheshire Arch., DNE 36; DVE/1BB/8, /1/KIII/15; see above, pp. 28, 64; below, p. 118.
50 BIA, HC.AB 17, fo. 51; 23 Oct. 1563.
51 HC.AB 6, fos. 75v, 106, 107v, 109, 148; S. T. Bindoff, *The House of Commons, 1509–1558* (3 vols. London: Secker & Warburg for the History of Parliament Trust, 1982), i. 697.
52 TNA, STAC 7/3/10.
53 BIA, CP.G 975A, Lady Ursula c Sir Rowland Stanley; CP.G 1042, Sir Rowland c Lady Ursula Stanley. It seems the case was resolved either at this point or soon after by Sir Rowland giving bonds for his behaviour, for which he was challenged again in 1565: Cheshire Arch., EDA 12/2, fos. 26, 89v, 91.
54 *Ibid.*
55 Shannon McSheffrey, 'Men and Masculinity in Late Medieval London Civic Culture: Governance, Patriarchy, and Reputation', in Jacqueline Murray (ed.), *Conflicted Identities and Multiple Masculinities: Men in the Medieval West* (New York, London: Garland, 1999), pp. 243–78.
56 Frances E. Dolan, 'Battered Women, Petty Traitors, and the Legacy of Coverture', *Feminist Studies*, 29 (2003), 249–77. See also Garthine Walker, *Crime, Gender and Social Order in Early Modern England* (New York: Cambridge University Press, 2003), p. 63, who also raises the point that the level of 'reasonable force' which could be used by the husband was undefined. In the later Stuart era, the use of reason was supposed to act as a check upon masculine violence; see Elizabeth Foyster, 'Male Honour, Social Control and Wife Beating in Late Stuart England', *Transactions of the Royal Historical Society*, 6th ser., 6 (1996), 215–24.
57 Walker, *Crime, Gender and Social Order*, p. 66.
58 R. H. Helmholz, *The Oxford History of the Laws of England*, vol. I: *The Canon Law and Ecclesiastical Jurisdiction from 597 to the 1640s* (Oxford: Oxford University Press, 2004), p. 554.
59 Cheshire Arch., EDA 12/2, fos. 89v, 90, 91.
60 BIA, HC.AB 6, fos. 79v, 133v, 180; HC.AB 7, fos. 1v, 97. For further on this case, see below, pp. 136–9.
61 *LP* iv. 2501, 6746; xii/2. 186 (50); R. B. Smith, *Land and Politics in the England of Henry VIII: The West Riding of Yorkshire, 1530–46* (Oxford: Clarendon Press, 1970), pp. 81, 147–50, 161, 189, 193–4.
62 *LP* iv. 6746. Interestingly, Robert Savile married Anne Hussey (widow of Matthew Thimbleby), and their son John was born in 1556. Nottinghamshire Archives, DD/SR/10/29, an indenture of 1553, identifies him as 'of Powlam, co. Lincs', suggesting he was already established there. This marriage enabled Robert to become an influential figure in Hussey's native Lincolnshire.
63 The matrimonial struggles were compounded by the political situation in the West Riding, where Savile and Sir Richard Tempest (a kinsman of Darcy's) were both trying to impose their authority on county government. Tempest also died in 1537, imprisoned in the Fleet. See Bindoff, *House of Commons, 1509–1558*, iii. 280–1, 430–1, for their political rivalry at this time. *The Plumpton Letters and Papers*, ed. Joan Kirby, Camden Society, 5th ser., 8 (1996), nos 240, 242.
64 Ormerod, *Chester*, ii. 414: 'Edward, son of Sibil (daughter of William Thomason *defunct.*), *alias* Edward Penleton, *alias* Edward Stanley, bastard son of Sir Roland', suggests some connection with Elizabeth Pendleton, the maid 'put away' for her pregnancy by Pitts.

65 Elizabeth Sothill inherited Fitzwilliam lands from her mother, Margery Fitzwilliam who, along with her sister Dorothy Copley was a coheiress of William Fitzwilliam of Sprotborough. This inheritance was a source of dispute; see for example, TNA, C 1/569/85 Savile and Copley v. Drury. William Fitzwilliam died in 1516, but Elizabeth Sothill and her second husband Richard Gascoigne were still engaged in litigation with Hugh Fitzwilliam in 1569/70, when he drew up a pedigree (Northampton, Northamptonshire Archives, F(M) roll/438) to help establish his claim to the lands.

6

The bastard children

IF ILLICIT SEXUAL RELATIONSHIPS before and after marriage continued to be significant among the northern English gentry and nobility, and if the mistresses of those men (and even the lovers of the women) in many cases enjoyed a relatively prominent position in society, then we must ask questions about the offspring of those relationships. Were these bastard children nonetheless treated as we understand their non-elite equivalents to have been – as the physical manifestations of a moral, religious, social and economic crisis for the individuals concerned and their neighbours? The evidence considered in this chapter will allow us to examine these questions in relation to the circumstances of the children's birth and infancy; to the support they received and any potential inheritance from their family; and to their eventual progress and role as individuals and members of their families and wider connections. There are particular potential lessons here for the overall arguments of this book about the nature of northern society and the ways in which its political culture might have changed in the early modern period, under the impact of religious, political, social and economic change. If all of these were driving towards a reduced tolerance of illicit relationships and bastard-bearing, then even if the more immediate aspects of enforcement in response to sexual relationships and pregnancies themselves might have been limited in their manifestations, then stigma directed towards individuals' bastard birth might have grown.

The evidence suggests that concealment of bastard births was more likely where the mother was of a higher social status than the father, and when the mother was the one whose participation in the relationship offended most directly against the bounds of marriage. There is, by contrast, very little evidence of the concealment where the father was a gentleman and the mother was not of gentle status. Evidence of this is to be found in the pattern of naming of the bastard child. In England the general custom was that a child's given name was aligned with those of godparents, but it is nonetheless true that there seems in many cases to have been a choice of godparent to allow for the selection of a particular name.[1] In these circumstances it is significant that a high proportion of male bastard children share names with either or both the father and legitimate siblings. Among female children, if we accept the argument that more atypical given names reflect greater licence being taken by a parent, and by extension less sense of responsibility shown to family tradition and expectation, then the relative rarity of atypical names among female bastards might suggest their value to the naming parents. Dorothy, daughter of Henry fourth earl of Derby, shared a name with Henry's mother; Elizabeth, daughter of Henry second earl of Cumberland, shared that name with an aunt and sister of her father. Surnames suggest a similar situation: children were known, at least later in life, by both their father's surname and another surname, usually that of their mother's family, or what appears to be a fostering family. This is therefore suggestive of the relative importance of the mistress's family, alongside the father's role. For example a property settlement of 1555 refers to 'Thomas son of Jane Danbie alias Thomas Brooke alias Thomas the Bastard son of the said Richard Brooke', and the identification of the mother is also clear in an enfeoffment from Derbyshire involving Sir Francis Leek and 'his illegitimate son Simon Leek, otherwise Simon Dawbney, son of Matilda Dawbney, widow.'[2] In the sample of wills used throughout this study, in twenty cases illegitimate children bore the same forenames as their fathers or other members of the immediate family. Sir Richard Cholmeley had a legitimate brother and an illegitimate son named Roger, and Edward Stanley, Lord Monteagle had legitimate and illegitimate sons named Thomas (possibly named for Thomas, first earl of Derby, Monteagle's father) and an illegitimate son Edward. The legitimate Thomas Stanley became Lord Monteagle after his father's death and fathered two daughters named Anne, one legitimate and the other illegitimate. Thirteen illegitimate sons bore the same name as their fathers, eight fathers had legitimate and illegitimate children each with the same name, and, of these, confusingly, three fathers themselves had the same name as their legitimate and illegitimate children (Sir Richard Holland, John Eden and John Hurleston).

If the economic issues surrounding illegitimacy and immorality among the poorer sections of society vexed the Tudor authorities and are reflected in surviving court records, maintenance of base-born children was also of concern to the gentry. The mechanisms of maintenance were, however, very different with gentlemen acquiring property and estates for their base-born children and passing them on through private legal settlement, or providing money for girls' marriage portions, for example. It cannot be denied that in some cases the response was one aimed at denying or limiting responsibility for the child. Wills in a couple of cases even provided for their disinheritance. In 1489, Sir Henry Pierrepoint willed 'Edmond, that calls him my bastard son, have neither lands nor tenements, nor goods that to me pertaineth and belongeth.'[3] A century later, in 1597, Roger Heyton testified in his will that property which had been in dispute did not belong to a man claiming to be Richard, son of Ferdinando Heyton, as the latter turned out to be 'but a bastard son of old Sir William Heyton'.[4] An accusation of bastardy could also be a route to overturning a previously agreed property settlement in favour of other family members, in spite of the consequential scandal. This was the route taken by John Fitzherbert esquire of Norbury, Derbyshire, who under Henry VIII 'in the open Sessions holden at Derby … to his greate shame and rebuke opynly shewid publisshed and declared that the saide Anne [his daughter, by then long-since married to Humphrey Wellys] was a Bastard'. At stake was the Fitzherbert inheritance, given that John was now over 70 and his wife 65, his son Nicholas was dead, and the other interested party was Sir Anthony Fitzherbert, the prominent judge and John's youngest brother.[5] The overwhelming proportion of the noble and gentry wills which refer to base-born individuals, however, do so to confirm financial or landed settlements upon base-born children or relatives, ranging in scale from the poorer gentleman providing livestock and crops, such as Walter Bradford of Houghton, gentleman, who left his illegitimate daughter Beatrix a cow, three quarters of malt and 'a bed with al thinges belongyng',[6] to those who provided a life interest in property, annuities, money for the marriages of daughters, or the education of sons, to Sir John Byron, who, lacking any legitimate heir, left all his landed property and interests to his illegitimate son John.

It is also possible to draw on other evidence, from property transactions and legal disputes, for example, to add to this picture of provision for illegitimate offspring. The most usual arrangements are those for illegitimate sons and daughters when there are legitimate heirs clearly identified. These are most usually in the form of annuities or simple cash gifts. John Egerton of Wrinehill on the Cheshire-Staffordshire border in 1515 enfeoffed a group headed by Master Richard Delves, clerk, Master Robert Foulehurst, clerk, and Sir John Aston with property to his own use, and after his death to pay annual sums to his wife and two daughters, the elder of whom was to receive in total 300 marks, and among others his three bastard sons 26s 8d each per annum.[7] Richard Wilbraham gave his daughter Elizabeth 'three score pounds to her marriage' in 1558.[8] Simple gifts and relatively modest monetary bequests were also given by fathers to sons. In 1562, Thomas Leyland bequeathed £6 and four silver spoons to his base son Roger, and Thomas, illegitimate son of George Trafford, received 'my best cofer, one crossbow, one raper to the same and one jacke, a sallet, a pair of splentes a gorget, a pair of slyves of metal, one long bow and all my saddles and bridles' as well as £6 13s 4d seed capital for investment.[9]

There seems no doubt that it was fathers who were most willing to acknowledge and attempt to provide for illegitimate children in this way. In some cases, however, a testator provided for a wider family of illegitimate relatives. In 1558 Richard Bowes bequeathed a gelding to 'Percival Bowes, base born son of my brother Sir Robert Bowes' and another horse to 'my cosyn Robert Bowes, base son of Sir George Bowes.' A more complicated family situation is illustrated by Thomas Forster, who left bequests to four illegitimate sons, three illegitimate nephews and his grandson (the son of one of his illegitimate sons).[10] Each of these cases suggests an acceptance of a wider circle of illegitimate kin. It is also striking that a significant proportion of the wills mentions more than one illegitimate child – sixteen with two, six with three, before we reach more unusual examples of more (Laurence Dutton and Luke Ogle with five each, Thomas Legh with seven and Thomas Forster with eight).[11] Out of ninety-six, twenty-six is a significant proportion, suggesting acceptance of bastard-bearing not just in the acknowledgement in the will, but in the repeat fathering of illegitimate children. The wills also illustrate interrelationships implying greater trust than simply recognition and the passage of a bequest. In nine cases illegitimate relatives were appointed as executors by their uncle, brother, parent or grandparent, including Cuthbert Halsall, who was appointed executor by his grandmother, Anne Halsall in 1589.[12] As we have already seen, an assumption, at least, of acceptance of illegitimate members by the testator's wife is also suggested by the seventeen wives who were chosen as executors for their husbands' estates and as a result expected to administer bequests to their spouse's base-born children, and the four women who were actually charged with bringing up their illegitimate step-children. There is a parallel assumption of acceptance to be found in the twenty-one cases where legitimate children were appointed as an executor and had at least a joint responsibility for administering a bequest to an illegitimate half-sibling. In five of these cases, the wife of the testator was also an executor – for example the executors of Robert, Lord Ogle who had to administer 'twenty head of kye and oxen' towards the marriage of 'my daughter Annas Ogle, bastard', and Jane and Anthony Lister, the wife and son of Laurence Lister, who had to administer forty shillings for 'Christopher Lister my bastard son'.[13] That said, female testators were also occasionally willing to recognise illegitimate family members, although only eight such examples appear in the sample. These tend to be grandmothers, suggesting that across the generations there was the potential for female acceptance; again as already discussed, there are just two stepmothers in this category – presumably a sign, if a limited one, that the illegitimate child is being recognised right across the family.[14]

Given this pattern of integration and wider kin support for illegitimate children, it is perhaps less surprising that their appearance as heirs to more substantial land, property and titles was more widespread than first appears. In the middle years of the sixteenth century, Sir Thomas Venables of Kinderton's determination to support the different bastard offspring of his two mistresses, Anne Broke and Anne Bostock, is evident across several decades, if with changing priorities. Early in the reign of Edward VI, he made a settlement which was to provide for the marriage portions of unmarried daughters and then, after his legitimate male heirs, was in favour of his brothers, John, Richard and Anthony, and then bastard sons William and Edward. Later, in settlements in 1562 and 1564, Thomas Venables, his illegitimate son by Broke, had precedence, followed by Edward, William and Cyprian, sons by Bostock. Then came Anthony, whose parentage is not identified in either document. It seems, therefore, that his family by Bostock was established first, and only in the early years of Elizabeth's reign did the Broke association appear and gain pre-eminence.[15] Edward was evidently well provided for, as his widow Eleanor was in a position to convey two messuages, five wichhouses, two gardens and one acre of land in Middlewich, Northwich and Newton to trustees including her brother-in-law Thomas Venables esquire in February 1571. William too had good support, as he was able in 1579 to lease a messuage and garden in Middlewich.[16] As outlined above, Sir John Byron bequeathed 'to John Byron, my base son, all my manors, lands leases etc.'[17] Sir John Pilkington left lands in Sowerbyshire, Greenhirst and Wistow to his son Robert in 1478.[18] In 1492, Henry, Lord Grey of Codnor effectively created an entail when he bequeathed the manor of Radcliffe-on-Trent to his bastard son Richard, and to his other two base sons both named Henry if the former died without heirs, and passed other manors to the two Henries.[19] The illegitimate son of Edward, Lord Grey of Powis and Jane Orwell also inherited manors, lordships and property under the terms of his father's will of 1544, with his base daughters Anne and Jane further featuring in default of male heirs.[20] The influence exerted by Jane Orwell's husband, John Herbert, in Buildwas and Welshpool was due to the Grey inheritance of his step-son.[21]

It was, by contrast, very unusual for illegitimate girls to inherit lands by will, but Ralph Worsley, having fathered one illegitimate and three legitimate daughters, sought to divide his estate between the two families (in addition to passing lands in Poultry, London to his nephew Hugh). He left his 'lands, tenements and hereditariments' in Lancashire to his base-born daughter Katherine with remainder to legitimate daughters Alice and (another) Katherine should she die without issue. His legitimate daughter Avice was not included in the succession to the Lancashire properties, as there seems to have been a dispute with her and her husband, Thomas Vawdrey. Conversely, the legitimate daughters Alice, Katherine and Avice benefitted from property in London; illegitimate Katherine was not included as they had been acquired from 'Nicholas Jennyns, late citizen and alderman [who] did gyve [them] unto me and unto Joane my late wyffe and to the heyres of our two bodyes lawfully begotten'.[22] Francis Sherington, husband of Worsley's base daughter, was an executor, along with his half-brothers-in-law Thomas Powell and Thomas Tutchett, thus suggesting inclusivity and integration within the family. In the middle of the sixteenth century, when Thomas de la Riviere died intestate and without legitimate heirs, his bastard daughter and her influential husband Roger, second son of Sir Richard Cholmondeley, were able to secure the inheritance of the manors of Brandsby and Brafferton in the East and North Ridings of Yorkshire.[23] Where illegitimate daughters were mentioned, it is often as part of a chain of inheritance, as in the example of Anne and Jane, daughters of Lord Grey of Powis. Being at the end of the inheritance queue did not, however, preclude base-born daughters from succeeding their fathers and brothers. Emanuel Scrope, earl of Sunderland died in 1630 leaving a widow, Elizabeth Manners, who died in 1653, no legitimate children and four young illegitimate children, John, Mary, Elizabeth and Annabella.[24] Although the earldom lapsed upon Emanuel Scrope's death, John inherited the Scrope estate in Bolton, North Yorkshire and after he died unmarried and without children in 1646, it passed to his sister Mary and her descendants. Property in Nottinghamshire was granted to Annabella Scrope, who in 1663 gained a warrant from Charles II, granting legitimacy to her and her siblings, although it seems unlikely that a marriage ever took place between Emanuel Scrope and her mother Martha Jeanes.[25]

As this example suggests, there were barriers which prevented illegitimate children from accessing some aspects of elite rank and position. Most titles expired upon the death of the last legitimate holder as evidenced by the Sunderland case and by the abortive efforts in the early seventeenth century of Robert Dudley, son of the earl of Leicester, to acquire titles previously held by members of the Dudley family.[26] While there is plenty of evidence for landed settlements and financial transactions to include illegitimates, it was very unusual for them to succeed to titles held by forebears. At most this was possible for the children of the illegitimate son, and to find many examples we have to look beyond the bounds of this study in the north. The earldom of Pembroke was (re)created in 1551 for William Herbert, son of Richard Herbert, illegitimate son of William Herbert, earl of Pembroke for example.[27] The obstacles were slightly different in the case of access to a newly created peerage. The main exceptions here were royal bastards, the most prominent base-born member of the peerage being Henry Fitzroy, duke of Richmond, the son of Henry VIII and Elizabeth Blount; it is noteworthy that the only other prominent acknowledged royal bastard active during this period, Arthur Plantagenet, son of Edward IV, also became a peer during the reign of Henry VIII, as Viscount Lisle.[28] Chris Given-Wilson and Alice Curteis have suggested that the status accorded to Richmond and Lisle (along with the marriage of Richard III's illegitimate daughter Katherine to the earl of Huntingdon in 1484) demonstrates an enhanced position within noble social circles for royal bastards, particularly when compared with those of earlier centuries, who did not benefit from such advancement, and that this may reflect attitudes to illegitimacy more generally. Michael Hicks has attempted to push this argument further, although its limits are highlighted by the relatively restricted extent of, for example, the influence of the Bastard of Bedford at the start of the fifteenth century, and of the limited visibility of Edward IV's other bastards a century later by comparison to the situation found in contemporary France and Burgundy.[29]

For a handful of other bastard-born males, hard work and a successful career elevated them to the ranks of the peerage. A survey of those recorded in *The Complete Peerage* between 1500 and 1640 indicates that four illegitimate men who gained peerages did so in their own right, and one is a highly relevant figure for our study. As a result of his success in law and politics, Thomas Egerton worked his way up from base son of Sir Richard Egerton of Ridley (Cheshire) and a servant named Alice Sparke, to the posts of solicitor-general (1581) and attorney-general (1592), a knighthood in 1594, creation as Baron Ellesmere and Lord Chancellor in 1603 and Viscount Brackley in 1616. Thomas Poynings, illegitimate son of Sir Edward Poynings, spent much of his military career in Calais before becoming a Baron.[30] Such remarkable men elevated the status of their families beyond the gentry or armigerous backgrounds into which they were born, but were rare in terms of the level of their distinguished careers and the resulting honours they enjoyed. Illegitimate sons born to peers also had to launch their own social trajectories. The politician and courtier Mountjoy Blount, the son of Charles Mountjoy, earl of Devonshire and Penelope Devereux did not inherit his father's comital title; he became Baron Mountjoy in the English peerage in 1627 and earl of Newport a year later.[31] During the reign of Henry VII, Charles Somerset, who was son of Henry Beaufort, duke of Somerset and his mistress Joan Hill, and therefore the king's cousin, and was also a career courtier and pillar of the regime in Wales, married the heir of William Herbert, earl of Huntingdon in 1492 and was created Lord Herbert in 1504. Under Henry VIII, after distinguished service in the French expedition of 1513, in February 1514 he was made earl of Worcester.[32] More accessible was creation for the sons of illegitimate children: the legitimate son of Sir Henry Savile did not have the social or financial success of his bastard half-brother Robert, who was knighted in 1594 and was able to build a house at Howley to rival the greatest in the country, spending, with his own son, something in the order of £30,000 on the project. Robert's Savile line progressed through the social hierarchy as his son John became Baron Savile of Pontefract and in turn his son Thomas was made earl of Sussex.[33]

Where illegitimate children were born as a result of the adultery of a wife (particularly to a marriage without other issue), the legal assumption that a child born in wedlock was the legitimate child of the husband could conflict with the reality that children fathered by other men stood to inherit titles or substantial property on the basis of the husband's landed wealth. In the rare cases where this happened, legal confusion and extensive litigation followed, with questions asked about intimate details such as the state of the marriage and the capacity of the husband to father a child decades or even centuries after the birth. *The Complete Peerage* suggests that Edward (1627–45) and Nicholas (1630–74) were sons of Elizabeth Howard, countess of Banbury by Edward, Lord Vaux rather than her first husband, William Knollys, earl of Banbury (Howard married Vaux shortly after Knollys' death). Nicholas acquired the Vaux lands by conveyance dated 1646 (to the detriment of Edward Vaux's brother Henry) and the earldom of Banbury.[34] The paternity of Frances Coke's son Robert Wright, alias Howard alias Villiers alias Danvers, born in 1624, also led to long-running disputes. Pressured by her father, Coke married John Villiers, Viscount Purbeck in 1617, but left him in 1621. After the birth of Robert, she and Sir Robert Howard appeared before High Commission and were found guilty of adultery. Sentenced to perform penance, she escaped punishment but became embroiled in lawsuits with the Villiers family, who no doubt focused upon their possible inheritance of Purbeck's estate (which partly derived from property settled upon Coke by her father at the time of her marriage) should he die childless. The lawsuits with the Villiers family were not resolved until 1678. Later descendants of Howard and Coke had the use of property granted to Frances Coke by her father until their final male descendant died childless in the late eighteenth century.[35]

With the exception of a few talented individuals, the ranks of the peerage were therefore closed to well-born bastard sons. Base-born girls were also acknowledged less frequently than boys, never acquired an honour in their own right, and appear as wives of peers only on two occasions during the years 1500–1640 – and in both cases the peers involved were relatively impoverished at the time of the marriage. Thomas, 8th Lord Clinton (d. 1517) married Jane Poynings, one of Sir Edward Poynings' seven illegitimate children, and sister of Thomas, Lord Poynings; and Arthur, Lord Grey of Wilton married Dorothy, daughter of Richard 9th Lord Zouche.[36] Although all the daughters of Emanuel, earl of Sunderland were married after 1640, it is worth examining their marital careers, as they provide some contrast to the observation that few illegitimate women married noblemen in the years 1500–1640. In addition to Mary and Annabella Scrope, who inherited extensive lands in Yorkshire and Nottinghamshire respectively, their sister Elizabeth married Thomas Savage, who succeeded his father to become Earl Rivers in 1654. Mary acquired a position at Court when she became a dresser to Queen Catherine of Braganza and her second marriage was to Charles Paulett, who became marquess of Winchester in 1675 (and duke of Bolton in 1689). Annabella did not marry a peer but was the mother of John, 1st Viscount Howe and so became the mother of one. These marriages took place prior to the legal legitimisation of the Scrope family by Charles II, but, perhaps rather more tellingly, after Mary and Annabella inherited their property from their brother.[37]

If the illegitimate daughters of peers did not generally succeed in achieving a place among the nobility by inheritance or marriage, many nonetheless found a place within gentle society. Surviving evidence of parental ambition (and societal constraints) can be found by identifying the husbands of illegitimate girls and / or assessing the generosity or otherwise of financial settlements made by fathers, expressed in wardship, portion and jointure. Wardship does not, at first sight, impact upon bastards, as they could not be considered heirs of the Crown's tenants-in-chief. However, wards could be purchased with a view to marrying them to illegitimate children, while giving the guardian control over a third of their lands during their minority. Elizabeth, bastard daughter of Thomas, second earl of Derby, married her father's ward Thomas Scarisbrick, whose land-holdings were near the Stanley family seat at Lathom in Lancashire.[38] Thomas was the second son of Gilbert Scarisbrick who died in 1501–2, but survived his elder brother James to succeed to the family patrimony.[39] At great expense, Edward Stafford, third duke of Buckingham purchased the wardship of Thomas Fitzgerald of Leixlip, half-brother to the earl of Kildare, whom he planned to marry to his illegitimate daughter Margaret.[40] Carole Rawcliffe argued that despite Kildare's treachery, the duke 'was no less anxious that his illegitimate daughter should do well for herself', like her half-siblings Elizabeth, Mary and Katherine who married the duke of Norfolk, Lord Bergavenny and the earl of Westmorland respectively. Wardship was undeniably controversial during the early modern period, with Sir Thomas Smith arguing that once a ward attained his majority and landed interests, he could expect to find 'woods decayed, stock wasted, land ploughed to the bare',[41] and an undesirable marriage might have been one of those legacies unfavourable to the ward. Coke argued that bastardy was a disparagement of blood and therefore a ward could refuse to marry an illegitimate spouse chosen by their guardian.[42] Coke's view was that such a marriage 'is not only a shame and infamie to the heire, but in him, to all his bloud and kindred.' However, in his study of wardship during the reign of Queen Elizabeth I, Joel Hurstfield found no examples of wards repudiating their marriages by arguing disparagement in the law courts, indicating that such problems were more theoretical than real.

Two generations later, the fourth earl of Derby's illegitimate daughter Dorothy married Sir Cuthbert Halsall, another prominent Lancashire landowner who, although illegitimate, was the sole heir of his father Richard. Her sister Ursula married John Salusbury of Lleweni, who held lands in Denbigh, close to Hawarden Castle, another of the earl's properties where his illegitimate family may have grown up. John's fortunes were at an extremely low ebb when, in approximately 1588, he married Ursula Stanley: his brother Thomas had been executed in 1586 for his role in the Babington plot against Queen Elizabeth. It has been argued that Salusbury's restoration to favour began with his alliance with the Stanleys: his brother-in-law William, fifth earl of Derby appointed him to the joint stewardship of Hawarden, Mold, Hope and Hopedale in 1595, and around the same time he began to make progress in establishing himself at Court. He showed loyalty to the crown during the Essex rebellion and was knighted in 1601; he and Ursula were the recipients of the dedication of Robert Chester's *Loues Martyr* of that year, which included verses by both Shakespeare and Jonson.[43] The social positions of the two illegitimate daughters of the second earl of Cumberland (1517–70) reflect those of Elizabeth, Dorothy and Ursula Stanley insomuch as they were married into endogamous northern families.[44] Elizabeth Clifford was married to Benjamin Lambert, whose father had been a steward of the first earl, and her sister Joan to Edward Birkbeck, who had responsibility for Clifford lands in Westmorland.[45] In the family of the earls of Northumberland, Isabel Percy, the daughter of the sixth earl's brother Sir Ingram, married Henry Tempest of Broughton in 1544. Her marriage was probably negotiated by her grandmother Katherine, countess of Northumberland after the death of Sir Ingram in 1538, as his will contains no reference to his daughter's (potential) marriage. Lady Northumberland bequeathed valuable silver and tapestries to Isabell with a view to her marriage and specified:

> Stephan Tempeste of Broughton, esquier, shulde have the order and governance of the saide Isabell Percie, with all her parte and porcon, to the entente that Henrie Tempeste, sone and here of the saide Steven shall marie and take to wif the said Isabell, according to the gret confidence and truste that shee doo putt in the saide Stephane and Anne his wif.[46]

A marriage settlement dated 1544 brought the countess's plan to fruition.[47] The Percy-Tempest marriage placed Isabell within the outer reaches of the Percy-Clifford orbit, as her aunt Margaret Percy was the second wife of Henry Clifford, first earl of Cumberland, who was also the supervisor of the countess of Northumberland's will. The Tempests were trusted advisers to the Cliffords, and the second earl of Cumberland was a supervisor of Stephen Tempest's will in 1549. He had provided legal advice to the earls for many years, and Isabell Percy's son, also named Stephen, became a faithful servant of George, third earl of Cumberland, culminating with the earl's sponsorship of Tempest's knighthood by James I.[48]

When it came to the gentry, the contrasting fortunes of illegitimate daughters might still be found good marriages, if less impressive ones than their illegitimate sisters. The Percies' Northumberland neighbour and political rival Sir John Forster also looked to the Yorkshire gentry when he married his illegitimate daughter Mary to Henry Stapleton, son of Sir Robert Stapleton, of Wighill in 1599. By the turn of the century, Stapleton's fortunes were in steep decline, prompted in part by Sir Robert's argument with the archbishop of York, Edwin Sandys.[49] The status of Mary Forster's husband nonetheless stands in contrast with that of the spouse of her legitimate half-sister, Juliana, who married Lord Francis Russell in 1571, a son of the second earl of Bedford, and whose son Edward became third earl in 1585.[50]

This pattern of illegitimate gentry daughters being able to achieve respectable marriages, if less prestigious ones than their legitimate siblings, is confirmed by an example from the first half of the sixteenth century in Derbyshire. Sir Godfrey Foljambe of Walton organised the marriages of his daughters 'begotten of Joane Mansfield' (presumably so described to distinguish them from his legitimate daughters, also named Benet and Katherine) prior to his death in 1541; Benet to Richard Assheby, son of William and his wife Joyes, and Katherine to Thomas Fitzrandolph.[51] The heralds recorded the marriage of Katherine to Fitzrandolph, and although the Assheby family do not appear in the visitations William was a Commissioner of the Peace for Leicestershire in 1531 and therefore of some stature.[52] Foljambe also had two legitimate daughters named Benet and Katherine, whose marriages took place a number of years before Sir Godfrey's death, the former marrying Sir John Dunham, the latter Thomas Nevile of Rolleston.[53]

Where there is surviving evidence for marriage portion provision, discrimination between legitimate and illegitimate daughters can again be detected throughout the period, although the distinctions between the base-born and other younger legitimate daughters is sometimes not as stark as might be expected. Anthony Browne, Master of the King's Horse, died in 1547 leaving four daughters. Mabel received 900 marks (£600), Lucy 800 marks (£533 6s 8d), Mary 400 marks (£266 13s 4d) but illegitimate daughter Anne the much lower sum of £100.[54] A brief survey of wills which include monetary bequests to illegitimate daughters among the gentry and nobility indicate cash sums of between £2 and £666 13s 4d, which could pay marriage portions, either in whole or part.[55] The most generous father, Richard Shirburn, provided his illegitimate daughter Margaret with 1000 marks (£666 13s 4d) in his will dated 1627. However, this amount is one-third of the £2000 he bequeathed to his legitimate daughter Katherine, to be paid via her husband William Pennington.[56] Erickson has delineated the amount of marriage portion according to social status, indicating that amounts of £5000 and more were paid by aristocratic fathers, £1000–£5000 by the gentry, £500–£1000 by the county gentry and £100–£500 by wealthier yeomen and tradesmen.[57] If we accept the sums of money mentioned in the wills as the total portion available to the illegitimate girls, Margaret Shirburn just fits into Erickson's 'county gentry' bracket, while her half-sister Katherine is firmly within the 'gentry'. Yet Margaret's portion is comparatively high, even compared with that of the illegitimate daughter of the aristocrat Lord Monteagle, Anne, who received £20 in 1558. This was 7.5% of the money granted to her legitimate half-sisters Elizabeth, Margaret and Anne, all of whom married outside the peerage and who each received £266 13s 4d. The only testator who did not discriminate directly between illegitimate and legitimate daughters was Richard Rawsthorne, who left £20 each to Agnes and Anne in 1592.[58] Another, Thomas Radclyffe, discriminated between his two illegitimate daughters Neoles who received 100 marks (£66 13s 4d) and Alice (£10); yet the former received the same amount of money as Radclyffe's legitimate unmarried daughter Katherine and the latter the same as the other four married legitimate daughters.[59] Interestingly, this is more than the five marks (£3 6s 8d) he bequeathed to John Radclyffe 'my bastard son', who received the same as 'Margaret Singleton, my servant'. Parity with other family members may be discerned; John Legh bequeathed £80 each to his illegitimate daughter Margaret and his mother, although his other (illegitimate) daughter Ellene received £100.[60] It was rare for illegitimate girls to receive £100 or more, with only five out of thirty-two fathers providing such a large sum. John Legh and his brother Thomas seem to have been generous in this respect, seemingly fathering a large number of illegitimate children but no legitimate ones. Thomas Legh left his three 'reputed' daughters £300 each in 1597; the others were Richard Wilbraham, who had already paid £40 part-payment of his daughter's portion when he left £60 in his will (dated 1558) to pay the balance, a total of £100; Alexander Houghton

£133 6s 8d in 1581; and Richard Shirburn £666 13s 4d for Margaret in 1627. Only Richard Shirburn had a legitimate daughter to provide for in addition to his illegitimate daughter, and it may be concluded that fathers without other financial commitments were willing and able to be more generous to their illegitimate daughters.[61]

In many cases, however, there was a large disparity between the amounts provided in wills for illegitimate girls and their legitimate half-sisters, with the former mainly receiving between 10 and 20 per cent of the total enjoyed by the latter. By Erickson's standard, the most generous provision for illegitimate girls in the wills was only just enough to make a marriage into the gentry, and, from the evidence of the marriages of the earls' daughters, even the Stanley and Clifford girls could expect to marry into the gentry as both Cuthbert Halsall and John Salusbury were only knighted after their marriages. A comparison between the earls' daughters reveals different social patterning as even within the gentry there were social distinctions; the Clifford sisters (illegitimate daughters of the second earl of Cumberland) and Elizabeth Stanley both married men who did not enter pedigrees in the visitation records whereas Ursula and Dorothy Stanley did. There are similarities, however: all five were based in the north of England and, as demonstrated, remained in the service of their legitimate half-siblings, suggesting closeness between the families.

This, then, posits the questions of whether the fortunes of these gentlemen were elevated (at least in part) by their marriage to an illegitimate daughter of the nobility and how free a choice the daughters had in choosing a husband. Certainly, for those marrying the daughters of the wealthiest aristocrats, social advancement and patronage were possible and appointments to stewardships and offices in the gift of the Clifford or Stanley families within reach. Illegitimate relatives populate the records of aristocratic families and were an important part of the noble and gentry landscape. The record books of the fourth earl of Derby record the visits of his illegitimate daughter Dorothy alongside those of her half-brother the future fifth earl and his family, for example.[62] As well as illegitimate daughters marrying their fathers' household officers, illegitimate sons were entrusted with the running of estates, with Anthony and Thomas, the illegitimate sons of the tenth Lord Clifford (d. 1523), both serving as Master Foresters of Craven, and Anthony also becoming steward of Cowling, Grassington, and Sutton.[63] Although writing about a later period, D. R. Hainsworth has argued that the position of steward required 'substance, education and experience drawn from the ranks of gentlemen'. Anthony and Thomas Clifford were responsible for managing extensive estates of some complexity, while also representing the (often absent) landowner.[64] Sir William Plumpton's bastard son Robert, familiarly known as 'Robinet', was his lawyer and man of business and dealt with everything from land purchases and family marriages to cloth buying. He also enjoyed a similarly positive business-like relationship with his brother Sir Robert (d. 1523).[65] Again, as in the case of illegitimate daughters marrying endogomously, situating base-born sons within the traditional family landholdings interlocked the interests of the legitimate line with that of the illegitimate and reinforced their county presence.

For illegitimate sons, a career in the church was considered acceptable by aristocratic parents, with some becoming remarkably successful. Edward, Lord Monteagle's illegitimate son Thomas was referred to in his father's will as the 'person of Baddisworth [Badsworth, Yorkshire]', the patronage of which was held by his kinsman the earl of Derby, and, earlier in his career, Thomas benefitted from the second earl of Derby holding the advowson of Winwick.[66] Arguably, his entire career owed much to his Stanley connections, as his most senior position, Bishop of Sodor and Man, was grounded firmly in Stanley territory.[67] The Savage family produced two generations of base-born churchmen, with Sir John Savage (d. 1492) fathering George, who in turn fathered a number of base sons (possibly including Edmund Bonner, the Marian bishop of London) and three daughters.[68] Christopher Haigh has pointed to both the 'double defect' of being a base son of a base-born father, but also the 'considerable social advantages and in particular influential connections in the Church', which allowed George Savage's sons to attend Oxford University and progress to successful clerical careers.[69] Furthermore, the legitimate side of the Savage family also boasted a prominent cleric, as Thomas, brother of John (and therefore uncle of George) became archbishop of York in 1501. Bonner's alleged illegitimate birth proved to be ammunition to political enemies, however; 'Lemuke Avale' attacked the bishop in print, alleging that his illegitimacy prevented him from being a true bishop, and compared him unfavourably with Cuthbert Tunstall, whose parents may have married after their son's birth.[70] Despite Bonner falling from power after the accession of Elizabeth I the pseudonymous author only felt able to attack the bishop's origins after his death in 1569, suggesting that it was impolitic to do so during his lifetime.

A career in the church was only available to women through convents and nunneries prior to the Reformation, and Barbara Harris has concluded 'very few aristocratic women entered convents'.[71] Claire Cross's findings are similar, concluding that the extension of kinship and 'client networks' through the marriages of daughters, supported by the economic structure of portion and jointure, were more desirable than consigning women to a convent.[72] Although neither Cross nor Harris refer to illegitimate women in particular, their conclusions may be applied to the evidence found in wills, as the pre-Reformation wills in the survey do not contain references to religious careers for illegitimate women being specified by their fathers.[73] While religious foundations may not have been a common path for noble or gentle women, the houses did often have aristocratic or gentry residents and, at the very least, had to retain or attract wealthy patronage. Illegitimate daughters were certainly not precluded from a religious life, as demonstrated by the prominent example of Cardinal Wolsey's daughter Dorothy Clansey, residing at Shaftesbury Abbey until its suppression in 1539.[74]

The extent of consensual inclusion and integration of bastard offspring in elite society should not be over-played, of course. For some of the more opportunistic members of society, the presence of a bastard could be used as a method of appropriating land to support their own families, with disruptive results. When William Singleton died in 1557, under the terms of his will he left his house, a mill and lands called 'Gamryddynge' to his wife Mary with remainder to his bastard son Robert.[75] Another relative, Anne Pilkington, had been seised of various lands and had an interest in 'Gamryddynge' until her death (sometime between 1557 and 1560), when they reverted to William's uncles Henry and

John Singleton. Sir John Southworth then seized the initiative, occupied Singleton property including Brockhole Hall, gained custody of Robert (and his goods), acquired Mary Singleton's interest for the use of Robert in 1559 and presumably arranged the later marriage of his daughter Anne to Robert. John Singleton launched a suit against Southworth in 1560 in the Duchy of Lancaster court, arguing that he had the reversion and remainder of the relevant properties as the heir of his elder brothers William and Henry. Southworth argued that the properties were devised by the will of William Singleton to Robert Singleton for life, and then to William's 'right heirs'. Decades later, Robert Singleton was established as a landholding member of gentry society as he is listed as a legitimate descendant of his father in the 1613 visitation of Lancashire.[76]

There is also the unavoidable fact that the complexity engendered by questionable and questioned legitimacy created the scope for disputes. In the 1530s, the active servant of the Talbot earls of Shrewsbury, Thomas Fitzwilliam alias Thomas Wortley, claimed to be the legitimate heir of his father, Sir Thomas Wortley, only to be opposed in a claim that affected a string of manors across South Yorkshire including Hemsworth, Wortley and Newhall by his sister Isabel Talbot, she asserting that he was 'engendered begottene and borne out of lawfull matrymonye'.[77]

Still, that base-born children were accommodated at the damaging expense of the legitimate family, creating subsequent financial problems and waste has been assumed by some historians and treated as profligacy – and the extent of this can be challenged. In his study of the Stanley family for example, Coward claims:

> Unfortunately, the Stanley estate had to pay for Henry's extra-marital happiness because when he became Earl of Derby, Henry decided to make provision for his illegitimate children. The eldest son Henry … received an estate in Ormskirk by virtue of a trust made in May 1582, and later lands in Broughton near Manchester were added to his estate.[78]

While Henry Stanley was the ultimate beneficiary of the trust made in 1582 (and his full brother Thomas was provided with estates in Childwall and Kirkby with the same conditions), he had to wait until the death of both his mother and father before he could take full control of his inheritance.[79] Henry also confirmed an annual payment of £100 per year, for seven years after his death, to his illegitimate daughter Dorothy. Yet it would be unfair to lay the blame for the Stanley's financial burden in later years to providing for the two families of Earl Henry. During his lifetime, Margaret Clifford, countess of Derby accrued large debts, and in his will he showed he could be generous: he bequeathed Gilbert Talbot, earl of Shrewsbury £100, and there were many smaller life-long annuities of £5–£10 per annum for servants over and above any bequests they had received under Earl Edward's will in 1572. The early death of the fifth earl, Ferdinando, leaving three daughters resulted in decades-long lawsuits, which proved expensive for William, the sixth earl. It could, therefore, be posited that any financial problems encountered by later earls of Derby were rooted in Henry Stanley's need to maintain an expensive lifestyle, Countess Margaret's debts and the legal expenses incurred in the wake of Earl Ferdinando's death rather than the acquisition of estates which benefitted Earl Henry for over a decade.[80]

For those who were expected to make their own way in the world, bequests could enable them to establish themselves in business or other professional career. In 1512, when he drafted his will, Sir Edward Howard expected at least one of his sons to embark upon a mercantile career, although he did take the precaution of ensuring some influential help:

> Whereas I have two bastards, I give the King's Grace the choice of them ... and him that the King's Grace chuseth I bequeath him my bark called 'Gennet' with all apparel and artillery and L li to begin his stock with; the other I bequeath to my special and trusty friend Charles Brandon, praying him to be a good master unto him and for because he hath no ship, I bequeath him C marks to set him forth in the world.[81]

Sir Ralph Bigod did not specify whether Arthur and John were his bastard sons when he made his will in 1515, but stipulated Arthur should be 'put and bondyne prentesse at a crafte in London and then to have v li to make him a stoke of and the encrease to remayn to his awne use' while John received the same education, but the sum of £3 6s 8d to start his business with.[82] Apprenticeships and mercantile activities were comparatively rare; where money was provided for schooling, many adopted the same approach as Lord Willoughby de Broke, who was less specific when he bequeathed his two sons £60 13s 4d 'for their promotion and living', to be given to them at the age of twenty-four. Their sister Margaret, on the other hand was granted the slightly larger individual sum of £66 13s 4d when she was eighteen.[83]

For some base-born landholders, some settlements were generous at first sight but came with encumbrances. Robert Duckinfield's legitimate children received annuities of either six or ten marks and 100 marks or £100 cash for the daughters' marriages, but his illegitimate son Robert received tenements and lands in Duckinfield and Stockport, worth just over £3 per year, out of which he had to pay his paternal grandmother an annuity of £1 13s. This sum of money did not revert to Robert after her death, as it then had to be paid to his father's 'heirs and assignees.'[84]

Acceptance within the family and society at large can be ascertained from will evidence, with, for example, Thomas Egerton benefitting from a bequest of £5 in the will of a distant cousin, Philip Egerton, and embarking upon a successful legal career.[85] Cuthbert Halsall seems to have been at the centre of a tight-knit nexus of well-born, illegitimate figures who collaborated over property transactions and intermarried over the course of generations. Cuthbert Halsall's great-grandmother Jane Stanley may have been descended from the illegitimate son of Sir John Stanley, brother of the first earl of Derby. The mistress of Henry Stanley, 4th earl of Derby was Joan Halsall, presumably a member of the extensive gentry family. Her children by Stanley also carried the name Halsall and are referred to as such in legal documents, with her eldest daughter Dorothy marrying Cuthbert Halsall; the couple often visited her father's household at Lathom or Knowsley, in Lancashire.[86] The trustees of a settlement made by Earl Henry in 1581 for the benefit of his illegitimate son Thomas are interesting as they include Sir Richard Sherbourne and Alexander Rigby, close associates of the earl, as well as Edward and Silvester Halsall (base sons of Henry Halsall). Cuthbert Halsall also acted with his brother-in-law in 1596, when Thomas Stanley alias Halsall alienated the manor of Kirkby to Sir Richard Molyneux. Beyond the familial intimacy, the public career of Cuthbert Halsall suggests wider community acceptance and respectability, as he was knighted in 1599, returned MP for Lancashire in 1614 and became mayor of Liverpool a year later.[87]

The same can be said to be true of collateral lines of bastard-bearing, where a number of base-born offspring were born to siblings and accepted into the ranks of the wider family. The will of Thomas Forster provides details of extensive bastardy by himself and two of his brothers.[88] Thomas fathered four illegitimate sons George, John, Hugh and Ralph and possibly a daughter; his younger brothers Sir John and Rowland were responsible for at least three spurious sons and two daughters and two sons respectively. In addition, Thomas's legitimate son, also named Thomas, was the father of an illegitimate son, Matthew, demonstrating cross generational as well as collateral bastardy.

The propensity of certain prominent families to bastardy has important implications for such offspring to maintain social prominence and noble, knightly or gentry status for the family (rather than individuals) over the course of several generations. As seen above, after several generations of numerous illegitimate Halsalls, the final male descendant Sir Cuthbert was able to hold high office within Lancashire, ally himself to the leading magnate in the county and be a regular visitor to Derby's household.[89] The Forsters were also able to maintain their endogamous influence through a base-born line, with Sir John's eldest base son Nicholas acting as High Sheriff of Northumberland in 1602 and his son Sir Claudius created a Baronet by James I.[90] The maintenance or even advance of family fortunes through illegitimacy could also occur in smaller families. A similar situation of social and political success for an illegitimate line of descent is traceable in the descendants of Sir Henry Savile (1499–1558). His legitimate son Edward died without any surviving children and his entailed estates passed to more distant kinsman by settlement dated 1559, yet the suppression of Kirkstall Abbey enabled Savile to acquire former monastic lands for his illegitimate son Robert. Robert Savile served as sheriff of Lincolnshire, was knighted in 1583 and purchased further lands in Yorkshire – and, as already noted, his son John was promoted to the Baronage, and his grandson Thomas to the earldom of Sussex, both being influential, national political figures, expanding the Savile family fortunes well beyond Yorkshire.[91]

While illegitimacy and illicit behaviour were condemned by contemporary observers, therefore, for some prominent gentry families, bastard branches (whether extensive or not) could extend influence, wealth and prestige for the family name. The evidence of the north of England suggests extensive acknowledgement of illegitimate offspring, allowing for their support through a variety of formal and informal means. This even included female offspring being supported to marry and establish themselves within a gentle milieu. This was part of the warp and weft of northern gentry society, and its added richness and potential complexity needs to be taken into account when describing the working of county political networks. The assumptions about male authority, honour and masculinity which underlay these networks and the place of bastard children in them also need to be reconsidered. It is therefore more understandable that some individuals of illegitimate birth were able to pursue prominent careers, in cases like Thomas Egerton even achieving the highest office and entering the peerage, and that alongside these men were many others who formed an important part of the society and politics of the elite in the north before the Civil War.

Notes

1. Scott Smith-Bannister, *Names and Naming Patterns in England, 1538–1700* (Oxford: Clarendon Press, 1997), esp. pp. 119–31 for consideration of the nobility.
2. Cheshire Arch., Brooke Family of Norton MSS, DBN/B/1/2; Derby, Derbyshire RO D187/2/18. See also John Legh's children Ellen Legh alias Ogden and Margaret Legh alias Downes, the latter the daughter of Ellen Stanley alias Baggiley, wife of Robert Stanley: *Lancashire and Cheshire Wills and Inventories from the Ecclesiastical Court, Chester*, ed. G. J. Piccope, Chetham Society, XXXIII, LI, LIV (1857–61), ii. 241–3.
3. *TE* iv. 43–5.
4. *Lancashire and Cheshire Wills and Inventories from the Ecclesiastical Court, Chester*, ii. 188–9.
5. TNA, C 1/590/56–8; J. H. Baker, 'Fitzherbert, Sir Anthony (*c*.1470–1538), *judge and legal writer*', *ODNB*, xix. 873–4; F. Boersma, 'Sir Antony Fitzherbert: A Biographical Sketch and Short Bibliography', *Law Library Journal*, 71 (1978), 387–400.
6. *TE* v. 283–7.
7. TNA, C 146/738.
8. *Lancashire and Cheshire Wills and Inventories from the Ecclesiastical Court, Chester*, i. 85–9.
9. *Ibid.*, i. 162–4; ii. 157–62.
10. *Wills and Inventories from the Archdeaconry of Richmond*, pp. 116–19; *Wills and Inventories from the Registry at Durham*, ii. 164–6.
11. *Lancashire and Cheshire Wills and Inventories from the Ecclesiastical Court, Chester*, i. 22–9; *Wills and Inventories from the Registry at Durham*, iii. pp. 160–1; *Lancashire and Cheshire Wills and Inventories at Chester*, 126–30; *Wills and Inventories from the Registry at Durham*, ii. pp. 164–5.
12. *TE*, vi. 166–8.
13. *Wills and Inventories Illustrative of the History, Manners, Language, Statistics etc of the Northern Counties of England from the Eleventh-Century Downwards, Part One*, ed. J. Raine, Surtees Society, II (1835), pp. 119–21, 306–7.
14. *TE* iii. 251; *Lancashire and Cheshire Wills from the Ecclesiastical Court at Chester*, iii. 54–7. For wives' involvement, see above, pp. 103–4.
15. Cheshire Arch., DVE/1/K III/15; /E II/16.
16. Cheshire Arch., DVE/1/M VI/16; /M VI/23.
17. *Lancashire and Cheshire Wills and Inventories 1572 to 1696 Now Preserved at Chester, With an Appendix of Lancashire and Cheshire Wills and Inventories Proved at York and Richmond 1542 to 1649*, ed. J. P. Earwaker, Chetham Society, New Series, 28 (Manchester, 1893), pp. 133–6.
18. *TE* iii. 238.
19. Nicholas Harris Nicolas, *Testamenta Vetusta: Being Illustrations from Wills of Manners, Customs etc as well of the Descents and Possessions of Many Distinguished Families. From the Reign of Henry the Second to the Accession of Queen Elizabeth* (2 vols. London: Nichols and Son, 1826), ii. 411–14; *CP*, vi. 130–3. There was some dispute over the implications of these dispositions: TNA, C 1/203/37, /39–41.

20 Nicolas, *Testamenta Vetusta*, ii. 723–4.
21 S. T. Bindoff, *The House of Commons, 1509–1558* (3 vols. London: Secker & Warburg for the History of Parliament Trust, 1982), ii. 339.
22 *Lancashire and Cheshire Wills and Inventories from the Ecclesiastical Court, Chester*, ed. Piccope, iii. 16–21.
23 TNA, C 1/1501/77; Sir Hugh tells us that there was a rumour that Roger himself was not the son of Sir Richard: *The Memoirs and Memorials of Sir Hugh Cholmley of Whitby, 1600–1657*, ed. Jack Binns, YASRS, 153 (2000), p. 65.
24 *CP*, xi. 551; Mervyn James, rev., 'Scrope, Emanuel, earl of Sunderland (1584–1630), *nobleman*', *ODNB*, xlix. 549.
25 *Calendar of State Papers Domestic: Charles II, 1663–4*, ed. Mary Anne Everett Green (London: Longman, 1862), p. 61. Arabella Scrope argued that her parents had undertaken a 'private marriage', although circumstantial evidence suggests otherwise. Scrope married Elizabeth Manners in 1609; the four children were born to Martha Jeanes during the mid-to-late 1620s, the youngest in 1629 shortly before his death. Elizabeth Manners survived until 1653, so the illicit relationship took place within her lifetime and given the regular childbearing of Martha Jeanes it seems unlikely that a sexual relationship between Jeanes and Scrope began before his marriage in 1609.
26 Simon Adams, 'Dudley, Sir Robert (1574–1649)', *ODNB*, xvii. 112–18.
27 *CP*, x. 405; Narasingha P. Sil, *William Lord Herbert of Pembroke (c. 1507–1570): Politique and Patriot* (Lewiston NY, Queenston ON: Edwin Mellen Press, 1988).
28 Beverley A. Murphy, *Bastard Prince: Henry VIII's Lost Son* (Stroud: Sutton, 2001). Arthur's title of Viscount Lisle (1523) had descended through his first wife's family, the Greys. *CP* v. 117; Chris Given-Wilson and Alice Curteis, *The Royal Bastards of Medieval England* (London: Routledge & Kegan Paul, 1984), pp. 162–73; Michael Hicks, 'The Royal Bastards of Medieval England', in Éric Bousmar, Alain Marchandisse, Christophe Masson and Bertrand Schnerb (eds), *La bâtardise et l'exercice du pouvoir en Europe du XIIIe au début du XVIe siècle* (Villeneuve-d'Ascq: Revue du Nord, 2015), pp. 369–86; Bertrand Schnerb, 'Des bâtards nobles au service du prince: l'example de la cour de Bourgogne (fin xive-début xve siècle)', *ibid.*, pp. 91–111; Laurent Hablot 'L'emblématique des bâtards princiers au xve siècle. Outil d'un nouveau pouvoir? *ibid.*, pp. 439–50; Bertrand Schnerb, 'Introduction bâtards et pouvoir: un theme de recherche', *ibid.*, pp. 7–10.
29 *Ibid.*, p. 174.
30 Egerton: *CP*, ii. 271–2; J. H. Baker, 'Egerton, Thomas, first Viscount Brackley (1540–1617), *lord chancellor*', *ODNB*, xvii. 1007–11. *CP* x. 668–9. Edward's brother Adrian, also illegitimate, was knighted by Elizabeth I. David Grummitt, 'Poynings, Thomas, first Baron Poynings (1512?–1545), *soldier and courtier*', *ODNB*, xlv. 183–4; Helen Miller, *Henry VIII and the English Nobility* (Oxford: Basil Blackwell, 1986), pp. 34–5, 184; M. A. Stevens, 'Poynings, Sir Adrian (1512?–1571), *soldier*', *ODNB*, xlv. 179.
31 *CP* ix. 549. He had already been granted the Irish title Baron Mountjoy in 1617. David L. Smith, 'Blount, Mountjoy, first earl of Newport (c.1597–1666), *courtier and politician*', *ODNB*, vi. 305–8.
32 *CP* viii. 200; Jonathan Hughes, 'Somerset [*formerly* Beaufort], Charles, first earl of Worcester (c. 1460–1526), *courtier and magnate*', *ODNB*, li. 572–3; Miller, *Henry VIII and the English Nobility*, pp. 15–17, 81–3, 86, 103, 107–10; W. R. B. Robinson, 'Early Tudor Policy Towards

Wales: The Acquisition of Lands and Offices in Wales by Charles Somerset, Earl of Worcester', *Bulletin of the Board of Celtic Studies*, 20 (1964), 422–7 and appendix.

33   Joan Kirby, 'Savile family (*per.* c. 1480–1644), *gentry*', *ODNB*, xlix. 96–8; Joan Kirby, 'Savile, John, first Baron Savile of Pontefract (1556–1630), *politician*', *ODNB*, xlix. 122–3; J. T. Cliffe, *The Yorkshire Gentry from the Reformation to the Civil War* (London: Athlone Press, 1969), p. 106; 'Papers Relating to the Delinquency of Lord Savile, 1642–1646', ed. James J. Cartwright, in *Camden Miscellany*, VIII, Camden Society, n.s., 31 (1879–83), p. 15; *The Diary of Sir Henry Slingsby of Scriven, Bart., Now First Published Entire from the Ms.: A Reprint of Sir Henry Slingsby's Trial, His Rare Tract, 'A Father's Legacy' Written in the Tower Immediately before his Death; and Extracts from Family Correspondence and Papers, with Notices, and a Genealogical Memoir*, ed. Daniel Parsons (London: Longman, Rees, Orme, Brown, Green, and Longman; J. Vincent, Oxford; Todd, York; and Wilson, Knaresborough 1836), p. 52.

34   *CP* i. 400–1 (Banbury); xii/2. 218–26 (Vaux); Harris Nicolas, *A Treatise of the Law on Adulterine Bastardy, with a Report of the Banbury Case, and of all Other Cases Bearing Upon the Subject* (London: W. Pickering, 1836), pp. 289–551. The legitimacy of Elizabeth Howard's sons, and therefore their right to succeed to the earldom, continued to be a vexed question. The matter came to court in the early 1640s after the death of Edward Knollys, in the 1660s during the political reorganisation of the Restoration, in the 1690s after Nicholas Knollys' son Charles was imprisoned for the death of Captain Philip Lawson, and in 1806–13, when Thomas Woods asked for a writ of summons to the House of Lords as the Earl of Banbury. The alienation of the Vaux estates appears not to have been contested by Henry Vaux.

35   Nicolas, *Adulterine Bastardy*, pp. 90–117. Thomas de Longueville, *The Curious Case of Lady Purbeck: A Scandal of the XVIIth Century* (London: Longmans, Green and Co., 1909).

36   Julian Lock, 'Grey, Arthur, fourteenth Baron Grey of Wilton (1536–1593), *lord deputy of Ireland and soldier*', *ODNB*, xxiii. 805–9.

37   *CP*, xi. 551; James, rev., 'Scrope, Emanuel'; see above, pp. 25, 119.

38   *VCH Lancs.*, iii. 267.

39   LRO, DDSC/19/8. Gilbert Scarisbrick was nominated for a knighthood shortly before his death.

40   *LP* iii. 497 (grant of wardship); C. S. L. Davies, 'Stafford, Edward, third duke of Buckingham (1478–1521)', *ODNB*, lii. 41–3, at p. 43, suggests that the Stafford-Fitzgerald marriage took place, whilst Carole Rawcliffe argues that it did not; *The Staffords: Earls of Stafford and Dukes of Buckingham, 1394–1521* (Cambridge: Cambridge University Press, 1978), p. 137. Lambeth, Lambeth Palace Library, Carew Manuscripts, MS 616, p. 46, does not mention Margaret in connection with the dispute over Sir Thomas's inheritance. However, in Stratford-upon-Avon, Shakespeare Centre Library (Shakespeare Birthplace Trust), Ferrers of Baddesley Clinton MSS, DR 3/306, is a bond of Dame Margaret Fitzgerald, widow of Sir Thomas Fitzgerald, for £100, dated 1534, possibly referring to Margaret Stafford.

41   Joel Hurstfield, *The Queen's Wards: Wardship and Marriage Under Elizabeth I* (London: Longmans, Green, 1958), p. 121.

42   Other disparagements included idiocy, deformity, marriage of an heir to a woman beyond childbearing years and, ironically given Thomas Fitzgerald's status, marriage to the child of an attainted traitor. Edward Coke, *The First Part of the Institutes of the Laws of England; or a Commentary Upon Littleton, Not the Name of the Author Only, but of the Law Itself*, ed. Francis Hargrave and Charles Butler, Vol. 1 (first American edn; 2 vols. Philadelphia: Robert H. Small, 1853), i. section 107.

43 John Williams, *Ancient and Modern Denbigh: A Descriptive History of the Castle, Borough and Liberties* (Denbigh: J. Williams, 1856), p. 167; P. W. Hasler, *The House of Commons, 1559–1603* (3 vols. London: HMSO for the History of Parliament Trust, 1981), iii. 336–7; Robert Chester, *Loues Martyr: Or, Rosalins Complaint: Allegorically Shadowing the Truth of Loue, in the Constant Fate of the Phoenix and Turtle. A Poeme Enterlaced with Much Varietie and Raritie; now First Translated out of the Venerable Italian Torquato Cæliano* (London: printed [by R. Field] for E. B[lount], 1601).
44 Note the presence of Elizabeth Stanley's grandson as a gentleman usher at the funeral of the third earl of Derby in 1572; he became the fourth earl's receiver general: *The Derby Household Books; Comprising an Account of the Household Regulations and Expenses of Edward and Henry Third and Fourth Earls of Derby Together with a Diary Containing the Names of the Guests who Visited the Latter Earl at his Houses in Lancashire*, ed. F. R. Raines, Chetham Society, XXXI (1853), p. 106.
45 R. T. Spence, *The Privateering Earl: George Clifford, 3rd Earl of Cumberland, 1558–1605* (Stroud: Alan Sutton, 1995), p. 16; Joseph Nicolson and Richard Burn, *The History and Antiquities of the Counties of Westmorland and Cumberland* (2 vols. London: printed for W. Strahan & T. Cadell, 1777), i. 399, suggests that Edward Birkbeck was granted Hornby Hall (near the Clifford seat at Brougham Castle) by the earl of Cumberland in 1553.
46 *North Country Wills, Being Abstracts of Wills Relating to the Counties of York, Nottingham, Northumberland, Cumberland and Westmorland at Somerset House and Lambeth Palace 1383 to 1550*, ed. J. W. Clay, Surtees Society, CXVI (1908), pp. 156–7 (Sir Ingram Percy), and *TE* vi. 166–8 (Katherine, countess of Northumberland). Isabel's position may have been complicated by her father and uncle's involvement in the Pilgrimage of Grace and by the sixth earl of Northumberland's decision to bequeath his property to the king rather than his family.
47 Thomas Dunham Whitaker, *The History and Antiquities of the Deanery of Craven, in the County of York* (London: printed by Nichols and Son; and sold by T. Payne … J. White … Hatchard … and Edwards …, 1805), p. 82; Joseph Foster, *Pedigrees of the County Families of Yorkshire* (3 vols. London: printed and published for the compiler by W. Wilfred Head, 1874), ii. 204.
48 For Stephen Tempest's will, see *TE* vi. 284–5; for the employment of grandfather and grandson in the household of the Cliffords, see R. T. Spence, *The Shepherd Lord of Skipton Castle, Henry Clifford, 10th Lord Clifford 1454–1523* (Skipton: Skipton Castle, 1994) p. 50; R. T. Spence, *Privateering Earl*, pp. 150, 187, 198.
49 Sarah L. Bastow, 'An Abortive Attempt to Defend an Episcopal Reputation: The Case of Archbishop Edwin Sandys and the Innkeeper's Wife', *History*, 97 (2012), 380–401.
50 Maureen M. Meikle, 'A Godly Rogue: The Career of Sir John Forster, an Elizabethan Border Warden', *Northern History*, 28 (1992), 126–63, at p. 135.
51 *North Country Wills*, pp. 175–8 (reference to Benet and Katherine as begotten of Joane Mansfield). *Dugdale's Visitation of Yorkshire: With Additions*, ed. J. W. Clay (3 vols. Exeter: W. Pollard & Co., 1899–1917), p. 187. Foljambe married Katherine Leake, who died in 1529, but did not appear to marry Mansfield. Neither Mansfield nor her two daughters by Foljambe appear in the visitations.
52 *LP* v. 166(10).
53 Benedicta or Benet was the name of Sir Godfrey's mother as well as his sister; there was, therefore, a family tradition of using this name. The marriage settlement negotiated between Sir Godfrey and Sir John Dunham is in Nottinghamshire Archives, Foljambe of Osberton MSS, DD/FJ/4/9/1.

54 West Sussex Record Office, SAS-BA/19. Interestingly there is similar discrimination between Browne's six legitimate younger sons who each received life annuities of 40 marks (£26 13s 4d) and his illegitimate son Charles, who received a £10 life annuity.

55 'Katine, filie mee bastard' was bequeathed xls (£2) by John Meoles in 1528: *Lancashire and Cheshire Wills and Inventories*, ed. Piccope, i. 8. Sir Piers Edgcomb bequeathed £1000 to his daughter Mary in 1530: Nicolas, *Testamenta Vetusta*, ii. 647–53. The wills are those used in the sample described at pp. 44–7 above, and from *Testamenta Vetusta*. It should be noted that this takes no account of the potentially significant less formal gifts during a father's lifetime, such as that of £10 in ready money, two goblets with covers of silver to value of £5 sterling, a salt of silver parcel gilt worth 30 shillings, a dozen silver spoons worth 40 shillings, and a mazer with a gilt band and a flower in the bottom, placed in trust for Isabel Wandell, daughter of Harry Staleham [Stateham?] by Joan, later? wife of Robert Hewicke of Nottingham: TNA, C 1/1010/44 (1538–44).

56 *Lancashire and Cheshire Wills and Inventories 1572 to 1696*, ed. Earwaker, pp. 199–200.

57 Amy Louise Erickson, *Women and Property in Early Modern England* (London: Routledge, 1993), pp. 86–8.

58 *Lancashire and Cheshire Wills and Inventories*, ed. Piccope, iii. 38–40.

59 *Lancashire and Cheshire Wills and Inventories*, ed. Piccope, ii. 163.

60 *Ibid.*, pp. 241–3.

61 For Houghton, see Henry Fishwick, *The History of Preston in Amounderness in the County of Lancaster* (Rochdale: J. Clegg, 1900), p. 261 (will). In *The Visitation of the County of the County Palatine of Lancaster, Made in the Year 1613 by Richard St. George Esq, Norroy King of Arms*, ed. F. R. Raines, Chetham Society, o.s., lxxxii (1871), p. 51, Alexander, 2nd son of Sir Richard Houghton is listed as *obit sine prole*. The bequest of 200 marks was revoked and Margaret's husband Roger Chrickelawe of Charnock does not appear in the above visitation.

62 *The Stanley Papers*, part II: *The Derby Household Books; Comprising an Account of the Household Regulations and Expenses of Edward and Henry, Third and Fourth Earls of Derby; Together with a Diary containing the Names of the Guests who Visited the latter Earl at his Houses in Lancashire, by William ffarington, Esquire, the Comptroller 1561–90*, ed. F. R. Raines, Chetham Society, o.s., xxxi (1853), pp. 35, 36, 57, 63, 72.

63 Spence, *Shepherd Lord*, pp. 41–2.

64 D. R. Hainsworth, *Stewards, Lords and People: The Estate Steward and his World in Later Stuart England* (Cambridge: Cambridge University Press, 1992), pp. 23–30.

65 *The Plumpton Letters and Papers*, ed. Joan Kirby, Camden Society, 5th ser., 8 (1996), letters 26, 150, 154, 173, 182.

66 http://db.theclergydatabase.org.uk/jsp/persons/index.jsp; A. B. Emden, *A Biographical Register of the University of Oxford, A.D. 1501–1540* (Oxford: Clarendon Press, 1974), pp. 535–6; LRO, Stanley, Earls of Derby Knowsley MSS, DDK/3/14.

67 J. R. Dickinson, *The Lordship of Man Under the Stanleys: Government and Economy in the Isle of Man, 1580–1704*, Chetham Society, 3rd ser., XLI (1996), p. 22.

68 *The Visitation of Cheshire in the Year 1580, Made by Robert Glover for William Flower with Numerous Additions and Continuations Including those from The Visitation of Cheshire made in the Year 1566; With an Appendix Containing The Visitation of a Part of Cheshire in the Year 1533 made by William Fellows for Thomas Benolte and a Fragment of The Visitation of the City of Chester in the Year 1591 made by Thomas Chaloner*, ed. J. P. Rylands, Harleian Society, XVIII (1882), p. 205.

69 C. A. Haigh, 'A Mid-Tudor Ecclesiastical Official: The Curious Career of George Wilmesley', *Transactions of the Historic Society of Lancashire and Cheshire*, 122 (1970), 1–24.
70 'Lemuke Avale', *A Commemoration or Dirige of Bastarde Edmonde Boner, alias Sauage, Vsurped Bisshoppe of London* ([London]: printed by P. O. [i.e. John Kingston], [1569]).
71 B. J. Harris, 'A New Look at the Reformation: Aristocratic Women and Nunneries, 1450–1540', *Journal of British Studies*, 32 (1993), 89–113.
72 Claire Cross, 'The Religious Life of Women in Sixteenth-Century Yorkshire', in William J. Sheils and Diane Wood (eds), *Women and the Church*, Studies in Church History, 27 (Oxford, 1990), pp. 307–24.
73 The only illegitimate girl with any kind of link to a religious house was Isabel Percy, who, along with her grandmother Katherine Countess of Northumberland, was a beneficiary of Katherine Nandyke's will in 1541. Nandyke was the final prioress of Wykeham, North Yorkshire, and a member of a Yorkshire gentry family. However, such an inclusion is not proof that Percy was destined for a religious foundation prior to the suppression. *TE* vi. 131–2.
74 A. F. Pollard, *Wolsey*, with an introduction by G. R. Elton (London: Collins, 1965), p. 307. For the suppression of Shaftesbury and Clansey's pension, see *LP* xiv/1. 586(2).
75 Fishwick, *History of Preston*, pp. 287–93. Sir John Southworth was also the supervisor of William Singleton's will. TNA DL 4/3/14.
76 *Visitation of the County Palatine of Lancaster Made in the Year 1613*, ed. Raines, p. 81. Fishwick cattily noted (*History of Preston*, p. 288) that Robert Singleton 'imposed himself upon Richard St George as son and heir, although in his father's will his illegitimacy is clearly stated.' This is reminiscent of Robert Holden's appearance in the same visitation (p. 18).
77 TNA, C 1/912/1–4.
78 Barry Coward, *The Stanleys, Lords Stanley and Earls of Derby 1385–1672: The Origins, Wealth and Power of a Landowning Family*, Chetham Society, 3rd ser., XXX (1983), pp. 31–2.
79 LRO, DDK/6/16a (Ormskirk); DDM/35/31 (Childwall and Kirkbie).
80 Coward, *Stanleys*; K. A. Walker, 'The Widowhood of Alice Spencer, Countess Dowager of Derby, 1594–1636', *Transactions of the Lancashire and Cheshire Historical Society*, 149 (2000), 1–18.
81 Nicolas, *Testamenta Vetusta*, pp. 533–4. Charles Brandon was created duke of Suffolk in 1514.
82 *TE* v. 55.
83 Nicolas, *Testamenta Vetusta*, p. 563.
84 *Lancashire and Cheshire Wills and Inventories*, ed. Piccope, ii. 24–8.
85 *Lancashire and Cheshire Wills and Inventories*, ed. Piccope, i. 144–8.
86 Coward, *Stanleys*, p. 32; *The Derby Household Books*, ed. F. R. Raines, pp. 35, 36, 57, 63, 72.
87 LRO, Molyneux, Earls of Sefton MSS, DDM/35/31 and DDM/35/32; *VCH Lancs.*, iii. 195.
88 *Wills and Inventories from the Registry at Durham*, ed. W. Greenwell, Surtees Society, XXXVIII (1860), ii. 302–4.
89 Although note his financial problems at the time of his death: TNA, PROB/11/161.
90 James Raine, *History and Antiquities of North Durham* (London: J. B. Nichols and Son, 1852), p. 306.
91 J. W. Clay, 'The Savile family', *Yorkshire Archaeological Journal*, 25 (1918–20), 1–47; see above, pp. 64–5, 109–10.

Conclusion

Probably the most prominent, bitterly fought and prolonged of all the disputes arising from mistress-keeping and bastardy upon which we have touched is that affecting Lady Ursula Stanley and her husband Sir Rowland. We have seen how it involved allegations of adultery on the part of both Lady Ursula and Sir Rowland, threats against her and her ejection from house and home, and challenges to the proper management of the household. Following the case through to its endings will help to draw out some of the overall conclusions to the evidence presented here.

After ten years, in the early 1570s, in spite of Sir Rowland giving bonds to his brother-in-law Sir Lawrence Smith for his conduct, the Stanley marriage was still in trouble; and it was again to interact with the politics and social life of Cheshire. In October, York High Commission proceeded against both husband and wife for their failure to cohabit. Sir Rowland indicated he was 'for his parte willinge to take his said wief', provided his bonds were brought in and cancelled; but Lady Ursula would not come in to court, and it seems that her brother was influential in shielding her from the censure of the court. Sir Lawrence Smith was summoned by special messenger to appear, bringing with him Lady Ursula and the bonds. As seen, it was soon recognised that action in York was unlikely to bring success, and from early 1572 there were attempts to transfer the case to Chester, attempts that continued into 1573.[1] Subsequently, in the summer of 1573, Lady Ursula sued Sir Rowland for a separation once again, this time in the court in Chester[2] and later in the same year Robert Fletcher wrote to the Archbishop Edmund Grindal, critical of Sir Rowland's choice of clergyman in the parish of Bebington (the advowson of which Stanley had purchased in 1571).[3] Fletcher and Sir Rowland had once been allies: in his suit in Star Chamber, Lady Ursula's alleged lover Richard Hurleston had reported that Sir Rowland connived to protect Fletcher when he was on trial for murder, ensuring the widow of the victim stayed silent. Hurleston reported that as a result 'the said Fletcher was … of the said death and murder of Hampton acquitted.'[4] Fletcher seems to have been something of a self-made man, originally from Ince, several miles from Hooton; he does not feature in the visitation records on his own account, but as the husband of Maud Poole, widow of Sir Thomas Grosvenor.[5] Fletcher was a defendant in a series of suits with the Cotton family and Sir Hugh Cholmondeley over the manor of Ince between 1558 and 1579; he had an interest in the manor of Bromborough along with Sir Rowland; and an entry in the pardon roll for 1559 places him in Sutton, virtually next door to Stanley's manor of Hooton.[6] However, by 1573, Fletcher found it both possible and politic to oppose Sir Rowland over the latter's nomination of one Myrrick to the advowson of Bebington and was willing to enlist some powerful help to do so. Sir Rowland's conduct in relation to his wife is given prominence in Fletcher's challenge. He wrote on 19 October 1573 to Grindal, mentioning 'Sir Rowlands behavior towchinge his vnorderlye vsinge before your grace for his wief and that also even now the Sute he maynteyneth against your Grace your cowrt and Mr Gylpyne which shalbe executed with extremyty by Chesshyer practises, yf so he be not prevented.'[7] Fletcher also mentioned Sir Rowland's 'prowd doinges and corrupt Religioon', hinting at Catholicism for the first time, and his attempts to obtain the shrievalty of Cheshire. Grindal then forwarded Fletcher's letter to Lord Burghley, also commenting upon his legal battles with Sir Rowland, who had sued the Archbishop using a writ of *quare impedit* at Chester when the latter favoured Luke Gilpin, the choice of competing claimants to the advowson, for Bebington, and strongly urging Burghley not to allow him to become sheriff.[8] Gilpin was a product of Trinity College Cambridge and had previously received preferment at Chesterton, a college living. His association with some of the most prominent protestant radicals is evident from the fact that he had penned verses prefixed to John Barthlet's *Pedegrewe of Heretiques* in 1566: Barthlet was a prominent envoy to the reformed communities in Switzerland, with George Withers, the following year. Gilpin himself was to be proctor at the University in 1574–75.[9] By contrast to this well connected protestant radical, Sir Rowland's candidate Myrrick, described by Grindal as an 'unlearned' doctor of laws who had lived long 'in concubinatu', is likely to be Rowland Meyrick, since 1559 bishop of Bangor, who had graduated DCL in 1537–8 and was notably condemned by Robert Ferrar for his indulgence of 'shameles whordome', or his brother Edmund, who was already chancellor of St Asaph and canon of Lichfield from 1558, and archdeacon of Bangor the following year, and also DCL (since 1567),[10] illustrating Sir Rowland's tendency to alienate mainstream opinion by associating with Welshmen[11] and with religious conservatives. Grindal also referred to Sir Rowland's failure to show respect to the Lord President of the Council in the North, Henry Hastings, earl of Huntingdon: 'for thatt now latelye he hath contemned diverse and sundrye processes, procedinge from my L. president and me, by vertue of the Ecclesiastical Commission: off which contempts we have determined aboute the ende off this terme to certiffie the whole board of the Cownsell, and to praye assistence. The sayd Sir Rowland wolde not vouchesafe to salute my L. President, att his late beyng in Chesshyre to take his vale off my L. off Essex: burdened (by lyke) with a gyltie Conscience.'[12] This was the departure, in the summer of 1573, of the undertaking by Walter Devereux to colonise Ulster which was widely supported, not least with a loan of £10,000 from the queen herself.[13] This was, in political and religious terms, a very sensitive time to make a protest against the Lord President and by implication against what was becoming a Protestant crusade in Ireland (and one Sir Lawrence Smith was directly involved in enabling).[14] Grindal successfully drew on the support of the Privy Council, which wrote on 21 December 1573 instructing the sheriff of Cheshire to visit Stanley and inform him 'how moche their Lordships mislike' his conduct, and threatening to take him into custody to be produced before the Council if he would not comply.[15]

Sir Rowland's failure to acknowledge the Lord President, coupled with his litigation with the archbishop, in which his marital problems seem to have interacted with the row over Bebington, may have contributed to the question-mark over his religion. By April 1574, the patience of Grindal and Hastings had been completely eroded: in a striking display of their joint indignation, York High Commission, unusually sitting with both present, committed Sir Rowland to York Castle, in spite of his efforts to claim privileges associated with the palatinate of Chester, the 'Chesshyer practises' of which Grindal had complained the year before.[16]

That sitting in York could be seen as epitomising the high point of the various challenges to elite sexual practices which various historians have seen running across the early modern period in the north of England. It seems a clear-cut and effective expression of concern about religious non-conformity, combined with a determination to achieve a reformation of manners, interacting with clear signs of the impact of new agencies and agents of central state power overwhelming the legacies of local particularism, in which many of the most active 'reformers' were 'new' men, rising on the back of the economic change of the period and bringing with them new attitudes to sex and social relationships. And at its very heart was a gentleman and his wife and their lovers and the bastard children he acknowledged, and their world seemed to be being upended by a revolution in so many of the contexts in which they lived.

Yet, little more than twelve months later, Archibishop Grindal had been recalled to the south and the impetus of this challenge to gentry mistress-keeping had been lost. Sir Rowland's position henceforth became more complicated, but he was by no means fatally damaged. Towards the end of the decade he was still known as one of the gentlemen of Cheshire 'whose houses are greatlie infected with Popery', but he was in a position to win a generous lease of the tithes of Stourton from Gilpin, as rector of Bebington, in August 1575, and most strikingly he was able to become sheriff of Cheshire, the office he had desired two years before, in November 1575.[17] A clear sign of Sir Rowland's confidence is to be found in an enfeoffment entered into during the year of his shrievalty.[18] The feoffees were a group united by a mixture of kinship and conservative religion. At their head was Sir Thomas Gerard of Kingsley and Bryn, Lancashire, and Etwall, Derbyshire, whose great-grandmother was Margaret, the daughter of Sir William Stanley of Hooton, and who served as sheriff of Lancashire in 1557–58 and MP for the shire in 1563. Both he and his wife were Catholics, and their younger son was the prominent Jesuit John Gerard; Sir Thomas employed Catholics to tutor his sons, and he had been implicated in a plot to free Mary Stuart from Tutbury Castle in 1571. He was only released two years later, and remained under suspicion.[19] There was then Ranulph Brereton of Handforth,[20] Robert Hesketh, Edward Torbock, Thomas Bunbury of Bunbury and Stanney,[21] John Poole junior of Nether Poole,[22] and John Egerton junior of Egerton and Oulton[23] esquires: the latter two were his sons-in-law, and also, in Egerton's case, his son William's wife Elizabeth's brother. Ursula was referred to as being *to that point* wife of Sir Rowland. But the most striking thing is that the beneficiaries of the enfeoffment included Edward, son of Sibil (daughter of William Thomason *defunct.*), alias Edward Penleton, alias Edward Stanley, bastard son of Sir Rowland, who was given priority over two of Sir Rowland's brothers, Edward and John.[24]

Sir Rowland was to die in 1612 at a very advanced age, allegedly the oldest knight in England, and his longevity seems to represent the resilience of the elite customs he epitomised. The gentry and nobility of the north of England maintained a pattern of relationships outside marriage, producing and recognising illegitimate offspring, throughout the early modern period. That behaviour was not fundamentally altered by economic change, nor did it become completely socially unacceptable as a result of novel religious beliefs and attitudes. There is clear evidence of the impact upon it of the Reformation, in the form of Protestantisation and new attitudes to Roman Catholicism. There is also evidence that elite sexual mores in the north of England were affected by the trend to what is called the 'reformation of manners'. This meant that many people were more intolerant of immorality, especially sexual immorality. Beginning most clearly from the 1540s, and with its greatest impact in the 1570s, voices were raised against gentry mistress-keeping, and towards the end of the century there was a renewed wave of concern about bastardy. When mistress-keeping, or a gentlewoman's immorality, or the production of a crop of bastards coincided with a suspect religious and/or political position (as was increasingly clearly the case with Sir Rowland Stanley) then it was more likely, if not inevitably, prone to attract censure. Yet this was not necessarily something which impacted particularly heavily on the elite; and there was a striking capacity for a double standard to operate whereby gentry adulterers could condemn lower-status adulterers, and those with a crop of illegitimate offspring could be in the vanguard of those pursuing the pregnant and unmarried, without apparent difficulty.

Elite masculinity may have developed, too, with many of the characteristics that have been observed in other contexts in England in the period, which helped to focus attention on male self-control and control over others in the household. Yet the commonly found emphasis there on the avoidance of falsehood could, in the north, still be combined with open affirmations of sexual virility and attractiveness to women expressed in the maintenance of mistresses and recognition of bastard children. Similarly, the evidence straightforwardly undermines an exaggerated view of a transition from a northern honour-based noble society characterised by extensive violence and mistress-keeping to an orderly civil society. At the same time, the alternative model of an honour society which was intrinsically resistant to the worst forms of violent disorder and more responsive to central control – and which might have been consistently more resistant to illicit sexual behaviour – is unwarranted.[25] Those codes of honour and norms of social behaviour which can be observed in association with the keeping of mistresses and interactions with illegitimate children suggest clear contrasts with other parts of England and perceptions of difference in conteporaries' eyes which they perceived as 'disorderly'.

This also interacted with the processes of the growth of the state which occurred in the north during this period. That interaction was seen most distinctively in the emergence of the ecclesiastical commissions, whereby laypeople and churchmen acted together under the monarch's warrant, it has been argued here not simply or primarily to challenge threats to the unity and coherence of the religious settlement but also to address adultery and sexual immorality. The Council in the North was also recruited into this campaign for some years, especially after the amendment to its responsibilities in 1561. The admitted strength of jurisdictional particularism in the north, on which some aspects of the developments of central influence were predicated, did not act as a bar to these changes. It was through a combination of High Commission, Council in the North, and a range of other instruments that Edmund Grindal and Henry, earl of Huntingdon led the most intense challenge to the mistress-keeping of the northern elite that the early modern period was to experience. And yet this challenge was short-lived, and elite sexual practices survived. In some ways the construction of the state in the gentry's own image meant that those who were now increasingly embedded in positons of wealth and influence in the north were those who sprang most directly from this culture of mistress-keeping and bastard-bearing. Sir Henry Savile is a prime example, with his ability to endow a parallel heir, in Robert Savile of Howley, who could rise through his children and grandchildren into the peerage, on the back of this legacy of the negotiation of the early modern state in the north.

Elite behaviour also interacted with the growth of the court. Norbert Elias's formulation of court culture disciplining the behaviour of the medieval nobility may provide a suggestive model for the routes by which untrammelled violence might be disciplined, for example through the etiquette of the joust or the duel, and ultimately tamed to the purposes of the royal state. In our case, however, a similar model proposing a check on sexual passions through the codes of courtly love still tends to leave us with evidence of those northerners who were drawn into court circles engaging in physical sexual relationships with others outside marriage and producing bastard children as a result, whatever the demands of the crown that they control themselves in the interests of order and harmony.

We are left, therefore, with a distinctive set of sexual behaviours and practices in the north of England, which are characterised by a congruence with other aspects of northern gentry and noble society with implications for other studies. Those sexual and associated social practices appear to fit with patterns of lordship and community in the locality, counties and wider regions of the north, sometimes reinforcing those solidarities, sometimes creating tensions within them. We can observe the ways in which illegitimate offspring became part of households, providing loyal service in key offices, and in which they and connections in which non-marital relationships were involved played a role in wider political networks. The careers of illegitimate children suggest that once they had been recognised and survived early childhood, and once they had demonstrated promise and ability, their capacity to contribute to family and wider networks was not in doubt, receiving patronage and being employed in responsible positions. 'Illegitimate' relationships had a capacity to work with the grain of the life cycle, not just of the male members of the elite, but also of the gentle- and noblewomen of the north. It was part of their adolescence, through their experience of service, at a crucial point in their lives in mixing with a network of others in a wider kin and client group, from whom sexual partners might be drawn. It was part of the process of moving into widowhood for women. The keeping of mistresses and production of bastard children was something which was, in many cases, recognised and even accepted in wider kinship networks, as represented in the arrangements for their support in wills and property settlements.

This was not, however, a manifestation of a different form of marriage to the one espoused by the church; but it was possibly a different approach to the difficulties of a marriage and opportunity to form another marriage – hence the fear of Edmund Bunny with which we began the book, and the centrality of divorce in the debates of the sixteenth century. Within those debates needs to be understood the potential for gentlemen and gentlewomen to wish to end failed marriages and replace them with other legitimated relationships which had already been established in adultery. We should therefore be prepared to qualify our simple overreliance on some of the stock figures of our social histories – the abused servant without agency, but equally the alternative marriage;[26] the coherence of a universal nuclear family unit and alliances straightforwardly based around the alliances made in marriage; the cross-generational structure of legitimate successions and relationships – and replace them with a richer, more complex society with illegitimate relationships and children at its heart.

Notes

1 BIA, HC.AB 6, fo. 79v, 133v, 180; HC.AB 7, fo. 1v, 97; see above, pp. 72–3, 82, 106–10.
2 Cheshire Arch., EDC 5/1573/25: sentence dated 29 Aug. 1573.
3 BL, Lansdowne MS 17, fos. 113–113v. Purchase: JRULM, RYCH/1455, /1587 (from Thomas Grene of Farnhill, Chesh.). On 6 Apr. 1571 Sir Rowland Stanley petitioned Edmund, archbishop of York, to admit Thomas Bennet, clerk, to be rector of Bebington in succession to the late Roger Sefton, clerk: RYCH/1456. The account of the incumbents and patronage of Bebington in George Ormerod, *The History of the County Palatine and City of Chester*, 2nd edn, revised and enlarged by Thomas Helsby (3 vols. London: Routledge, 1882), ii. 439 is particularly sketchy, showing the institution of Roger Sefton in Oct. 1556, when John Grice was patron, *pro hac vice*, but then nothing clear, other than a possible reference to Luke Gilpin as former rector in 1581, taken from Piccope's notes.
4 TNA, STAC 7/3/10.
5 *The Visitation of Cheshire in the Year 1580, Made by Robert Glover, Somerset Herald, for William Flower, Norroy King of Arms*, ed. John Paul Rylands, Harleian Society, XVIII (1882), p. 192. Sir Rowland's great-grandfather Sir William Stanley's wife was Agnes, daughter of Robert Grosvenor: JRULM, RYCH/1430.
6 TNA, C 1/1416/46, C 3/33/16, C 3/39/19, C 3/43/1, C 3/42/85 (Ince); Cheshire Arch., DMB/103/10 (Bromborough); *CPR, 1558–60*, p. 178.
7 BL, Lansdowne MS 17, fos. 113–113v (printed in *The Cheshire Sheaf*, 3rd ser., IV (1902), 111–13; 121).

8   BL, Lansdowne MS 17 fos. 112, 114 (printed in John Strype, *The History of the Life and Acts of the Most Reverend Father in God, Edmund Grindal, the First Bishop of London, and the Second Archbishop of York and Canterbury Successively, in the Reign of Queen Elizabeth: To which is Added, an Appendix of Original MSS. Faithfully Transcribed out of the Best Archives; Whereunto Reference is Made in the History* (Oxford: Clarendon Press, 1821), pp. 265–7). Patrick Collinson, *Archbishop Grindal 1519–1583: The Struggle for a Reformed Church* (London: Jonathan Cape, 1979), p. 209.

9   John Venn and J. A. Venn, *Alumni Cantabrigiensis: A Biographical List of all Known Students, Graduates and Holders of Office at the University of Cambridge from the Earliest Times to 1900. Part 1: From the Earliest Times to 1751* (4 vols. Cambridge: Cambridge University Press, 1922–7), ii. 18; Charles Henry Cooper and Thompson Cooper, *Athenae Cantabrigienses* (2 vols. Cambridge: Deighton, Bell and Macmillan, 1858–61), ii. 17; Brett Usher, 'Bartlett [Barthlet], John (fl. 1562–1567), Church of England clergyman and author', *ODNB*; John Barthlet, *The Pedegrewe of Heretiques. Wherein is Truely and Plainely Set Out, the First Roote of Heretiques Begon in the Church, Since the Time and Passage of the Gospell, Together with an Example of the Ofspring of the Same* (London: H. Denham for L. Harryson, 1566), fos. iv–iv^v.

10 Joseph Foster, *Alumni Oxoniensis: The Members of the University of Oxford 1500-[1886]: Their Parentage, Birthplace, and Year of Birth, with a Record of their Degrees: Being the Matriculation Register of the University* (8 vols. in 4, Oxford: Parker and Co., 1887–92), iii. 1006–7; Mihail Dafydd Evans, 'Meyrick, Rowland (1504/5–1566), bishop of Bangor', *ODNB*; John Foxe, *Actes and Monuments of these Latter and Perillous Dayes* (London: printed by Iohn Day, dwellyng ouer Aldersgate, 1563), p. 1166.

11 An openness to engagement with the Welsh gentry was not new in the family; Sir Rowland's mother was Grace, the daughter of Sir William Griffith, chamberlain of North Wales: JRULM, RYCH/1680. Was Sir Rowland's own forename a result of these earlier connections with potential godparents of the name amongst the Welsh gentry?

12 BL, Lansdowne MS 17, fo. 113.

13 R. C. Morton, 'The Enterprise of Ulster', *History Today*, 17 (1967), 114–21; Walter Bourchier Devereux, *Lives and Letters of the Devereux Earls of Essex, in the Reigns of Elizabeth, James I., Charles I., 1540–1646* (2 vols. London: John Murray, 1853), i. chs 2–6, esp. pp. 26–33; Nicholas P. Canny, *The Elizabethan Conquest of Ireland: A Pattern Established, 1565–76* (Hassocks: Harvester, 1976), esp. pp. 88–90, 118–31, 134–5; Ciaran Brady, *The Chief Governors: The Rise and Fall of Reform Government in Tudor Ireland, 1536–1588* (Cambridge: Cambridge University Press, 1994), pp. 144–6, 251–2, 256–7.

14 *Calendar of State Papers Domestic, 1547–1580*, pp. 288, 291, 292, 294.

15 *Acts of the Privy Council of England*, ed. J. R. Dasent *et al.* (46 vols. London: HMSO, 1890–1964), vol. 8: *1571–1575*, p. 170.

16 BIA, HC.AB 7, fo. 204.

17 JRULM, RYCH/1588. Grindal, at the start of the affair, observed that Sir Rowland's only motivation in presenting to the living was that he 'mighte have the proffettes': BL, Lansdowne MS 17, fo. 114.

18 Ormerod, *Chester*, ii. 414 (20 Feb. 1576).

19 Ormerod, *Chester*, ii. 132; P. W. Hasler, *The House of Commons, 1558–1603* (3 vols. HMSO for the History of Parliament Trust, 1981), ii. 186.

20 Son of Sir Urian; o.s.p., and no wife recorded in Ormerod, *Chester*, ii. 644. 'Henricus Bierton de hanford, knight' (a mistake for Sir Urian, who d. 19 Mar. 1576/77) had been listed as a

positively unfavourable justice in 1564 – 'A Collection of Original Letters from the Bishops to the Privy Council, 1564', ed. Mary Bateson, in *Camden Miscellany* IX, Camden Society, n.s., 53 (1895), p. 75.

21 Ormerod, *Chester*, ii. 395.
22 John Poole, son of Thomas and Mary is not shown as marrying her in Ormerod, *Chester*, ii. 423; but in the pedigree of Stanley, he appears as husband of Mary and so Sir Rowland's son-in-law.
23 Born 1551, and did not succeed until 1590: Ormerod, *Chester*, ii. 629.
24 Sir Rowland's son's surname, Penleton – possibly for Pendleton – raises the possibility of a role for Elizabeth Pendleton, the maid dismissed by Lady Ursula for fornication with Robert Pitts, as either the child's mother, or as part of a foster family for the child.
25 Recent accounts of the workings of honour in political society might place more emphasis on the role of sexual relationships in their models; e.g. Brendan Kane, *The Politics and Culture of Honour in Britain and Ireland, 1541–1641* (Cambridge: Cambridge University Press, 2010); Courtney Thomas, '"The Honour & Credite of the Whole House": Family Unity and Honour in Early Modern England', *Cultural and Social History*, 10 (2013), 329–45.
26 R. C. Richardson, 'A Maidservant's Lot in Early Modern England', *History Today*, 60 (2) (Feb. 2010), 25–31. In spite of the arguments of Ruth Mazo Karras, *Unmarriages: Women, Men and Sexual Unions in the Middle Ages* (Philadelphia: University of Pennsylvania Press, 2012), we find no evidence of people consciously and brazenly living in relationships at odds with the idea that sex outside marriage was wrong.

Bibliography

Unprinted primary sources

Borthwick Institute of Archives, York

HC.AB Court of High Commission: Act Books
CP Cause Papers

British Library, London

Lansdowne MS 17

Cheshire Archives, Chester

DBN Brooke Family of Norton
DVE Vernon and Warren Family
EDA 12 Court of High Commission
EDC 1 Consistory Court: Court Books
EDC 2 Consistory Court: Depositions Books
EDC 5 Consistory Court: Court Papers
ZDCAS Chester Archaeological Society

Cumbria Archive Service, Carlisle Record Office

DRC 3/1 Court of High Commission: Court Book 1571–72

Derbyshire Record Office, Derby

D187 Woolhouse and Hallowes of Glapwell

Durham Cathedral Archives

DCD/D/SJB/7, Durham Cathedral Muniments, High Commission Court book, 1614–17

Durham University Library

DDR/A/ACN/1, Archdeaconry of Northumberland Court Book, 1619–24
DDR/A/ACN/2, Archdeaconry of Northumberland Court Book, 1619–22
DDR/EJ/CCA/1/1, Durham Consistory Act Books main series, 1530–38
DDR/EJ/CCA/1/2, Durham Consistory Act Books main series, 1567–72
DDR/EJ/CCA/1/3, Durham Consistory Act Books main series, 1576–80
DDR/EJ/CCA/1/4A, Durham Consistory Act Books main series, 1580–89
DDR/EJ/CCA/1/8, Durham Consistory Act Books main series, 1610–14
DDR/EJ/CCA/1/12, Durham Consistory Act Books main series, 1632–36
DDR/EJ/CCA/2/1, Durham Consistory Act Books ex-officio cases, 1578–80
DDR/EJ/CCA/3/2, Durham Consistory cases from the Archdeaconry of Northumberland, 1560–70
DDR/EJ/CCD/1/2, Durham Consistory Deposition Book, 1565–73
DDR/EJ/CCD/1/5, Durham Consistory Deposition Book, 1589–90
DDR/EJ/CCD/1/9, Durham Consistory Deposition Book, 1607–11
DDR/EJ/CCD/1/11, Durham Consistory Deposition Book, 1618–22
DDR/A/ACN/1, Archdeaconry of Northumberland Court Book, 1619–24
DDR/A/ACN/2, Archdeaconry of Northumberland Court Book, 1619–22
Durham Dean and Chapter Library, Hunter MSS, vol. 16, High Commission Court Book, 1628–39
Durham Dean and Chapter Library, Hunter MSS, vol. 17, High Commission Deposition Book, 1626–38

East Sussex Record Office, Brighton

AMS 315
SAS/D/125; /128

Hereford Record Office

F8/11/466

John Rylands University Library of Manchester

Arley Charters, 12/19
Brooke of Mere, box 1/1/32
Rylands Charters

Lambeth Palace Library

Carew Manuscripts, MS 616
Talbot Papers, MS 3199
Shrewsbury MSS 694–710

Lancashire Record Office, Preston

ARR/2/4/4/148 Archdeaconry of Richmond, Consistory Court Cause Papers, c. 1561–1836
DBB Parker Family of Browsholme MSS

DDF Farington of Worden, Leyland MSS
DDIN Blundell of Ince Blundell Muniments
DDK Earls of Derby Knowsley MSS
DDL Finch, Johnson & Lynn, Solicitors of Preston MSS
DDM Molyneux, Earls of Sefton MSS
DDSC Scarisbrick Muniments
DDTA Tatton of Cuerden MS
DP/449 Purchased Documents, Parker of Browsholme MSS
QDD/11 Lancashire Courts of Quarter Session, Enrolment, Registration and Deposit
QSB Lancashire Courts of Quarter Session, Recognizances, Recognizance Rolls

Leeds University Library

Ripon Cathedral MS 37 Edmund Bunny, 'Of Divorce for Adultery and Marrying Again' (1595)

Leicestershire, Leicester and Rutland Record Office

16 D 66 /461 Braunstone Estate Documents

The National Archives of the United Kingdom, Kew

C 1 Court of Chancery: Six Clerks Office: Early Proceedings, Richard II to Philip and Mary
C 78 Chancery and Supreme Court of Judicature, Chancery Division: Six Clerks Office and successors: Decree Rolls
PROB 11 Prerogative Court of Canterbury and related Probate Jurisdictions: Will Registers
SP 12 Secretaries of State: State Papers Domestic, Elizabeth I
STAC 2 Court of Star Chamber: Proceedings, Henry VIII
STAC 7 Court of Star Chamber: Proceedings, Elizabeth, Addenda
STAC 8 Court of Star Chamber: Proceedings, James I

Northamptonshire Archives, Northampton

F(M) Fitzwilliam (Milton) Charters

Nottinghamshire Archives, Nottingham

DD/FJ Foljambe of Osberton MSS
DD/SR Savile of Rufford: Deeds and Estate Papers

Parliamentary Archives, Westminster

HL/PO/PB/1/1542/34&35H8n32 Act for the declaration of Elizabeth Burgh's children to be bastards
HL/PO/PB/1/1542/34&35H8n39 Act whereby the Lady Parr's children be made bastards
HL/PO/PB/1/1542/34&35H8n40 Act for heirs of Lady Draycote's lands

HL/PO/PB/1/1543/35H8 Act for Thomas Lord Burgh
HL/PO/PU/1/1533/25H8n21, An Act concerning the Exoneration of the King's Subjects from Exactions and Impositions heretofore paid to the See of Rome; and for having Licences and Dispensations within this Realm, without suing further for the same

Shakespeare Centre Library (Shakespeare Birthplace Trust), Stratford-upon-Avon

DR 3/306 Ferrers of Baddesley Clinton MSS

University of Nottingham Manuscripts and Special Collections

AN/PB Archdeaconry of Nottingham, Presentment Bills
Ne D 1802 Estate and Official Papers of the Newcastle Family of Clumber Park

West Sussex Record Office, Chichester

Ep/I/10 Chichester Diocese Court Act Books 1556–57, 1576–79, 1582–88
SAS-BA/19

West Yorkshire Archive Service, Leeds

RD/A/1 Archdeaconry of Richmond and the Diocese of Ripon and Leeds: Consistory Court, 1543–48
RD/A/2 Archdeaconry of Richmond and the Diocese of Ripon and Leeds: Consistory Court, 1570–73

Printed primary sources

The Act Book of the ecclesiastical court of Whalley 1510–1538, ed. Alice M. Cooke, Chetham Society, n.s., 44 (1901).
The Acts of the High Commission Court Within the Diocese of Durham, ed. W. Hylton Dyer Longstaffe, Surtees Society, XXIV (1858).
Acts of the Privy Council of England, ed. J. R. Dasent *et al.* (46 vols. London: HMSO, 1890–1964).
Anne Clifford's Great Books of Record, ed. J. L. Malay (Manchester: Manchester University Press, 2015).
Aubrey, John *Brief Lives, Chiefly of Contemporaries*, ed. Andrew Clark (2 vols. Oxford: Clarendon Press, 1898).
Avale, Lemuke', *A Commemoration or Dirige of Bastarde Edmonde Boner, alias Sauage, Vsurped Bisshoppe of London* ([London]: printed by P. O. [i.e. John Kingston], [1569]).
Barthlet, John *The Pedegrewe of Heretiques. Wherein is Truely and Plainely Set Out, the First Roote of Heretiques Begon in the Church, Since the Time and Passage of the Gospell, Together with an Example of the Ofspring of the Same* (London: H. Denham for L. Harrysson, 1566)
Bedfordshire Wills, 1480–1519, ed. Patricia Bell, Publications of the Bedfordshire Historical and Record Society XLV (Bedford, 1966).
Bedfordshire Wills 1484–1533, ed. Patricia Bell, Publications of the Bedfordshire Historical and Record Society LXXVI (Bedford, 1997).

Bedfordshire Wills Proved in the Prerogative Court of Canterbury, 1383–1548, ed. Margaret McGregor, Publications of the Bedfordshire Historical and Record Society LVIII ([Bedford], 1979).

Blackstone, William *Commentaries on the Laws of England, Book the Second. By Sir William Blackstone, Knt. one of His Majesty's Justices of the Common Pleas. 12th Edition with the last corrections of the author; and with notes and additions by Edward Christian, Esq. Barrister at Law, and Professor of the Laws of England in the University of Cambridge* (London: printed by A. Strahan and W. Woodfall, Law-Printers to the King's Most Excellent Majesty, for T. Cadell, in The Strand, 1794).

The Border Papers: Calendar of Letters and Papers Relating to the Affairs of the Borders of England and Scotland Preserved in Her Majesty's Public Record Office London, ed. Joseph Bain (2 vols. Edinburgh: H. M. General Register House, 1894–96).

Bunny, Edmund *Of Diuorce for Adulterie, and Marrying Againe: That There is no Sufficient Warrant so to do. VVith a Note in the End, that R.P. Many Yeeres Since was Answered* ('Oxford' [i.e. London]: printed by Ioseph Barnes, 1610).

Calendar of the Manuscripts of the Most Hon. The Marquis of Salisbury K.G. ... Preserved at Hatfield House, Hertfordshire, ed. R. A. Roberts, M. S. Giuseppi and G. Dyfnallt Owen, Historical Manuscripts Commission, 9 (24 vols. London: HMSO, 1883–1973).

Calendar of Patent Rolls ... Edward VI (London: HMSO, 1924–29).

Calendar of the Proceedings of the Committee for Advance of Money, 1642–1656, ed. Mary Anne Everett Green (3 vols. (paginated through); London: HMSO, 1888).

Calendar of State Papers: Domestic Series. The Reign of Charles I, ed. John Bruce and William Douglas Hamilton (23 vols. London: HMSO, 1858–97).

Calendar of State Papers: Domestic Series. The Reign of Charles II, ed. Mary Anne Everett Green, F. H. B. Daniell and F. Bickley (28 vols. London: Longman, Green, Longman & Roberts; HMSO, 1860–1939).

Calendar of State Papers: Domestic Series. The Reign of James I, ed. Mary Anne Everett Green (5 vols. London: Longman, Brown, Green, Longmans & Roberts, 1857–72).

Calendar of State Papers: Domestic Series of the Reign of Mary I, 1553–1558, ed. C. S. Knighton (London: Public Record Office, 1998).

Calendar of State Papers, Domestic Series, of the Reigns of Edward VI, Mary and Elizabeth, 1547–80, ed. Robert Lemon (London: Longman, Brown, Green, Longmans, & Roberts, 1856).

The Cely Letters, 1472–1488, ed. A. Hanham, Early English Text Society, 273 (London: Oxford University Press, 1975).

Certain Sermons or Homilies (1547): And, A Homily against Disobedience and Wilful Rebellion (1570): A Critical Edition, ed. Ronald B. Bond (Toronto: University of Toronto Press, 1987).

Chester, Robert *Loues Martyr: Or, Rosalins Complaint: Allegorically Shadowing the Truth of Loue, in the Constant Fate of the Phoenix and Turtle. A Poeme Enterlaced with Much Varietie and Raritie; now First Translated out of the Venerable Italian Torquato Cæliano* (London: printed [by R. Field] for E. B[lount], 1601).

The Christen State of Matrimony: Moost Necessary [and] Profitable for all the[m], that Entend to Liue Quietly and Godlye in the Christe[n] State of Holy Wedlock Newly set Forth in Englyshe (London: printed in the house of John[n], Mayler for John[n] Gough, '1546' [i.e. 1543]).

Chroniques, des îles de Jersey, Guernesey, Auregny, et Serk: auquel on a ajouté un abrégé historique des dites îles, ed. George S. Syvret (Guernsey: Thomas James Mauger, 1832).

Coke, Edward, *The First Part of the Institutes of the Laws of England; or a Commentary Upon Littleton, Not the Name of the Author Only, but of the Law Itself*, ed. Francis Hargrave and Charles Butler Vol. 1 (first American edn; 2 vols. Philadelphia: Robert H. Small, 1853).

'A Collection of Original Letters from the Bishops to the Privy Council, 1564', ed. Mary Bateson, in *Camden Miscellany* IX, Camden Society, n.s., 53 (1895).

The Constitutions and Canons Ecclesiastical (Made in the Year 1603, and Amended in the Year 1865) to which are Added the Thirty-Nine Articles of the Church of England (London: S.P.C.K., 1900).

Copley, Anthony *Wits fittes and fancies Fronted and entermedled with presidentes of honour and wisdome. Also: Loves Ovvl. An idle conceited dialogue betwene loue, and an olde man* (London: by Richard Iohnes, at the sign of the rose and crowne nexxt aboue S. Andrews, 1595).

The Court Rolls of the Honor of Clitheroe in the County of Lancaster, vol. III, ed. William Farrer (Edinburgh: Ballantyne Press, 1913).

The Courts of the Archdeaconry of Buckingham 1483–1523, ed. E. M. Elvey, Buckinghamshire Record Society, 19 (1975).

Dalton, Michael *The Countrey Iustice Containing the Practise of the Iustices of the Peace out of their Sessions. Gathered, for the Better Helpe of such Iustices of Peace as Haue not been much Conuersant in the Studie of the Lawes of this Realme. Newly Corrected and Inlarged* (London: printed [by Adam Islip] for the Societie of Stationers, 1619).

Daniel, Samuel *Delia. Containing Certaine Sonnets: With the Complaint of Rosamond* (London: printed by I[ohn] C[harlewood] for S. Watersonne, 1592).

Daniel, Samuel *The Poeticall Essayes of Sam. Danyel* (London: printed by P. Short for Simon Waterson, 1599).

Depositions and Other Ecclesiastical Proceedings from the Courts of Durham: Extending from 1311 to the Reign of Elizabeth, ed. James Raine, Surtees Society, XXI (1845).

The Derby Household Books; Comprising an Account of the Household Regulations and Expenses of Edward and Henry Third and Fourth Earls of Derby Together with a Diary Containing the Names of the Guests who Visited the Latter Earl at his Houses in Lancashire, ed. F. R. Raines, Chetham Society, XXXI (1853).

The Diaries of Lady Anne Clifford, ed. D. J. H. Clifford (Stroud: Alan Sutton, 1990).

The Diary of Sir Henry Slingsby of Scriven, Bart., Now First Published Entire from the Ms.: A Reprint of Sir Henry Slingsby's Trial, His Rare Tract, 'A Father's Legacy' Written in the Tower Immediately before his Death; and Extracts from Family Correspondence and Papers, with Notices, and a Genealogical Memoir, ed. Daniel Parsons (London: Longman, Rees, Orme, Brown, Green, and Longman; J. Vincent, Oxford; Todd, York; and Wilson, Knaresborough 1836).

Dugdale, William *The Visitation of the County of Yorke, begun in Ao Dni MDCLXV and finished Ao Dni MDCLXVI*, ed. R. Davis, Surtees Society, XXXVI (1859).

Dugdale's Visitation of Yorkshire: With Additions, ed. J. W. Clay (3 vols. Exeter: W. Pollard & Co., 1899–1917).

Edgar, Thomas *The Lavves Resolutions of Womens Rights: Or, The Lavves Prouision for Woemen A Methodicall Collection of Such Statutes and Customes, with the Cases, Opinions, Arguments and Points of Learning in the Lavv, as Doe Properly Concerne Women. Together with a Compendious Table, Whereby the Chiefe Matters in this Booke Contained, May be the More Readily Found* (London: printed by [Miles Flesher for] the assignes of Iohn More Esq. and are to be sold by Iohn Groue, 1632).

Extracts from the Records of the Merchant Adventurers of Newcastle-upon-Tyne, ed. F.W. Dendy, vol. 1, Surtees Society, XCIII (1895).

Feet of Fines of the Tudor Period, ed. Francis Collins, Yorkshire Archaeological Society, Record Series, 2, 5, 7–8 (1887–90).

Foxe, John *Actes and Monuments of these Latter and Perillous Dayes* (London: printed by Iohn Day, dwellyng ouer Aldersgate, 1563).

Furnivall, F. J. *Child Marriages, Divorces and Ratifications etc in the Diocese of Chester, A.D. 1561–6*, Early English Text Society, 108 (1897).

Gossip from a Muniment-room, Being Passages in the Lives of Anne and Mary Fitton, ed. Anne Emily Newdigate-Newdegate (London: Nutt, 1898).

Hainault, Jean de *The Estate of the Church: with the Discourse of Times, from the Apostles Vntill this Present: Also of the Liues of all the Emperours, Popes of Rome, and Turkes: As Also of the Kings of Fraunce, England, Scotland, Spaine, Portugall, Denmarke, &c. With all the Memorable Accidents of their Times*, trans Simon Patrick (London: printed by Thomas Creede, 1602).

The Injunctions and Other Ecclesiastical Proceedings of Richard Barnes Bishop of Durham from 1575 to 1587, ed. James Raine, Surtees Society, XXII (1850).

Lancashire and Cheshire Cases in the Court of Star Chamber, ed. R. Stewart-Brown, RSLC, 71 (1916).

Lancashire and Cheshire Wills and Inventories 1563 to 1807 Now Preserved at Chester, ed. J. P. Rylands, Chetham Society, n.s., 37 (1897).

Lancashire and Cheshire Wills and Inventories 1572 to 1696 Now Preserved at Chester, with an Appendix of Lancashire and Cheshire Wills and Inventories Proved at York and Richmond 1542 to 1649, ed. J. P. Earwaker, Chetham Society, n.s., 28 (1893).

Lancashire and Cheshire Wills and Inventories at Chester, with an Abstract of Wills now Lost or Destroyed Transcribed by the late G. J. Piccope, M.A., ed. J. P. Earwaker, Chetham Society, n.s., 3 (1884).

Lancashire and Cheshire Wills and Inventories from the Ecclesiastical Court, Chester, ed. G. J. Piccope, Chetham Society, XXXIII, LI, LIV (1857–61).

Lancashire Inquisitions Returned into the Chancery of the Duchy of Lancaster and now Existing in the Public Record Office, London, Stuart Period Part I, 1–11 James I, ed. J. P. Rylands, RSLC, III (1879).

Lancashire Inquisitions Returned into the Chancery of the Duchy of Lancaster and now Existing in the Public Record Office, London, Stuart Period Part III, 20–23 James I, ed. J. P. Rylands, RSLC, XVII (1888).

Letters and Papers, Foreign and Domestic, of the Reign of Henry VIII, Preserved in the Public Record Office, the British Museum, and Elsewhere in England, ed. J. S. Brewer, J. Gairdner and R. H. Brodie (London: HMSO, 1862–1910); Addenda, I (London: HMSO, 1929–32).

Letters of John Chamberlain, ed. Norman Egbert McClure, Memoirs of the American Philosophical Society, XII, pts. 1–2 (2 vols. Philadelphia: The American Philosophical Society 1939).

The Letters of Lady Anne Bacon, ed. Gemma Allen, Camden Society, 5th ser., 44 (2014).

Letters Written by John Chamberlain during the Reign of Queen Elizabeth, ed. Sarah Williams, Camden Society, LXXIX (1861).

Leycester, Peter *Historical Antiquities in Two Books the First Treating in General of Great-Brettain and Ireland: The Second Containing Particular Remarks Concerning Cheshire* (London: printed by W. L. for Robert Clavell, 1673).

Lincoln Wills, Volume. I, *A.D. 1271–1526*, ed. C. W. Foster, Lincoln Record Society 5 (Lincoln, 1914).

Lincoln Wills, Volume. II, *A.D. 1505–May 1530*, ed. C. W. Foster, Lincoln Record Society 10 (Lincoln, 1918 for 1914).

Lincoln Wills, Volume. III, *A.D. 1530–1532*, ed. C. W. Foster, Lincoln Record Society 24 (Lincoln, 1930).

'A List of the Freeholders in Cheshire in the Year 1578', ed. William Fergusson Irvine, in *Miscellanies, IV*, RSLC, XLIII (1902).

Lynch, Margaret *Life, Love, and Death in North-east Lancashire, 1510 to 1537: A Translation of the Act Book of the ecclesiastical court of Whalley*, Chetham Society, 3rd ser., XLVI (2006).

Materials for a History of the Reign of Henry VII, ed. William Campbell (2 vols. London: Longman & Co., 1873–77).

The Memoirs and Memorials of Sir Hugh Cholmley of Whitby, 1600–1657, ed. Jack Binns, Yorkshire Archaeological Society, Record Series, 153 (2000).

The Memoirs of Sir George Courthop, 1616–1685', ed. S. C. Lomas, in *Camden Miscellany*, XI, Camden Society, 3rd ser., 13 (1907).

Nicolas, Nicholas Harris *Testamenta Vetusta: Being Illustrations from Wills of Manners, Customs etc as well of the Descents and Possessions of Many Distinguished Families. From the Reign of Henry the Second to the Accession of Queen Elizabeth* (2 vols. London: Nichols and Son, 1826).

North Country Wills, Being Abstracts of Wills Relating to the Counties of York, Nottingham, Northumberland, Cumberland and Westmorland at Somerset House and Lambeth Palace 1383 to 1550, ed. J. W. Clay, Surtees Society, CXVI (1908).

Oxford Church Courts: Depositions, 1592–1596, ed. Jack Howard Drake (Oxford: Oxfordshire County Council, 1998).

Overbury, Thomas *New and Choise Characters, of Seuerall Authors Together with that Exquisite and Unmatcht Poeme, The Wife / Written by Syr Thomas Ouerburie; With the Former Characters and Conceited Newes, all in one Volume* (London: T. Creede for L. L'isle, 1615).

Papers Relating to the Delinquency of Lord Savile, 1642–1646', ed. James J. Cartwright, in *Camden Miscellany*, VIII, Camden Society, n.s., 31 (1879–83).

The Parish Registers of Mirfield, Part I: *Baptisms, Marriages & Burials 1559–1700*, ed. William Brigg, Yorkshire Parish Register Society, LXIV (1919).

The Parish Registers of Otley, Co. York, Part I: *1562 to 1672*, ed. W. Brigg, Yorkshire Parish Record Society, 33 (1908).

The Parish Registers of Saint Mary Stockport, Containing the Baptisms, Marriages and Burials from 1584–1620, ed. E. W. Bulkeley (Stockport: Swain and Co., 1889).

The Paston Letters, ed. James Gairdner (6 vols. reprinted in 1; Gloucester: Alan Sutton, 1983).

Paston Letters and Papers of the Fifteenth Century, ed. Norman Davis (2 vols. Oxford: Oxford University Press, 2004–5).

Pleadings and Depositions in the Duchy Court of Lancaster in the Time of Henry VIII, ed. H. Fishwick, RSLC, XXXV (1897).

The Plumpton Letters and Papers, ed. Joan Kirby, Camden Society, 5th ser., 8 (1996).

The Protestant [Domestick] Intelligence: Or, News Both from City & Country, no. 18; Friday, 5 Sept. 1679.

The Register of John Morton, Archbishop of Canterbury, 1486–1500, ed. Christopher Harper-Bill, Canterbury and York Society, 75, 78, 89 (1987–2000).

The Register of the Parish of Mirfield, Part I: *Baptisms, Marriages & Burials 1559–1700*, ed. William Brigg, Yorkshire Parish Register Society, LXIV (1919).

The Registers of the Cathedral Church of Manchester: Christenings, Burials and Weddings, 1573–1616, ed. John Owen, Henry Brierley, Mrs. Brierley and Miss Wrigley, LPRS, 31 (1908).

The Registers of the Parish Church of Cartmel in the County of Lancaster: Christenings, Burials and Weddings, 1559–1661, ed. Henry Brierley, LPRS, 28 (1907).

The Registers of the Parish Church of Colne in the County of Lancaster: Christenings, Weddings, and Burials, 1599–1653, ed. Thomas Backhouse Ecroyd, LPRS, 17 (1904).

The Registers of the Parish Church of Croston in the County of Lancaster: Christenings 1543–1721; Weddings 1538–1685; Burials 1538–1684, ed. Henry Fishwick, LPRS, 6 (1900).

The Registers of the Parish Church of Ormskirk in the County of Lancaster, Part 1: *Christenings, Burials and Weddings 1557–1626*, ed. Josiah Arrowsmith, LPRS, 13 (1902).

The Registers of the Parish of Burnley in the County of Lancaster: Christenings, Weddings, and Burials, 1562 to 1653, ed. William Farrer, LPRS, 2 (1899).

St. George, Richard, and St. George, Henry *Pedigrees Made at the Visitation of Chester, 1613*, ed. George J. Armytage and J. Paul Rylands, RSLC, LVIII (1909).

Sheils, W. J. *Archbishop Grindal's Visitation 1575 Comperta et Acta Book*, Borthwick Texts & Calendars: Records of the Northern Province (York: Borthwick Institute of Historical Research, University of York, 1977).

Somerset Medieval Wills (2nd Series), 1501–1530, with Some Somerset Wills Preserved at Lambeth, ed. F. W. Weaver, Somerset Record Society 19 (Taunton, 1903).

Somerset Medieval Wills (3rd Series), 1531–1558, ed. F. W. Weaver, Somerset Record Society 21 (Taunton, 1905).

Smith, Henry *A Preparatiue to Marriage: The Summe Whereof was Spoken at a Contract, and Inlarged After. Whereunto is Annexed A Treatise of the Lords Supper: And Another of Vsurie* (London: printed by R. Field for Thomas Man, 1591).

The Stanley Papers, part II: *The Derby Household Books; Comprising an Account of the Household Regulations and Expenses of Edward and Henry, Third and Fourth Earls of Derby; Together with a Diary containing the Names of the Guests who Visited the Latter Earl at his Houses in Lancashire, by William ffarington, Esquire, the Comptroller 1561–90*, ed. F. R. Raines, Chetham Society, o.s., xxxi (1853).

Testamenta Eboracensia, A Selection of Wills from the Registry at York, parts II–VI, ed. J. Raine and J. W. Clay, Surtees Society, XXX, XLV, LIII, LXXIX, CVI (1855, 1865, 1868, 1884, 1902).

Tudor Church Reform: The Henrician Canons of 1535 and the Reformatio Legum Ecclesiasticarum, ed. Gerald Bray, Church of England Record Society, 8 (2000).

Tudor Royal Proclamations, ed. Paul L. Hughes and James F. Larkin (3 vols. New Haven CT: Yale University Press, 1964–69).

Vergil, Polydore *Anglica Historia*, ed. Denys Hay, Camden Society, 3rd ser., 74 (1950).

The Visitation of Cheshire in the Year 1580, Made by Robert Glover for William Flower with Numerous Additions and Continuations Including those from The Visitation of Cheshire made in the Year 1566; With an Appendix Containing The Visitation of a Part of Cheshire in the Year 1533 made by William Fellows for Thomas Benolte and a Fragment of The Visitation of the City of Chester in the Year 1591 made by Thomas Chaloner, ed. J. P. Rylands, Harleian Society, XVIII (1882).

The Visitation of the County Palatine of Lancashire Made in the Year 1567 by William Flower Esq, Norroy King of Arms, ed. F. R. Raines, Chetham Society, LXXXI (1870).

The Visitation of the County Palatine of Lancaster Made in the Year 1613 by Richard St George Esq, Norroy King of Arms, ed. F. R. Raines, Chetham Society, o.s., LXXXII (1871).

The Visitation of Lancashire and a Part of Cheshire Made in the Twenty Fourth Year of the Reign of King Henry the Eighth A. D. 1533, ed. William Langton, Chetham Society, XCVIII, CX (1876–82).

The Visitation of Yorkshire in the Years 1563 and 1564 Made by William Flower, Norroy King of Arms, ed. C. B. Norcliffe, Harleian Society, XVI (1881).

The Visitation of Yorkshire, made in the Years 1584–85, by Robert Glover, Somerset Herald; to Which is Added the Subsequent Visitation made in 1612, by Richard St. George, Norroy King of Arms, ed. Joseph Foster (London: privately printed, 1875).

Warner, William *Albions England a Continued Historie of the same Kingdome, from the Originals of the First Inhabitants thereof: and most the Chiefe Alterations and Accidents there Hapning: Vnto, and in, the Happie*

Raigne of our now most Gracious Soueraigne Queene Elizabeth. VVith Varietie of Inuentiue and Historicall Intermixtures. First Penned and Published by VVilliam VVarner: and now Reuised, and newly Inlarged by the same Author (London: printed by the widow Orwin, for I[oan] B[roome], 1597).

The Wentworth Papers, 1705–1739: Selected from the Private and Family Correspondence of Thomas Wentworth, Lord Raby, Created in 1711 Earl of Strafford, ed. James Joel Cartwright (London: Wyman and Sons, 1883).

Wills and Inventories from the Registry at Durham, ed. W. Greenwell, J. C. Hodgson and H. M. Wood, Surtees Society, XXXVIII, CXII, CXLII (1860, 1906, 1929), ii–iv.

Wills and Inventories from the Registry of the Archdeaconry of Richmond, Extending Over Portions of the Counties of York, Westmorland, Cumberland and Lancaster, ed. J. Raine, Surtees Society, XXVI (1853).

Wills and Inventories Illustrative of the History, Manners, Language, Statistics etc of the Northern Counties of England from the Eleventh-Century Downwards, Part One, ed. J. Raine, Surtees Society, II (1835).

Yorkshire Star Chamber Proceedings, ed. William Brown, H. B. McCall and John Lister, Yorkshire Archaeological Society, Record Series, 41, 45, 51, 70 (1909–27).

Secondary sources

Adair, Richard *Courtship, Illegitimacy and Marriage in Early Modern England* (Manchester: Manchester University Press, 1996).

Archer, Ian W. *The Pursuit of Stability: Social Relations in Elizabethan London* (Cambridge: Cambridge University Press, 1991).

Armstrong, C. A. J. 'An Italian Astrologer at the Court of Henry VII, in E. F. Jacob (ed.), *Italian Renaissance Studies: A Tribute to the late C. M. Ady* (London: Faber and Faber, 1960), pp. 433–54.

Arundale, R. L. 'Edmund Grindal and the Northern Province', *Church History Quarterly* CLX (1959), 182–99.

Baines, Edward *The History of the County Palatine and Duchy of Lancaster*, ed. James Croston (5 vols. Manchester: John Heywood, 1888–93).

Barley, M. W. 'Castle Howard and the Village of Hinderskelfe, N. Yorkshire', *Antiquaries Journal*, 58 (1978), 358–60.

Barnes, Thomas G. 'A Cheshire Seductress, Precedent, and a "Sore Blow" to Star Chamber', in Morris S. Arnold et al. (eds), *On the Laws and Customs of England: Essays in Honour of Samuel E. Thorne* (Chapel Hill NC: University of North Carolina Press, 1981), pp. 359–82.

Bastow, Sarah 'An Abortive Attempt to Defend an Episcopal Reputation: The Case of Archbishop Edwin Sandys and the Innkeeper's Wife', *History*, 97 (2012), 380–401.

Bennett, Michael J. 'A County Community: Social Cohesion amongst the Cheshire Gentry, 1400–25', *Northern History*, 8 (1973), 24–44.

Bennett, Michael J. *Community, Class, and Careerism: Cheshire and Lancashire Society in the Age of Gawain and the Green Knight* (Cambridge: Cambridge University Press, 1983).

Bernard, G. W. *Anne Boleyn: Fatal Attractions* (New Haven CT, London: Yale University Press, 2010).

Berry, William *County Genealogies: Pedigrees of the Families in the County of Sussex* (London: Sherwood, Gilbert, and Piper, 1830).

Bindoff, S. T. *The House of Commons, 1509–1558* (3 vols. London: Secker & Warburg for the History of Parliament Trust, 1982).

Boersma, F. 'Sir Antony Fitzherbert: A biographical Sketch and Short Bibliography', *Law Library Journal*, 71 (1978), 387–400.

Bousmar, Éric, Marchandisse, Alain, Masson, Christophe and Schnerb, Bertrand (eds), *La bâtardise et l'exercice du pouvoir en Europe du XIIIe au début du XVIe siècle* (Villeneuve-d'Ascq: Revue du Nord, 2015).

Brady, Ciaran *The Chief Governors: The Rise and Fall of Reform Government in Tudor Ireland, 1536–1588* (Cambridge: Cambridge University Press, 1994).

Brigden, Susan *Thomas Wyatt: The Heart's Forest* (London: Faber and Faber, 2012).

Bruce, Yvonne '"That which Marreth All": Constancy and Gender in The Virtuous Octavia', *Medieval & Renaissance Drama in England*, 22 (2009), 42–59.

Brundage, James A. *Law, Sex, and Christian Society in Medieval Europe* (Chicago: University of Chicago Press, 2014).

Burn, John Southerden *The Star Chamber: Notices of the Court and Its Proceedings, with a Few Additional Notes of the High Commission* (London: J. R. Smith, 1870).

Bush, M. L. *The European Nobility* (2 vols. Manchester: Manchester University Press, 1983–88).

Butler, Sara M. 'Lies, Damn Lies and the Case of St Lucy: Cases of Judicial Separation from the Medieval Court of York', in Philippe Romanski and Aïssatou Sy-Wonyu (eds), *Trompe-l'oeil* (Rouen: C.É.L.C.L.A., Université de Rouen, 2002), pp. 1–16.

Canny, Nicholas P. *The Elizabethan Conquest of Ireland: A Pattern Established, 1565–76* (Hassocks: Harvester, 1976)

Capp, Bernard 'The Double Standard Revisited: Plebeian Women and Male Sexual Reputation in Early Modern England', *Past & Present*, 162 (1999), 70–100.

Capp, Bernard *When Gossips Meet: Women, Family, and Neighbourhood in Early Modern England* (Oxford: Oxford University Press, 2003).

Capp, Bernard 'Bigamous Marriage in Early Modern England', *Historical Journal*, 52 (2009), 537–56.

Carlson, Eric Josef 'Marriage Reform and the Elizabethan High Commission', *Sixteenth Century Journal*, 21 (1990), 437–52.

Carlton, Charles 'The Widow's Tale: Male Myths and Female Reality in 16th and 17th Century England', *Albion*, 10 (1978), 118–29.

Carlton, Katharine and Thornton, Tim 'Illegitimacy and Authority in the North of England, c. 1450–1640', *Northern History*, 48 (2011), 23–40.

Carpenter, Christine *Locality and Polity: A Study of Warwickshire Landed Society, 1401–1499* (Cambridge: Cambridge University Press, 1992).

Clark, Ira 'The Widow Hunt on the Tudor-Stuart Stage', *Studies in English Literature, 1500–1900*, 41 (2001), 399–416.

Clark, Margaret 'Northern Light? Parochial Life in a "Dark Corner" of Tudor England', in Katherine French, Gary G. Gibbs and Beat A. Kümin (eds), *The Parish in English Life 1400–1600* (Manchester: Manchester University Press, 1997), pp. 56–73.

Clark, Peter *English Provincial Society from the Reformation to the Revolution: Religion, Politics, and Society in Kent, 1500–1640* (Hassocks: Harvester Press, 1977).

Clay, J. W. 'The Savile Family', *Yorkshire Archaeological Journal*, 25 (1920), 1–47.

Cliffe, J. T. *The Yorkshire Gentry from the Reformation to the Civil War* (London: Athlone Press, 1969).

C[okayne], G. E. *The Complete Baronetage* (5 vols. Exeter: William Pollard, 1900–9).

C[ockayne], G. E. and White, G. H. *The Complete Peerage* (14 vols. London and Stroud: St Catherine Press; Sutton, 1910–59, 1998).

Collinson, Patrick *Archbishop Grindal 1519–1583: The Struggle for a Reformed Church* (London: Jonathan Cape, 1979).

Collinson, Patrick 'Elizabethan and Jacobean Puritanism as Forms of Popular Religious Culture', in Christopher Durston and Jacqueline Eales (eds), *The Culture of English Puritanism, 1560–1700* (Basingstoke: Macmillan, 1996), pp. 32–57.

Contamine, Philippe *La noblesse au royaume de France de Philippe le Bel à Louis XII: essai de synthèse* (Paris: presses universitaires de France, 1997).

Cooper, Charles Henry and Cooper, Thompson *Athenae Cantabrigienses* (2 vols. Cambridge: Deighton, Bell and Macmillan, 1858–61).

Coward, Barry *The Stanleys, Lords Stanley and Earls of Derby, 1385–1672: The Origins, Wealth and Power of a Landowning Family*, Chetham Society, 3rd ser., XXX (1983).

Cox Marjorie with Hopkins, L. A. *A History of Sir John Deane's Grammar School, Northwich, 1557–1908* (Manchester: Manchester University Press, 1975).

Crawford, Julie *Mediatrix: Women, Politics, and Literary Production in Early Modern England* (Oxford: Oxford University Press, 2014).

Crawford, Patricia 'The Construction and Experiences of Maternity in Seventeenth-Century England', in Valerie A. Fildes and Dorothy McLaren (eds), *Women as Mothers in Pre-industrial England* (London: Routledge, 1990), pp. 3–38.

Cross, Claire 'Sin and Society: The Northern High Commission and the Northern Gentry in the Reign of Elizabeth', in Claire Cross, David Loades and J. J. Scarisbrick (eds), *Law and Government under the Tudors: Essays Presented to Sir Geoffrey Elton … on … his Retirement* (Cambridge: Cambridge University Press, 1986), pp. 195–209.

Cross, Claire 'The Religious Life of Women in Sixteenth-Century Yorkshire', in William J. Sheils and Diane Wood (eds), *Women and the Church*, Studies in Church History, 27 (Oxford, 1990), pp. 307–24.

Cust, Richard 'Honour and Politics in Early Stuart England: The Case of Beaumont v Hastings', *Past & Present*, 149 (1995), 57–94.

Dabhoiwala, Faramerz 'The Construction of Honour, Reputation and Status in Late Seventeenth- and Early Eighteenth-Century England', *Transactions of the Royal Historical Society*, 6th ser., 6 (1996), 201–13.

Da Silva, Francisco Vaz 'Sexual Horns: The Anatomy and Metaphysics of Cuckoldry in European Folklore', *Comparative Studies in Society and History*, 48 (2006), 396–418.

Davies, C. S. L. 'Richard III, Henry VII and the Island of Jersey', *The Ricardian*, 9 (1991–4), 334–42.

Devereux, Walter Bourchier *Lives and Letters of the Devereux Earls of Essex, in the Reigns of Elizabeth, James I, Charles I, 1540–1646* (2 vols. London: John Murray, 1853).

Dibdin, Lewis *English Church Law and Divorce*: Part I, *Notes on the Reformatio legum ecclesiasticarum*; Part II, *Notes on the Divorce and Remarriage of Sir John Stawell* by Sir Charles E. H. Chadwyck Healey; with appendices (London: J. Murray, 1912).

Dickinson, Roger J. *The Lordship of Man Under the Stanleys: Government and Economy in the Isle of Man, 1580–1704*, Chetham Society, 3rd ser., XLI (1996).

Dolan, Frances E. 'Battered Women, Petty Traitors, and the Legacy of Coverture', *Feminist Studies*, 29 (2003), 249–77.

Donahue, Charles *Law, Marriage, and Society in the Later Middle Ages: Arguments about Marriage in Five Courts* (Cambridge: Cambridge University Press, 2007).

Doubleday, H. Arthur and Page, William (eds), *The Victoria History of the County of Bedford* (4 vols. London: Constable, 1904–14).

Draper, Peter *The House of Stanley; Including the Sieges of Lathom House, With Notices of Relative and Co-Temporary Incidents, & etc.* (Ormskirk: T. Hutton, 1864).

Druitt, Herbert and Smith, Sydney *A Manual of Costume as Illustrated by Monumental Brasses* (London: Alexander Moring Ltd, The De la More Press, 1906).

Durant, David N. *Bess of Hardwick: Portrait of an Elizabethan Dynast* (revised paperback edn, London: Peter Owen, 1999).

Elias, Norbert *Die höfische Gesellschaft: Untersuchungen zur Soziologie des Königtums und der höfischen Aristokratie* (Neuwied: Luchterhand, 1969).

Elton, G. R. *Reform and Renewal: Thomas Cromwell and the Common Weal* (Cambridge: Cambridge University Press, 1973).

Emden, A. B. *A Biographical Register of the University of Oxford, A.D. 1501–1540* (Oxford: Clarendon Press, 1974).

Erickson, Amy Louise *Women and Property in Early Modern England* (London: Routledge, 1993).

Everitt, Alan *The Community of Kent and the Great Rebellion, 1640–60* (Leicester: Leicester University Press, 1966).

Farrer, William and Brownbill, J. (eds), *The Victoria History of the County of Lancaster* (8 vols. London: Constable and Co., 1906–14).

Finch, Andrew 'Repulsa uxore sua: Marital Difficulties and Separation in the Later Middle Ages', *Continuity and Change*, 8 (1993), 11–38.

Fishwick, Henry *The History of Preston in Amounderness in the County of Lancaster* (Rochdale: J. Clegg, 1900).

Fissell, Mary E. *Vernacular Bodies* (Oxford: Oxford University Press, 2006).

Fissell, Mary 'Remaking the Maternal Body in England, 1680–1730', *Journal of the History of Sexuality*, 26 (2017), 114–39.

Fletcher, Anthony *Reform in the Provinces: The Government of Stuart England* (New Haven CT, London: Yale University Press, 1986).

Foster, Joseph *Pedigrees of the County Families of Yorkshire* (3 vols. London: printed and published for the compiler by W. Wilfred Head, 1874).

Foster, Joseph *Alumni Oxonienses: The Members of the University of Oxford 1500–[1886]: Their Parentage, Birthplace, and Year of Birth, with a Record of their Degrees: Being the Matriculation Register of the University* (8 vols. in 4; Oxford: Parker and Co., 1887–92).

Foyster, Elizabeth 'Male Honour, Social Control and Wife Beating in Late Stuart England', *Transactions of the Royal Historical Society*, 6th ser., 6 (1996), 215–24.

Foyster, Elizabeth A. *Manhood in Early Modern England: Honour, Sex and Marriage* (London, Harlow: Longman, 1999).

Gay, E. F. 'The Temples of Stowe and Their Debts: Sir Thomas Temple and Sir Peter Temple, 1603–1653', *Huntington Library Quarterly*, 2 (1939), 399–438.

Given-Wilson, Chris and Curteis, Alice *The Royal Bastards of Medieval England* (London: Routledge & Kegan Paul, 1984).

Goldberg, P. J. P. 'Gender and Matrimonial Litigation in the Church Courts in the Later Middle Ages: The Evidence of the Court of York', *Gender & History*, 19 (2007), 43–59.

Gowing, Laura 'Gender and the Language of Insult in Early Modern London', *History Workshop*, 35 (1993), 1–21.

Gowing, Laura *Domestic Dangers: Women, Words and Sex in Early Modern London* (Oxford: Clarendon Press, 1996).

Gowing, Laura 'Ordering the Body: Illegitimacy and Female Authority in Seventeenth-Century England', in Michael J. Braddick and John Walter (eds), *Negotiating Power in Early Modern Society: Order, Hierarchy and Subordination in Britain and Ireland* (Cambridge: Cambridge University Press, 2001), pp. 43–62, nn.255–7.

Greenwood, William *The Redmans of Levens and Harewood: A Contribution to the History of the Levens Family of Redman and Redmayn in Many of its Branches* (Kendal: Titus Wilson, 1905).

Gunn, S. J. 'The Courtiers of Henry VII', *EHR*, 108 (1993), 23–49.

Hablot, Laurent 'L'emblématique des bâtards princiers au xve siècle. Outil d'un nouveau pouvoir?' in Éric Bousmar, Alain Marchandisse, Christophe Masson and Bertrand Schnerb (eds), *La bâtardise et l'exercice du pouvoir en Europe du XIIIe au début du XVIe siècle* (Villeneuve-d'Ascq: Revue du Nord, 2015), pp. 439–50.

Haigh, C. A. 'A Mid-Tudor Ecclesiastical Official: The Curious Career of George Wilmesley', *Transactions of the Historic Society of Lancashire and Cheshire*, 122 (1970), 1–24.

Haigh, C. A. 'Slander and the Church Courts in the Sixteenth Century', *Transactions of the Historic Society of Lancashire and Cheshire*, 78 (1975), 1–13.

Haigh, C. A. 'Finance and Administration in a New Diocese: Chester, 1541–1641', in Rosemary O' Day and Felicity Heal (eds), *Continuity and Change: Personnel and Administration of the Church of England, 1500–1642* (Leicester: Leicester University Press, 1976), pp. 145–66.

Haigh, Christopher *Reformation and Resistance in Tudor Lancashire* (Cambridge: Cambridge University Press, 1975).

Hainsworth, D. R. *Stewards, Lords and People: The Estate Steward and his World in Later Stuart England* (Cambridge: Cambridge University Press, 1992).

Hammer, Paul E. J. 'Sex and the Virgin Queen: Aristocratic Concupiscence and the Court of Elizabeth I', *Sixteenth Century Journal*, 31 (2000), 77–97.

Harris, B. J. 'A New Look at the Reformation: Aristocratic Women and Nunneries, 1450–1540', *Journal of British Studies*, 32 (1993), 89–113.

Harris, Barbara J. *English Aristocratic Women, 1450–1550: Marriage and Family, Property and Careers* (Oxford: Oxford University Press, 2002).

Harris, B. E., Lewis C. P. and Thacker, A. T. (eds), *The Victoria History of the County of Chester* (4 vols. in 5 parts, continuing; Oxford / Woodbridge: published for the Institute of Historical Research by Oxford University Press / Boydell & Brewer, 1979).

Harriss, Gerald 'Political Society and the Growth of Government in Late Medieval England', *Past & Present*, 138 (1993), 28–57.

Hasler, P. W. *The House of Commons, 1558–1603* (3 vols. HMSO for the History of Parliament Trust, 1981).

Hatcher, John 'Understanding the Population History of England 1450–1750', *Past & Present*, 180 (2003), 83–130.

Heal, Felicity and Holmes, Clive *The Gentry in England and Wales, 1500–1700* (Basingstoke: Macmillan, 1994).

Heath, Peter 'The Medieval Archdeaconry and Tudor Bishopric of Chester', *Journal of Ecclesiastical History*, 20 (1969), 243–52.

Heller, Henry *Iron and Blood: Civil Wars in Sixteenth-Century France* (Montreal; Buffalo: McGill-Queen's University Press, 1991).

Helmholz, R. H. *Marriage Litigation in Medieval England* (Cambridge: Cambridge University Press, 1974).

Helmholz, R. H. *The Oxford History of the Laws of England*, vol. 1: *The Canon Law and Ecclesiastical Jurisdiction from 597 to the 1640s* (Oxford: Oxford University Press, 2004).

Henning, Basil Duke *The House of Commons, 1660–1690* (3 vols. London: Secker & Warburg for the History of Parliament Trust, 1983).

Hewitt, David 'Some Cases from the Defamation Jurisdiction of the Archdeaconry Court of Richmond', *The Journal of Legal History*, 19 (1998), 251–69.

Hicks, Michael 'Heirs and Non-Heirs: Perceptions and Realities amongst the English Nobility, c. 1300–1500', in Frédérique Lachaud and Michael Penman (eds), *Making and Breaking the Rules: Succession in Medieval Europe, c. 1000–c. 1600* (Turnhout, Belgium: Brepols, 2008), pp. 191–200.

Hicks, Michael 'The Royal Bastards of Medieval England', in Éric Bousmar, Alain Marchandisse, Christophe Masson and Bertrand Schnerb (eds), *La bâtardise et l'exercice du pouvoir en Europe du XIIIe au début du XVIe siècle* (Villeneuve-d'Ascq: Revue du Nord, 2015), pp. 369–86.

Hill, C. *Society and Puritanism in Pre-Revolutionary England* (London: Secker and Warburg, 1964).

Hindle, Steve *The State and Social Change in Early Modern England, c. 1550–1640* (Basingstoke: Palgrave, 2000).

Hindle, Steve *On the Parish? The Micro-Politics of Poor Relief in Rural England, c. 1550–1750* (Oxford: Clarendon Press, 2004).

Hollingsworth, T. H. 'The Demography of the English Peerage', supplement to *Population Studies*, 18 (1964).

Houlbrooke, Ralph A. *Church Courts and the People during the English Reformation, 1520–1570* (Oxford, New York: Oxford University Press, 1979).

Houlbrooke, Ralph A. *The English Family, 1450–1700* (London, New York: Longman, 1984).

Hoyle, R. W. 'Faction, Feud and Reconciliation amongst the Northern English Nobility, 1525–1569', *History*, 84 (1999), 590–613.

Hunter, Joseph *Antiquarian Notices of Lupset, the Heath, Sharlston, and Ackton, in the County of York* (London: printed by J. B. Nichols and Son, 1851).

Hurstfield, Joel *The Queen's Wards: Wardship and Marriage Under Elizabeth I* (London: Longmans, Green, 1958).

Ingram, Martin *Church Courts, Sex and Marriage in England, 1570–1640* (Cambridge: Cambridge University Press, 1987).

Ingram, Martin *Carnal Knowledge: Regulating Sex in England, 1470–1600* (Cambridge: Cambridge University Press, 2017).

Ives, E. W. *The Life and Death of Anne Boleyn: 'The Most Happy'* (Malden MA, Oxford: Blackwell, 2005).

James, Mervyn *English Politics and the Concept of Honour, 1485–1642* (Past & Present Supplement, 3) (Oxford: Past & Present Society, 1978).

James, Mervyn *Society, Politics and Culture: Studies in Early Modern England* (Cambridge: Cambridge University Press, 1986).

James, Susan E. 'A Tudor Divorce: The Marital History of William Parr, Marquess of Northampton', *Transactions of the Cumberland and Westmorland Antiquarian and Archaeological Society*, 90 (1990), 199–204.

James, Susan E. *Kateryn Parr: The Making of a Queen* (Aldershot: Ashgate, 1999).

Johnston, Nathaniel 'History of the Family of Foljambe', *Collectanea Topographica et Genealogica*, i (1834), 91–111, 333–61; ii (1835), 68–90.

Jones, Whitney R. D. *The Tudor Commonwealth, 1529–1559: A Study of the Impact of the Social and Economic Developments of Mid-Tudor England upon Contemporary Concepts of the Nature and Duties of the Commonwealth* (London: Athlone Press, 1970).

Kane, Brendan *The Politics and Culture of Honour in Britain and Ireland, 1541–1641* (Cambridge: Cambridge University Press, 2010).

Karras, Ruth Mazo *Unmarriages: Women, Men and Sexual Unions in the Middle Ages* (Philadelphia: University of Pennsylvania Press, 2012).

Kushner, Nina *Erotic Exchanges: The World of Elite Prostitution in Eighteenth-Century Paris* (Ithaca: Cornell University Press, 2013).

Laslett, Peter *Family Life and Illicit Love in Earlier Generations: Essays in Historical Sociology* (repr. with corrections, Cambridge: Cambridge University Press, 1980).

Laslett, Peter 'Long-term Trends in Bastardy in England', in *Family Life and Illicit Love in Earlier Generations: Essays in Historical Sociology* (repr. with corrections, Cambridge: Cambridge University Press, 1980), pp. 102–59.

Laslett, Peter, Oosterveen, Karla and Smith, Richard M. (eds), *Bastardy and its Comparative History: Studies in the History of Illegitimacy and Marital Nonconformism in Britain, France, Germany, Sweden, North America, Jamaica and Japan* (London: Edward Arnold for the Cambridge Group for the History of Population and Social Structure, 1980).

Laughton, Jane *Life in a Late Medieval City: Chester, 1275–1520* (Oxford: Windgather Press, 2008).

Leneman, Leah 'Wives and Mistresses in Eighteenth-Century Scotland', *Women's History Review*, 8 (1999), 671–92.

Levine, David and Wrightson, Keith 'The Social Context of Illegitimacy in Early Modern England', in Peter Laslett, Karla Oosterveen and Richard M. Smith (eds), *Bastardy and Its Comparative History: Studies in the History of Illegitimacy and Marital Nonconformism in Britain, France, Germany, Sweden, North America, Jamaica and Japan* (London: E. Arnold, 1980), Part I: Britain, pp. 158–75.

Longueville, Thomas de *The Curious Case of Lady Purbeck: A Scandal of the XVIIth Century* (London: Longmans, Green and Co., 1909).

MacCulloch, Diarmaid *The Later Reformation in England, 1547–1603* (2nd edn, Basingstoke: Palgrave 2001).

McDougall, Sara 'The Opposite of the Double Standard: Gender, Marriage, and Adultery Prosecution in Late Medieval France', *Journal of the History of Sexuality*, 23 (2014), 206–25.

McIntosh, Marjorie Keniston *Controlling Misbehavior in England, 1370–1600* (Cambridge: Cambridge University Press, 1998).

Macfarlane, Alan *Marriage and Love in England: Modes of Reproduction 1300–1840* (Oxford: Basil Blackwell, 1986).

McNabb, Jennifer 'Ceremony versus Consent: Courtship, Illegitimacy, and Reputation in Northwest England, 1560–1610', *Sixteenth Century Journal*, 37 (2006), 59–81.

McSheffrey, Shannon 'Men and Masculinity in Late Medieval London Civic Culture: Governance, Patriarchy and Reputation', in Jacqueline Murray (ed.), *Conflicted Identities and Multiple Masculinities: Men in the Medieval West* (New York: Garland, 1999).

McSheffrey, Shannon *Marriage, Sex, and Civic Culture in Late Medieval London* (Philadelphia: University of Pennsylvania Press, 2006).

Marchant, Ronald A. *The Church under the Law: Justice, Administration and Discipline in the Diocese of York, 1560–1640* (Cambridge: Cambridge University Press, 1969).

Marcombe, David 'The Durham Dean and Chapter: Old Abbey Writ Large?' in Rosemary O' Day and Felicity Heal (eds), *Continuity and Change: Personnel and Administration of the Church of England, 1500–1642* (Leicester: Leicester University Press, 1976), pp. 125–45.

Matthew, H. C. G. and Harrison, Brian (eds), *The Oxford Dictionary of National Biography* (61 vols. Oxford: Oxford University Press, 2004).

Meikle, Maureen M. 'A Godly Rogue: The Career of Sir John Forster, an Elizabethan Border Warden', *Northern History*, 28 (1992), 126–63.

Miller, Helen *Henry VIII and the English Nobility* (Oxford: Basil Blackwell, 1986).

Morrill, J. S. *The Revolt of the Provinces: Conservatives and Radicals in the English Civil War, 1630–1650* (London, New York: Allen and Unwin; Barnes & Noble, 1976).

Morton, R. C. 'The Enterprise of Ulster', *History Today*, 17 (1967), 114–21.

Muir, Kenneth *Life and Letters of Sir Thomas Wyatt* (Liverpool: Liverpool University Press, 1963).

Murphy, Beverley A. *Bastard Prince: Henry VIII's Lost Son* (Stroud: Sutton, 2001).

Neill, Michael '"In Everything Illegitimate": Imagining the Bastard in Renaissance Drama', *The Yearbook of English Studies*, 23 (1993), 270–92.

Neill, Michael 'Bastardy, Counterfeiting, and Misogyny in The Revenger's Tragedy', *Studies in English Literature, 1500–1900*, 36 (1996), 397–416.

Nicholson, Joseph and Burn, Richard *The History and Antiquities of the Counties of Westmorland and Cumberland* (2 vols. London: printed for W. Strahan; and T. Cadell, 1777).

Nicolas, Harris *A Treatise of the Law on Adulterine Bastardy, with a Report of the Banbury Case, and of all Other Cases Bearing Upon the Subject* (London: W. Pickering, 1836).

Oakes, Elizabeth '"The Duchess of Malfi" as a Tragedy of Identity', *Studies in Philology*, 96 (1999), 51–67.

Orme, Nicholas *From Childhood to Chivalry: The Education of the English Kings and Aristocracy 1066–1530* (London, New York: Methuen, 1984).

Ormerod, George *The History of the County Palatine and City of Chester*, 2nd edn, revised and enlarged by Thomas Helsby (3 vols. London: Routledge, 1882).

Outhwaite, R. B. *The Rise and Fall of the English Ecclesiastical Courts, 1500–1860* (Cambridge: Cambridge University Press, 2006).

Page, William (ed.), *The Victoria History of the County of York: North Riding* (3 vols. London: Constable and Co., 1914–25).

Palmer, William 'Scenes from Provincial Life: History, Honor, and Meaning in the Tudor North', *Renaissance Quarterly*, 53 (2000), 425–48.

Phillips, C. B. and Smith, J. H. *Lancashire and Cheshire from AD 1540* (London: Longman, 1994).

Phillips, Roderick *Untying the Knot: A Short History of Divorce* (Cambridge: Cambridge University Press, 1991).

Pollard, A. F. *Wolsey*, with an introduction by G. R. Elton (London: Collins, 1965).

Pollock, Linda A. 'Honor, Gender and Reconciliation in Elite Culture, 1570–1700', *Journal of British Studies*, 46 (2007), 3–29.

The Prose Works of Fulke Greville, Lord Brooke, ed. John Gouws (Oxford: Clarendon Press, 1986).

Raine, James *History and Antiquities of North Durham* (London: J. B. Nichols and Son, 1852).

Rawcliffe, Carole *The Staffords: Earls of Stafford and Dukes of Buckingham, 1394–1521* (Cambridge: Cambridge University Press, 1978).

Reid, R. R. *The King's Council in the North* (London: Longmans, Green and Co., 1921).
Richardson, R. C. 'A Maidservant's Lot in Early Modern England', *History Today*, 60 (2) (Feb. 2010), 25–31.
Rickman, Johanna *Love, Lust, and License in Early Modern England: Illicit Sex and the Nobility* (Aldershot: Ashgate, 2008).
Robinson, W. R. B. 'Early Tudor Policy Towards Wales: The Acquisition of Lands and Offices in Wales by Charles Somerset, Earl of Worcester', *Bulletin of the Board of Celtic Studies*, 20 (1964), 422–7 and appendix.
Scarisbrick, J. J. 'Wolsey and the Common Weal', in E. W. Ives, Robert J. Knecht and J. J. Scarisbrick (eds), *Wealth and Power in Tudor England: Essays Presented to S. T. Bindoff* (London, Atlantic Highlands, N.J.: Athlone Press, 1978), pp. 45–67.
Schnerb, Bertrand 'Des bâtards nobles au service du prince: l'example de la cour de Bourgogne (fin xive-début xve siècle)', in Éric Bousmar, Alain Marchandisse, Christophe Masson and Bertrand Schnerb (eds), *La bâtardise et l'exercice du pouvoir en Europe du XIIIe au début du XVIe siècle* (Villeneuve-d'Ascq: Revue du Nord, 2015), pp. 91–111.
Schnerb, Bertrand 'Introduction bâtards et pouvoir: un theme de recherche', in Éric Bousmar, Alain Marchandisse, Christophe Masson and Bertrand Schnerb (eds), *La bâtardise et l'exercice du pouvoir en Europe du XIIIe au début du XVIe siècle* (Villeneuve-d'Ascq: Revue du Nord, 2015), pp. 7–10.
Schutte, Kimberly 'Marrying Out in the Sixteenth Century: Subsequent Marriages of Aristocratic Women in the Tudor Era', *Journal of Family History*, 38 (2013), 3–16.
Sellers, M. *The York Mercers and Merchant Adventurers 1356–1917*, Surtees Society, CXXIX (1918).
Shagan, Ethan *Popular Politics and the English Reformation* (Cambridge: Cambridge University Press, 2003).
Sharpe, J. A. *Defamation and Sexual Slander in Early Modern England: The Church Courts at York*, Borthwick Publications, 58 (York: Borthwick Institute of Historical Research, 1980).
Sherborn, Charles Davies *A History of the Family of Sherborn* (London: Mitchell and Hughes, 1901).
Sil, Narasingha P. *William Lord Herbert of Pembroke (c.1507–1570): Politique and Patriot* (Lewiston NY; Queenston ON: Edwin Mellen Press, 1988).
Skidmore, Chris *Death and the Virgin: Elizabeth, Dudley and the Mysterious Fate of Amy Robsart* (London: Weidenfeld & Nicolson, 2010).
Smith, R. B. *Land and Politics in the England of Henry VIII: The West Riding of Yorkshire, 1530–46* (Oxford: Clarendon Press, 1970).
Smith-Bannister, Scott *Names and Naming Patterns in England, 1538–1700* (Oxford: Clarendon Press, 1997).
Somerset, Anne *Unnatural Murder: Poison at the Court of James I* (London: Weidenfeld & Nicolson, 1997).
Somerville, Robert 'The Duchy and County Palatine of Lancaster', *Transactions of the Historic Society of Lancashire and Cheshire*, 103 (1951), 59–67.
Spence, Richard T. *The Shepherd Lord of Skipton Castle: Henry Clifford, 10th Lord Clifford 1454–1523* (Skipton: Skipton Castle, 1994).
Spence, Richard T. *The Privateering Earl: George Clifford, 3rd Earl of Cumberland, 1558–1605* (Stroud: Alan Sutton Publishing, 1995).
Spence, Richard T. *Lady Anne Clifford: Countess of Pembroke, Dorset and Montgomery (1590–1676)* (Stroud: Sutton, 1997).
Starkey, David *et al.* (eds), *The English Court: From the Wars of the Roses to the English Civil War* (London: Longman, 1987).

Stone, Lawrence *The Family, Sex and Marriage in England 1500–1800* (London: Weidenfeld & Nicolson, 1977).

Stone, Lawrence *The Family, Sex and Marriage in England, 1500–1800*, 2nd edn (Harmondsworth: Penguin, 1979).

Stone, Lawrence *Road to Divorce: England, 1530–1987* (Oxford: Oxford University Press, 1990).

Stretton, Tim *Women Waging Law in Elizabethan England* (Cambridge: Cambridge University Press, 2005).

Stretton, Tim 'Marriage, Separation and the Common Law in England, 1540–1660', in Helen Berry and Elizabeth Foyster (eds), *The Family in Early Modern England* (Cambridge: Cambridge University Press, 2007), pp. 18–39.

Strype, John *The History of the Life and Acts of the Most Reverend Father in God, Edmund Grindal* (London: printed for John Wyat and John Hartley, 1710).

Strype, John *The History of the Life and Acts of the Most Reverend Father in God, Edmund Grindal, the First Bishop of London, and the Second Archbishop of York and Canterbury Successively, in the Reign of Queen Elizabeth* (Oxford: Clarendon Press, 1821).

Strype, John *Annals of the Reformation and Establishment of Religion and Other Various Occurrences in the Church of England During Queen Elizabeth's Happy Reign: Together with an Appendix of Original Papers of State Records and Letters* (4 vols. in 7; Oxford: Clarendon Press, 1824).

Thomas, Courtney '"The Honour & Credite of the Whole House": Family Unity and Honour in Early Modern England', *Cultural and Social History*, 10 (2013), 329–45.

Thomas, Keith 'The Double Standard', *Journal of the History of Ideas*, 20 (1959), 195–216.

Thornton, Tim *Cheshire and the Tudor State, 1480–1560* (Woodbridge: Boydell, 2000).

Thornton, Tim 'Fifteenth-Century Durham and the Problem of Provincial Liberties in England and the Wider Territories of the English Crown', *Transactions of the Royal Historical Society*, 6th ser., 11 (2001) 83–100.

Thrush, Andrew and Ferris, John P. (eds), *The House of Commons, 1604–29* (6 vols. Cambridge: Cambridge University Press, 2010).

Tyler, Philip 'The Significance of the Ecclesiastical Commission at York', *Northern History*, 2 (1967), 27–44.

Usher, Rowland G. *The Rise and Fall of the High Commission* (Oxford: Clarendon Press, 1913).

Venn, John and Venn, J. A. *Alumni Cantabrigienses: A Biographical List of all Known Students, Graduates and Holders of Office at the University of Cambridge, from the Earliest Times to 1900* (2 parts in 10 vols. Cambridge: Cambridge University Press, 1922–54).

Virgoe, Roger 'The Divorce of Sir Thomas Tuddenham', *Norfolk Archaeology*, 34 (1969), 406–18.

Walker, Garthine 'Expanding the Boundaries of Female Honour in Early Modern England', *Transactions of the Royal Historical Society*, 6th ser., 6 (1996), 235–45.

Walker, Garthine *Crime, Gender and Social Order in Early Modern England* (New York: Cambridge University Press, 2003).

Walker, Greg 'Rethinking the Fall of Anne Boleyn', *Historical Journal*, 45 (2002), 1–29.

Walker, K. A. 'The Widowhood of Alice Spencer, Countess Dowager of Derby, 1594–1636', *Transactions of the Lancashire and Cheshire Historical Society*, 149 (2000), 1–18.

Walsham, Alexandra '"Yielding to the Extremity of the Time": Conformity, Orthodoxy and the Post-Reformation Catholic Community', in Peter Lake and Michael C. Questier (eds), *Conformity and Orthodoxy in the English Church, c. 1560–1660* (Woodbridge: Boydell, 2000), pp. 211–36.

Walzer, Michael *The Revolution of the Saints: A Study in the Origins of Radical Politics* (Cambridge MA: Harvard University Press, 1965).

Wark, K. R. *Elizabethan Recusancy in Cheshire*, Chetham Society, 3rd ser., XIX (1971).
Warnicke, Retha M. *The Rise and Fall of Anne Boleyn: Family Politics at the Court of Henry VIII* (New York: Cambridge University Press, 1989).
Warnicke, Retha M. 'The Conventions of Courtly Love and Anne Boleyn', in Charles Carlton, Robert L. Woods, Mary L. Robertson and Joseph S. Block (eds), *State, Sovereigns and Society in Early Modern English History: Essays in Honour of A. J. Slavin* (Stroud: Sutton, 1998), pp. 103–18.
Watson, Emma 'The Court of High Commission and Religious Change in Elizabethan Yorkshire', in Christopher Dyer, Andrew Hopper, Evelyn Lord and Nigel Tringham (eds), *New Directions in Local History since Hoskins* (Hatfield: University of Hertfordshire Press, 2011), pp. 172–85.
Watts, John '"Common Weal" and "Commonwealth": England's Monarchical Republic in the Making', in Andrea Gamberini, Jean-Philippe Genet and Andrea Zorzi (eds), *The Languages of Political Society: Western Europe, 14th–17th Centuries* (Rome: Viella Libreria Editrice, 2012), pp. 147–63.
Whitaker, Thomas Dunham *The History and Antiquities of the Deanery of Craven, in the County of York* (London: printed by Nichols and Son; and sold by T. Payne … J. White … Hatchard … and Edwards …, 1805).
Williams, John *Ancient and Modern Denbigh: A Descriptive History of the Castle, Borough and Liberties* (Denbigh: J. Williams, 1856).
Williamson, G. C. *George, Third Earl of Cumberland (1558–1605): His Life and Voyages* (Cambridge: Cambridge University Press, 1920).
Williamson, George *Lady Anne Clifford, Countess of Dorset, Pembroke & Montgomery, 1590–1676: Her Life, Letters and Work, Extracted from all the Original Documents Available, Many of which are here Printed for the First Time* (Kendal: Titus Wilson and Son, 1922).
Wood, Andy 'Social Drama and Rituals of Rebellion', in Stuart Carroll (ed.), *Cultures of Violence: Interpersonal Violence in Historical Perspective* (Basingstoke: Palgrave Macmillan, 2007), pp. 99–116.
Wood, Andy 'Subordination, Solidarity, and the Limits of Popular Agency in a Yorkshire Valley, c. 1596–1615', *Past & Present*, 93 (2007), 41–72.
Wrightson, Keith *English Society, 1580–1680* (London: Routledge, 1982).
Wrigley, E. A. and Schofield, R. S. *The Population History of England, 1541–1871: A Reconstruction* (London: Edward Arnold for the Cambridge Group for the History of Population and Social Structure, 1981).
Youngs, Deborah *The Life Cycle in Western Europe, c. 1300–c. 1500* (Manchester: Manchester University Press, 2006).

Databases / websites

theclergydatabase.org.uk/jsp/search/index.jsp
portrait miniature painted by Laurence Hilliard of Margaret, Countess of Cumberland (d. 1616), after Earl George's death, inscribed with 'Constant in the Midst of Inconstancey': https://collections.vam.ac.uk/item/O1067940/miniature-portrait-of-a-lady-portrait-miniature-hilliard-laurence/

Unpublished dissertations

Matthews, Helen Sarah, 'Illegitimacy and English Landed Society c. 1285–c. 1500' (unpubl. Ph.D. diss., Royal Holloway University of London, 2013).
Tyler, Philip, 'The Ecclesiastical Commission for the Province of York 1561–1641' (unpubl. D.Phil. diss., Oxford University, 1965).
Watson, Jack Brierley, 'Lancashire Gentry 1529–58' (unpubl. M.A. diss., London Univ., 1959).

Index

Adair, Richard 1, 44, 48–9, 85
adultery 5, 16, 17–18, 19, 21, 22–3
Aldersey, Margaret *see* Stanley, Margaret
Anne, queen consort of James VI and I 101
annulment 74
anticlericalism 4–5
Antwerp 92
apprentices 3, 24, 34n.46, 103, 128
Arthur, prince of Wales 9
Ashton, Maurice 39, 62
Ashton, Sir Ralph, of Whalley 26
Ashton-under-Lyne (Lancs.) 62
Askwith, Timothy 105
Assheley, Gilbert, gent. 21
astrology 9, 14
Atherton, Rauf 42
Athie, Christopher 40, 54n.14, 105
Aubrey, John 87
Audley, Tobias 88
Augustus, emperor of Rome 101
Awde, Edward 18, 90
Awde, Margery 18, 90
Ayton, Robert 103

Bacon, Lady Anne 42, 60
Bacon, Nicholas 27, 49, 58n.57
Baker, Matthew 8
Barentyne, Sir William, of Little Haseley 65
Barnby, Charles 18, 68–9, 77n.61
Barnes, Richard, bishop of Carlisle (1575–87) 29, 36nn.80–1
Barnham, Alice, widow of Francis Bacon, Viscount St Albans 87
Barston, Margaret, wife of Peter 67
Barston, Margery 64–5, 67, 76n.34, 92, 109–10
Barston, Peter 67
Barthlet, John 137
    Pedegrewe of Heretiques 137
Barton, John 85–6, 95n.28
Bebington (Chesh.) 136–7, 138, 141n.3

Beckwith (née Cholmeley), Elizabeth, wife of Roger, esq. 70
Beckwith, Roger, esq. 66, 70, 78n.65
Becon, Thomas 5
Beconsall, Adam 66
Bedford, Richard, the 'Bastard of Bedford' 120
Bedfordshire 45
bigamy 50
Bigod, Agnes, wife of Sir Ralph 103
Bigod, Arthur 103
Bigod, Sir Ralph 103
Bigod family 128
Bilsbie, Gile 50, 74
Bindloss (née Dockray), Alice 83–4, 90–1
Bindloss, Robert 83–4, 90–1, 95n.19
Birkbeck, Edward 123
Birkbeck (née Clifford), Joan 123
Blount, Elizabeth 120
Blount, Mountjoy, Baron Mountjoy and 1st earl of Newport 120
Blundell, Robert 41, 62
Bold, Richard 27
Bold, Thomas 27
Boleyn, Anne, queen, consort of Henry VIII 12
Boleyn, George, Viscount Rochford 6
Boleyn (née Parker), Jane, Lady Rochford, wife of George, Lord Rochford 6
Bolton Percy (Yorks.) 16
Bonner, Edmund 126
Booth, Dorothy, wife of John 103, 104
Booth (née Warburton), Lady Elizabeth 87
Booth, John 103, 104
Booth, Mary 103
Booth, Richard 103
border, Anglo-Scottish 27–8, 41
Bostock, Anne 64, 118
Bostock, Elena 29
Bostock, Ralph 29
Boteler, Elizabeth 24–5
Boteler, Sir Thomas 24

Bourchier, Henry, earl of Essex 89
Bowes, Sir George 117
Bowes, Richard 117
Bowes, Sir Robert 117
Bradshaw, William, gent. 21
Brandling, Sir Robert 92
Brandling family 92
Brandon, Charles, 1st duke of Suffolk 128
Brandon, Frances, duchess of Suffolk 87
brass, monumental 104
Brereton, Sir Randle 30
Brereton, Ranulph, of Handforth 138
Brereton, Richard 104, 112n.32
Brereton, Sir Urian 72, 142–3n.20
Britton, Eleanor 68
Broke, Anne 106, 118
Brooke, Elizabeth *see* Wyatt, Elizabeth
Brooke, Richard 81
Brooke, Sir Richard, of Norton 88, 116
Brooke, Thomas, of Norton 88–9
Brooke family 88–9
brothels 6
Bucer, Martin 16
Buckingham, archdeaconry of 8
Bullinger, Heinrich 5
  The Christen State of Matrimony (1543) 5
Bulmer, Elizabeth *see* Sothaby, Elizabeth
Bulmer, Francis, of Brampton 65, 76n.36
Bulmer, Thomas, of Scarborough, gent. 29
Bunbury, Thomas, of Bunbury and Stanney 138
Bunny, Edmund 16, 18, 141
Burdet, Henry, of Penistone, gent. 29
Burfitt, George 26, 71
Burgh, Lady Elizabeth 51, 89–90, 97n.60
Burgh, Sir Thomas 89–90, 102–3
Burgh, Thomas, Lord Burgh 89–90, 97n.60
Butler, Sir Thomas, of Bewsey 21
Byron, Sir John 47, 117, 118

Calais 42, 120
Calvin, Jean 16
Cambridge, University of 137
  see also Trinity College
canon law 16, 18
Capp, Bernard 5, 73
Carey, Sir John 27
Carlisle, bishop of *see* Barnes, Richard; Robinson, Henry
Carlisle, diocese of 41, 104
Carr, Agnes 63
Carr, Jane 28
Carr, Robert, earl of Somerset 52
Carr, Thomas 63
Carr, William, of Giggleswick 83–4, 90–1
Catholicism 4–5, 24, 72–3, 137, 138, 139
Cavendish (née Boughton), Elizabeth, dowager countess of Devonshire 89
Cecil, Sir Robert 102, 111n.19

Cecil, William, Lord Burghley 27, 68, 137
Cely letters 42
Chamberlain, John 42, 67
Chancery 45, 68
Chancery, York 38
Charles II, king of England 110n.5
Cheshire 22, 25, 29, 44–5, 66, 72, 108, 136
Chester 24, 48, 72, 105, 108, 136, 137
  Chester Castle 66
  Chester Cathedral 26
Chester, diocese of 21, 36n.79, 40, 41, 106
  see also Downham, William
Chester Consistory 25, 105
Chester High Commission 30, 40, 65, 66, 70, 73, 106
Chester palatinate 24–5, 138
Chichester, diocese of 46, 57
child marriages 58
Childwall (Lancs.) 64
Cholmeley, Sir Richard 116
Cholmondeley, Sir Hugh 137
Cholmondeley, Sir Richard 119
Cholmondeley, Roger 119
churchwardens 46
Cistercian monasteries 23
Cleopatra 101
Clifford, Anthony 125
Clifford (née Pudsey), Lady Florence 80–1
Clifford, Frances, dau. of George, 3rd earl of Cumberland 43
Clifford, George, 3rd earl of Cumberland 60, 101, 102, 111n.15, 123
Clifford, George, son of George, 3rd earl of Cumberland 43
Clifford, Henry, 10th Lord Clifford 43, 80–1, 94n.4, 125
Clifford, Henry, 1st earl of Cumberland 123
Clifford, Henry, 2nd earl of Cumberland 43, 116, 123
Clifford, Lady Anne *see* Sackville (née Clifford), Anne, countess of Dorset
Clifford (née Russell), Margaret, countess of Cumberland, alias Lady Margaret Clifford 60, 101–2, 111n.15
Clifford, Rosamund 100
Clifford, Thomas 125
Clifford family 52
Clinton, Thomas, 8th Lord Clinton 121
Clitheroe (Lancs.) 23, 50
  castle 23
  church 23, 50, 73
  honor of 41–2, 54n.21
Coke, Frances *see* Villiers, Frances
commonweal / commonwealth 3, 4
concealment of bastardy 115–16
concubines 21
conduct books 107
consanguinity 19

consistory courts 21
Constable, Michael 64
Constable, Sir Robert 25
Constable, Thomas 25
Constable, William 19–20
Cooke, Margery 72, 107–8
Corbet, Sir Andrew 106
Cotton family 136–7
Council in the North 22–3, 31, 137, 140
court 2, 5, 8, 13n.32, 51–2, 102, 140
Courthope, John 81–2, 94n.7
courtly love 8, 140
Croft, Laurence 91
Crofts, Elizabeth 89
Crofts, Sir Henry 89
Crofts family 89
Cromwell, Thomas 88
Cross, Claire 28, 38–9, 49, 65, 126
Croston (Lancs.) 41, 62
  parish church 26
cruelty 18
cuckold, cuckoldry 99, 102, 110
Cumbria 29

Dalton, Michael 26
  The Countrey Iustice 26
Danbie, Simon 50
dancing 24
Daniel, Samuel 100, 101–2, 111n.15
  The Complaint of Rosamund 100
  Letter from Octavia to her Husband Marcus Antonius 101
Daniell, Elizabeth 66
Daniell, Mary 63, 66
Daniell, Thomas, of Over Whitley 65–6
Daniell, Thomas, of Tabley 65
Darcy, Thomas, Lord Darcy 109, 113n.63
Darrell, Elizabeth 8
Davenport, William, of Bramall Hall (Chesh.) 9
de la Riviere (née Lascelles), Anne 85–6
de la Riviere, Thomas 85–6, 95n.28, 119
defamation 63
Dekker, Thomas 88
  Keep the Widow Waking 88
demography 2–3
Deventer 72
Devereux, Robert, 2nd earl of Essex 42, 52, 60, 102
Devereux, Walter, 1st earl of Essex 137
diaries 43
Dickson, John 73, 79n.90
Digby (née Stanley), Venetia, wife of Kenelm 55
dissolution of the monasteries 4
divorce 16, 18–19, 44, 105, 141
Dixon, Elizabeth 105
Dixon, Janet 40, 105
Dobbison, Margaret 63, 66

'double standard' 2, 5, 107, 93n.3, 110
Doughtie, Henry 20
dower 73–4, 86, 88, 93, 102, 108
Downes, Margaret *see* Leigh, Margaret
Downham, William, bishop of Chester (1561–77) 29, 36n.79
drama 99
Draycott, Elizabeth 89–90
Draycott, John 89–90
Draycott, Sir Philip 89–90
Draycott family 51, 90
Dudley (née Robsart), Amy, wife of Robert, earl of Leicester 78n.74
Dudley, Robert 119
Dudley, Robert, earl of Leicester 78n.74
duel, duelling 13n.32, 140
Durham 104, 105
Durham, Co. 17, 21, 65, 68
Durham, diocese of 34n.52, 40–1
Durham consistory 20, 28, 40, 62, 63
Durham High Commission 28, 40, 103, 104, 105
Durham palatinate 24–5
Dutton, John 61, 103
Dutton, Laurence 44, 117
Dynham, Sir Roger 8

East March *see* border, Anglo-Scottish
Ecclesiastical Commission 47, 100, 140
  see also High Commission
Ecclesiastical Commission, Chester (1543) 40, 47
Eden, John, junior 63
Eden, John, senior 63, 66, 116
Eden, Margaret, wife of John, junior 66
Edinburgh 36n.71
Edrington, William 104
Edward VI, king of England 5
Egerton, John, of Egerton and Oulton 138–9
Egerton, John, of Wrinehill 117
Egerton, Philip 128
Egerton, Sir Ralph 52
Egerton, Richard 52
Egerton, Sir Richard 120
Egerton, Thomas, viscount Brackley 52, 120, 128, 130
Eleanor of Aquitaine 100
Elias, Norbert 13n.32, 140
Elizabeth I, queen of England 8, 32n.13, 51, 72–3, 137
Elsdon, Anne 88
Elston, Elizabeth *see* Holden (née Elston), Elizabeth
Elston, Richard 50
enclosure 4
English Civil War 9
entails 2
Erasmus, Desiderius 16
Eure, Sir Ralph 103
Everingham (née Lynley), Lady Agnes 71, 81

Index

Fairfax, Gabriel 20
family 2, 7
Faringdon, Henry 27
Faringdon, Margaret 27
Faringdon, William 27
femininity 100, 105
fertility 2
Fitton, Mary 55n.24
Fitzgerald, Thomas, of Leixlip 122
Fitzherbert, Sir Anthony 117
Fitzherbert, John, esq. 116–17
Fitzroy, Henry, 1st duke of Richmond 120
Fitzwilliam, Hugh 114n.65
Fitzwilliam, Margery 114n.65
Fitzwilliam, William, of Sprotborough 114n.65
Fitzwilliam family 110, 114n.65
Fletcher, Robert 72, 136–7
Foljambe (née Wray), Lady Elizabeth, wife of Sir Francis 29, 81–2, 90, 97n.9
Foljambe, Sir Francis 29, 81–2, 90
Foljambe, Sir Godfrey and family 123–4, 133n.51, 133n.53
fornication 5, 16, 17, 18, 19, 21, 22, 23, 39, 102, 143n.24
Forster, George 117
Forster, Thomas 44, 117, 129
Forster family 123, 128
Foster, Alexander 41
Foster, Ellyn 41
fostering 40, 91, 116
France 8, 100
Frenche, Laurence, of Budworth 66–7

gambling 24
Gascoigne, Margaret 18
Gascoigne, Richard 114n.65
Gascoigne, William, of Caley 48, 57n.47, 73
Gee, Henry 24
gender 5
Gerard, Jane, wife of Thomas, of Bryn 22
Gerard, John 138
Gerard, Sir Thomas, of Kingsley and Bryn 21–2, 70, 138
Gerard, William, of Bryn 21
Gill, John 29, 95n.20
Gilpin, Luke 137, 138, 141n.3
Gouge, William 107
Gower (née Fairfax), Mary 70, 83, 89
Gowing, Laura 5, 64
Graham family 36n.69
Great Haseley (Oxfordshire) 104
Gregson, Ellen 25–6, 35n.56, 39, 54n.6
Gressingham (Lancs.) 91
Greville, Fulke 100
Grey, Arthur, Lord Grey of Wilton 121
Grey, Edward, Lord Grey of Powis 118, 119
Grey, Henry, Lord Grey of Codnor 118

Grindal, Edmund, archbishop of York (1570–75) 18, 23, 25, 28, 29–30, 45, 72, 108, 136–8, 140, 141n.3, 142n.17
Grosvenor, Sir Thomas 136
guilds, trade 23–4

Halsall family 37n.83, 52, 85, 117–18, 122, 128–9
Halsall (née Molyneux), Anne, wife of Henry 52
Halsall, Cuthbert 52, 117, 122, 125, 128–9
Halsall, Cuthbert, alias Norreys 52
Halsall (née Stanley), Dorothy 116, 122, 125, 127, 128
Halsall, Edward 52
Halsall, Gilbert 52
Halsall, Henry 52
Halsall, Joan (mistress of Henry, 4th earl of Derby) 48, 64, 128
Halsall, Richard 52
Halsall, Silvester 52
Halsall, Sir Thomas 52
handkerchiefs 68, 77n.53
Hart, Sir John, of Lullington (Kent) 67
Hartilpoole, Elizabeth 66, 76n.43
Hartilpoole, William, of St James', Clerkenwell (Middlesex) 66
Hastings, Henry 3rd earl of Huntingdon 23, 25, 137–8, 140
Haughton, Isabel 50, 74
Hawkesworth, Sir Richard 26, 29, 70–1, 105
Heiton, William 40, 66
Helmholz, R. H. 17, 71
Henry II, king of England 100
Henry VIII, king of England 5, 6, 8, 16, 25, 72, 120
heralds 43, 50
Herbert, Edward, Lord Herbert of Cherbury 6
Herbert, William, earl of Huntingdon (d. 1491) 120
Herbert, William, earl of Pembroke (d. 1570) 119
heresy 18, 22
Hesketh, Robert 138
Hesketh, Robert (1560–1620) 27, 42, 52
Hesketh, Thomas 26
Hesketh family 52–3, 59n.73
Hexhamshire 21
Heydon, John 42
Heyton, Roger 116
Heyton, William 116
Heywood, Dorothy, of Laverton 82
Heywood, Fabian 82
High Commission, southern 25, 26
  see also Chester; Durham; Ecclesiastical Commission; York
Hilliard, Laurence 111n.15
Hobbes, Robert, abbot of Woburn 45
Hobbys, William 14

Holden (née Elston), Elizabeth 50, 58, 74
Holden, George 63
Holden, Rafe 49–50, 58, 74
Holden, Robert 50
Holford, Sir George 67
Holland, Katherine 85
Holland, Sir Richard 103, 116
honour 2, 5, 9–10, 52, 64, 74, 129–30, 139, 143n.25
Hooton (Chesh.) 82, 107, 136, 137
Houghton, Alexander 124–5
Houghton, Elizabeth 17–18
Houghton, Margaret 17–18
Houlbrooke, Ralph 7, 46, 48
Howard, Sir Edward 128
Howard (née de Vere), Frances, countess of Surrey 87
Howard, Frances, countess of Essex 52
Howard, Sir Robert 52, 121
Howard family 70, 121, 132n.34
Howe, John, 1st Viscount Howe 121
Huddleston, Anthony, of Millom 17, 65, 66, 76n.43, 104
Huddleston, Ferdinando, of Millom 63
Huddleston, Sir John, of Millom 65
Huddleston, Mary, wife of Anthony 65, 66, 104
Huddleston, William, of Millom 66, 76n.43, 104
Hull (Yorks.) 50
Hurleston, John 116
Hurleston, John, of Idenshaw (Chesh.) 104
Hurleston, John, son of John of Idenshaw (Chesh.) 104, 112n.32
Hurleston, Richard 72, 82, 106–8, 136
Hussey, John, Lord Hussey 109
Hutton, Matthew, archbishop of York (1595–1606) 18, 23, 51

Ince (Chesh.) 106, 136, 137
incest 17–18, 21, 22, 65
Ingram, Martin 3, 4, 17, 46, 48
inheritance 116–19, 126–8, 130n.19, 132n.34, 133n.55, 134n.54
Ireland 22, 137
Ireland, Laurence 102, 112n.24
Isle of Man 102, 112n.23

Jackson, Agnes, wife of Robert 104
James VI and I, king of England and Scotland 27, 51, 101
Jeanes, Martha 119
Jennyns, Nicholas 119
Jersey 8–9
Jesuits 79n.80, 138
jewellery 67–8
jointure 2, 74, 86, 88, 93, 102, 108
Jonson, Ben 122
joust 140
Justices of the Peace 26

Kaye, John, of Okenshaw, esq. 29, 92, 93
Kellett, George 91
Kendal (Westmorland) 84, 90
Kenyon, Alice, wife of John 26
King's Bench 8
Kirkby (Lancs.) 64, 129
Kirkstall (Yorks.) 109, 129
Knollys (née Howard), Elizabeth, countess of Banbury 52, 121
Knollys, William 1st earl of Banbury 121
Knowsley (Lancs.) 60, 102

Lambert (née Clifford), Elizabeth 123
Lancashire 22, 23, 26, 30, 44–5, 102, 138
Lancaster, duchy of 24, 42
Lancaster palatinate 24–5
Langdale, Robert 81
Latows, Anne, wife of Ralph 17, 65, 104
Leek, Sir Francis 116
Legh, Edward, of Baguley 72, 85
Legh, Ellen see Ogden, Ellen
Legh, Jane, wife of Edward, of Baguley 72
Legh, John 61, 124
Legh (née Langley), Katherine, wife of Thomas Legh 103
Legh, Margaret, wife of Piers (d. 1589) 22
Legh, Piers 22
Legh, Thomas 44, 103, 117
Legh family 130n.2
Leicestershire 60
Leigh, Elizabeth, widow of Thomas Leigh 48, 89
Leigh, Margaret, alias Downes 61, 130n.2
Leigh, Thomas 105
Leke (née Foljambe), Jane 85
Leke, Sir John 85, 95n.25
Lewis of Caerleon 14
life cycle 2–3, 60, 140–1
Lincolnshire 45, 113n.62
Lincolnshire Rebellion 10
lineage 5
Lister, Laurence 118
Lloyd, Henry 82, 108
London 3, 4, 8, 9, 25, 81, 103
  court of aldermen 9
  St Clements Eastcheap 25
Lyngfield, John, alias John Hunter 89

Maddyson, Peter 18, 90
magistrates 83, 91–2
Manchester 62
manorial courts 41
Mark Antony 101
Markham (née Roos), Lady Anne 87–8, 96nn.39,42
Markham, Sir Griffin 87–8
marriage 1, 2, 41
marriage disparagement 132n.42
marriage portion 88–9, 93, 124–5

Mary I, queen of England 22, 73
masculinity 100, 105, 129–30, 139
Massey, George 104, 112n.32
Mawdesley, Robert 47
Medwall, Henry 14n.43
  Fulgens and Lucrece 14n.43
mental incapacity 19
Merchant Adventurers Guild of Newcastle 24
Merchant Adventurers Guild of York 24
Meyrick, Rowland, bishop of Bangor (1559–66) 137
Middleton, Edward 48, 57, 89
Midgley, James 84
Milburne, John, of Hinderskelfe, gent. 70, 83, 89
military leadership 106
'Millenax' [Molyneux?], Gilbert, of Sefton? 21
Millom (Cumberland) 65, 104
Mirfield (Yorks.) 41, 62
Molyneux, Thomas 24–5
monasticism 4–5
Musgrave, Sir Simon 27
Musgrave, Thomas 27–8, 36n.70

Needham, Sir Robert, of Shavington Hall (Shropshire) 106
Nelson, Alice 47
Nelson, Frances, wife of William 18, 68–9, 77n.61
Nelson, William 18, 69
Neville, Henry, 5th earl of Westmorland 18, 32
Neville (née Cholmeley), Jane, countess of Westmorland 18
Neville, Katherine, duchess of Norfolk 88
Newcastle (Northumberland) 24, 27
Norres, Beatrice 102, 112n.24
Norres, William, of Speke 102
Northern Rebellion (1569) 10, 29
Northumberland, archdeaconry 40
Norwich, diocese of 46
Nottingham, archdeaconry of 21
Nowell, Laurence 23, 34n.43

Octavia 101
office-holding 1, 22, 137
Ogden, Ellen, alias Legh 61, 130n.2
Ogle, Luke 44, 117
Ogle, Robert, Lord Ogle 118
Oglethorpe, Thomas 71, 81
Ormskirk (Lancs.) 26–7, 64, 85
Overbury, Sir Thomas 86
  The Wife 86

palatinates 25, 31
  see also Chester; Durham; Lancaster
parish 69
parish registers 41, 61–2, 85
Parker, Elizabeth *see* Risheton, Elizabeth, alias Parker

Parker, Katherine 91–2
parliament 89–90
Parr (née Bourchier), Lady Anne 51, 89–90, 97n.59
Parr, William, 1st marquess of Northampton 89, 102–3, 112n.25
Parron, William 9, 14
Paston, Edmund 42
Paston, John II 42, 55
Paston, John III 42
Paston, Margaret 42
Paston, William (II or III) 55
Paston letters 42
paternity 40
Paulett, Charles, 6th marquess of Winchester and 1st duke of Bolton 121
Paylor, Sir Edward, of Thoralby Hall 17, 65, 76n.36
penance 66
Pendleton, Edward *see* Edward Stanley
Pendleton, Elizabeth 107, 113n.64, 143n.24
Peniston, Elizabeth *see* Stanford, Elizabeth
Penistone (née Temple), Lady Martha, wife of Sir Thomas 43, 67
Percy, Eleanor, wife of Sir Richard Holland 103
Percy, Sir Ingram 43, 47, 61, 123, 133n.46
Percy, Isabel *see* Tempest (née Percy), Isabel
Percy (née Spencer), Katherine, countess of Northumberland 44, 123, 133n.46, 135n.73
physicians 14
Pierrepont, Sir Henry 116
Pilgrimage of Grace 10, 23, 109
Pilkington, Sir John 47, 118
Pitts, Robert 82, 107, 113n.64, 143n.24
Plantagenet, Arthur, Viscount Lisle 120
Plumpton, Anne, wife of Henry Scrope 25
Plumpton, Sir Edward 25, 35n.53
Plumpton, Isabel 56n.33
Plumpton, Robert 125
Plumpton, Sir Robert 125
Plumpton, Sir William 42, 125
Poole, John, of Nether Poole, junior 138–9, 143n.22
Poole, Mary, wife of John 143n.22
Potter, James 83–4, 90
poverty 3
Poynings, Sir Edward 120, 121
Poynings, Thomas 120
Privy Council 29, 138
Protestantism 4–5, 10, 16, 24, 30, 37n.92, 72–3, 137, 139
purse 68, 77n.53
Pykeringe, Thomas 48, 57n.48

Radcliffe, Sir John 85
rape 1
Readshaw, Mary 69
recusancy 22

Redman (née Gascoigne), Bridget, wife of Matthew 40, 48, 57n.47, 73
Redman, Matthew 40, 73, 79n.89
Reformation 4–5, 30–1, 139
'reformation of manners' 3, 4, 16, 31, 138, 139
Rhodes, Isabella, wife of Robert 70–1, 105
Rhodes, John 71, 105
Rhodes, Richard 105
Richard III 120
Richmond, archdeaconry of 18, 21, 63
Ridley, Agnes, wife of John 104
Ridley, Anne 105
Ridley, Joan 26, 71
Ridley, John 104
Ridley, William 105
Rishton, Alice 70
Rishton (née Stanley), Anne 28, 50–1, 67, 73–4
Rishton (née Parker), Elizabeth 28, 50–1, 73–4, 79n.92
Rishton (née Towneley), Helen 50
Rishton, Jeffrey 70
Rishton, John 51
Rishton, Ralph, of Ponthalgh (Lancs.) 28, 50–1, 73–4, 79n.92
Rishton, William 50
Robinson, Henry, bishop of Carlisle (1598–1616) 30, 36n.70
Rossell, Mary 91–3
Rosthorne, Edward, of Holcombe near Bury 62
Russell, Francis, 2nd earl of Bedford 60
Russell family 101

Sackville (née Clifford), Anne, countess of Dorset 43, 51–2, 54, 55n.29, 60, 67, 77n.51, 101
Sackville, Richard, 3rd earl of Dorset 43, 67
Saltmarsh, Edward 61
Salusbury, John, of Lleweni 122, 125
Salusbury (née Stanley), Ursula 122, 125
Sands, William, of Graithwaite 62
Sandys, Edwin, archbishop of York (1577–88) 26, 35n.62, 83, 123
Savage family 126
Savile, Dorothy 92, 93, 98n.74
Savile (née Sothill), Elizabeth, wife of Sir Henry 65, 67, 109–10, 114n.65
Savile, Sir Henry 42, 64–5, 67, 76n.34, 109, 120, 129, 140
Savile, John, Baron Savile 120, 129
Savile, Katherine 28, 92, 97n.75
Savile, Margaret 19
Savile, Sir Robert, son of Sir Henry 92, 109, 113n.62, 120, 129, 140
Savile, Thomas, 1st earl of Sussex 120, 129
Savile, Thomas, gent. 28
Scarisbrick, Edward 27
Scarisbrick (née Stanley), Elizabeth 43, 122, 125, 133n.44
Scarisbrick, Henry 27

Scarisbrick, James 43
Scarisbrick, Thomas 43, 122
Scotland, the Scots 27–8, 36nn.69–72, 41, 69, 106, 108
see also border, Anglo-Scottish
Scott, James, 1st duke of Monmouth 110n.5
Scrope family 119, 121, 131n.25
Scrope, Lady Elizabeth 44
Scrope, Emanuel, 1st earl of Sunderland 25, 35n.54, 119, 121
Scrope, Henry 25
Scrope, Lord 27–8, 36n.69
separation 74
servants, service 3, 46, 60–1, 65, 66, 67, 71, 73, 79n.88, 140–1
sexuality 5
Shaftesbury Abbey 126
Shakespeare, William 122
Shirburn, Hugh, esq. 23
Shirburn, Margaret, alias Stegson 35n.56
Shirburn, Sir Richard 25–6, 35n.56, 39, 54n.6, 124, 125
Singleton family 126–7, 135n.76
Sinningthwaite nunnery 86
Smith, Henry 80
A Preparative to Marriage 80
Smith, Sir Lawrence, of Chester 72–3, 108, 136, 137
Somerset 45
Somerset, Charles, Lord Herbert and 1st earl of Worcester 120
Sothaby, Elizabeth, alias Elizabeth Bulmer, wife of Francis Bulmer 17, 65
Sothill, Alice 67
Sothill, Thomas 67, 109
Sothill family 109
Southworth, Sir John 127
Sparke, Alice 52
Stafford family 122, 132n.40
Stafford, Edward, 3rd duke of Buckingham 122
Stafford, William, son of Thomas, esq. of Tattenhoe (Beds.) 45
Standish, Thomas 17–18
Stanhope, Anne 87
Stanley, Alice, dowager countess of Derby 102
Stanley, Anne, alias Rishton *see* Rishton, Anne
Stanley, Anne, bastard dau. of Sir Rowland 109
Stanley, Anne, wife of James 67
Stanley (née Hart), Anne 51, 58–9
Stanley, Edward 79n.80, 139
Stanley, Edward, alias Edward Pendleton 109, 113n.64, 139, 143n.24
Stanley, Edward, Lord Monteagle 43, 116, 125–6
Stanley, Elizabeth, wife of William (son of Sir Rowland) 139
Stanley (née de Vere), Elizabeth, countess of Derby, wife of William, 6th earl of Derby 42, 52, 60, 102, 104

Stanley, Ellen, alias Baggily, wife of Robert
    Stanley 61
Stanley, Ferdinando, 5th earl of Derby 86
Stanley, George, Lord Strange 21, 67
Stanley, Grace, wife of Sir William (d. 1547)
    142n.11
Stanley, Henry (bastard son of Henry, 4th earl of
    Derby) 64, 127
Stanley, Henry, 4th earl of Derby 27, 48, 64,
    116, 125, 127, 128
Stanley, James, 7th earl of Derby 102, 112n.23
Stanley, Sir James, of Crosshall 21, 22, 51, 66–7,
    70, 77n.45
Stanley, John 79n.80, 139
Stanley, John, son of Sir Rowland 109
Stanley (née Clifford), Margaret, countess of
    Derby 48, 127
Stanley (née Smith), Lady Ursula, wife of Sir
    Rowland 72–3, 78n.75, 79n.83, 81–2, 90,
    106–10, 136–7, 139, 143n.24
Stanley (née Vernon), Margaret, wife of Sir
    Edward 55
Stanley, Margaret, dau. of Sir William, of Hooton
    138
Stanley (née Aldersey), Margaret, wife of Sir
    Rowland 78n.75, 109
Stanley, Peter 26
Stanley, Robert 61
Stanley, Sir Rowland, of Hooton 25, 72–3,
    78n.75, 79n.83, 81–2, 90, 106–8, 113n.64,
    136–9, 141n.3, 142n.11
Stanley, Thomas (bastard son of Henry, 4th earl of
    Derby) 64, 127
Stanley, Thomas, 1st earl of Derby 51, 67
Stanley, Thomas, 2nd earl of Derby 21, 43, 122
Stanley, Thomas, bishop of Sodor and Man
    (bastard son of Edward, Lord Monteagle)
    116, 125–6
Stanley, Thomas, Lord Monteagle 43
Stanley, Sir William, of Hooton (d. 1546) 72
Stanley, Sir William (d. 1630), son of Sir
    Rowland 72, 109, 139
Stanley, William, 5th earl of Derby 122
Stanley, William, 6th earl of Derby 60, 102, 104
Stanley, William, of Hooton d. 1546 72
Stanleys, earls of Derby 72
Star Chamber 25, 27, 35n.62, 65, 82, 85, 136
state-building 3–4, 16, 22, 100, 140
Staveley, Anna, wife of William, gent. 29, 95n.20
Steele, Gervase 19
stoic philosophy 101–2
Stokes, Adrian 87
Strype, John 30, 72
Stuart, Mary, queen of Scots 138
Suffolk, archdeaconry of 46–7

Talbot, Cecily, wife of Thomas 67
Talbot, Edmund, of Bashall 67
Talbot, George, 6th earl of Shrewsbury 68
Talbot, Gilbert, 7th earl of Shrewsbury 68
Talbot, Sir Thomas, of Bashall 50–1
Talbot family, earls of Shrewsbury 127
Tattersall, William 28
Tempest, Henry, of Broughton 43, 123
Tempest (née Percy), Isabel 43, 123, 133n.46,
    135n.73
Tempest, Sir Richard 113n.63
Tempest, Stephen 43
Tempest, Sir Thomas 65
Temple, Sir Thomas 67
Terling (Essex) 1, 41
testicles 5–6
Tetloe, Laurence 28, 62, 71
The Court of Good Counsell 107–8
The Lawes Resolutions of Womens Rights 87, 92–3
The Married Woman's Case 107–8
Thirlby, Thomas, bishop of Norwich (1550–54)
    46
Thomason, Sibyl, dau. of William 109, 113n.64
Thomasyn, Ellen 72, 73, 107–9
Thornburgh, John, of Cartmel, gent. 62
Thornton, Dorothy, wife of Richard 104,
    105
Thornton, John 23
Thornton, Richard 104, 105
Thurgoland, Richard, gent. 62
Thwaite, Robert, of Bossall, gent. 29
Todd, Alice 64
Todd, John 63
Todd family 63–4
Torbock, Edward 138
Towneley, Agnes 23
Towneley, Richard 41–2
Towneley family 41–2
Townsend, Lady Dorothy 30
Trafford, George 117
Trinity College, Cambridge 137
Tuddenham, Sir Thomas 42
Tunstall, Cuthbert, bishop of Durham (1530–52;
    54–1558) 126

Underhill, John 87
unemployment 3
Usher, Mathew 20

vagabonds 70
Vaisey, John, gent. 99–100
Varnam, Jane 28, 106
Vaughan, Sir Hugh 8–9
Vaux, Edward, Lord Vaux (d. 1661) 52, 121
Vavasour, Sir John 26, 29
Vawdrey, Margaret 72, 85
Vawdrey, Robert, of Riddings 72, 85, 95n.26
Vawdrey, Thomas 119
Venables (née Brereton), Elizabeth, wife of
    Thomas 64

Venables, Matilda, wife of Sir Thomas, of Kinderton 106
Venables, Sir Thomas, of Kinderton 28, 65, 106, 118
Venables, William, of Kinderton 51, 66–7
Vernon, Elizabeth 42
Villiers (née Coke), Frances, Viscountess Purbeck 52, 121
Villiers, John, Viscount Purbeck 52, 121
visitations 21, 29, 36n.79

Wales, the Welsh 137, 142n.11
Walter, Lucy 110n.5
Warburton, Sir Peter 66–7
wardship 122
Warner, William 100
  Albion's England 100
Warriner, Richard 90–1
Watson, Margaret, dau. of Henry, 5th earl of Westmorland 18
Webster, John
  Duchess of Malfi, The 88
Weighall, Anna 64
Weighall family 63–4
Wellys, Humphrey 116
Wentworth, Thomas, earl of Strafford 86
Wentworth, William 86
Westminster, palace of 8
Whalley (Lancs.) 23
  abbey 23
  church 23, 26
Wharton, Roger 80–1, 94n.4
whores 8, 24, 69
widows, widowhood 47, 86–9, 141
Wilbraham, Richard 117, 124
Wilkinson, Agnes 91
Wilkinson, William 91
William, Hugh ap 82

Willoughby de Broke, Lord 128
Willoughby, Katherine 87
wills 1, 43–7, 60, 141
Woburn abbey (Beds.) 45
Wolsey, Thomas, Cardinal 109, 126
Woodhouse, Sir Roger, of Kimberley (Norfolk) 46
Woodruff, Anne, of Woolley 83
Woodville, Sir John 88
Wormley, Anne 40
Wormley, Simon 40, 66
Worsley, Ralph 119
Wortley, Sir Thomas 127
Wrightington, Richard 27
Wriothesley, Henry, 3rd earl of Southampton 42
Wyatt (née Brooke), Elizabeth, wife of Sir Thomas 8
Wyatt, Thomas 8
Wynstanley, John, gent. 21
Wyrall, Edward 62
Wyrall, Katherine 61

York 18, 24, 70, 104
  castle 138
  Minster 26
  Walmgate Bar 70
York, archbishop of 21
  see also Grindal, Edmund; Hutton, Matthew; Sandys, Edwin; Young, Thomas
York, archdiocese of 21, 41
York consistory 19, 23, 25, 27, 50, 105, 107
York High Commission 17, 20, 21, 22, 25, 26, 27, 28, 29–31, 34n.52, 38–40, 43, 50–1, 62, 65, 68–9, 70, 72, 73, 83, 104, 106, 108, 136, 138, 140
Yorkshire 16, 26, 44, 65
Young, Thomas, archbishop of York (1561–68) 18, 32

EU authorised representative for GPSR:
Easy Access System Europe, Mustamäe tee 50,
10621 Tallinn, Estonia
gpsr.requests@easproject.com

www.ingramcontent.com/pod-product-compliance
Lightning Source LLC
Chambersburg PA
CBHW071205240426
43668CB00032B/2102